PSYCHOLOGY, EDUCATION, GODS, AND HUMANITY

PSYCHOLOGY, EDUCATION, GODS, AND HUMANITY

cb

LAURENCE SIMON

Westport, Connecticut
London

Library of Congress Cataloging-in-Publication Data

Simon, Laurence R., 1940–
    Psychology, education, gods, and humanity / Laurence Simon.
      p.   cm.
    Includes bibliographical references and index.
    ISBN 0–275–96058–7 (alk. paper)
    1. Psychology—Study and teaching (Higher).   I. Title.
BF77.S56   1998
150′.71′1—dc21   98–11136

British Library Cataloguing in Publication Data is available.

Library of Congress Catalog Card Number: 98–11136
ISBN: 0–275–96058–7

First published in 1998

Praeger Publishers, 88 Post Road West, Westport, CT 06881
An imprint of Greenwood Publishing Group, Inc.

Printed in the United States of America

The paper used in this book complies with the
Permanent Paper Standard issued by the National
Information Standards Organization (Z39.48–1984).

10 9 8 7 6 5 4 3 2 1

To Jeremy, with love, from Papa Larry

CONTENTS

INTRODUCTION

For the past three decades and more I have pursued what I had believed to be two separate careers: college professor at a community college of the City University of New York and clinical psychologist in a variety of venues including hospital psychiatric clinics and private practice. The two aspect of my professional life seemed separate because as a professor I taught a wide variety of courses to undergraduate students and as a therapist I treated mentally ill patients in order to cure their psychological afflictions. I knew that many of my students were (and had been) patients and that many of my patients were, had been, and if I had anything to do about it, would be students. But when I was at the college or at the clinic I felt that the two places were essentially different and that there was little overlap existed in my two professional roles. As the years went by, more rapidly than I had ever imagined or wished that they would, the walls began to crumble between these two aspects of my identity. I began to see many similarities between the theories that I taught and used to guide my clinical work and the recognition that as human beings my students and patients bore more similarities than differences. This book represents my attempt at telling the story of the collapse of the walls that separated my two identities and the integration that followed the traumas and joys of the collapse!

The transformations that marked my professional identity took place slowly over the course of many years as the result of much reading and a variety of life experiences. In many ways my personal reorganization followed the revolution taking place throughout the academic and intellectual communities defined by the word postmodernism. The postmodern mode of thinking involves a general attack on established intellectual authority and as such represents the natural outgrowth of the rise of science and democratic institutions of human governance. Science and democracy are historically linked in numerous ways and are both responsible for the emergence of humanism as a moral philosophy. Modernism reflects the scientific attitude of learning through direct observations of naturalistic phenomena as well as the scientific insistence of a rejection of supernatural phenomena. Postmodern attitudes also reflect the democratic and humanistic notion that all human beings have a voice and opinions that are worth hearing and that no individual possesses any innate, supernatural qualities that make them authorities whose opinions and viewpoints are inherently superior to those of others. This idea of intellectual equality has increased necessary scientific skepticism for some and created chaos for others. For some, science had finally grown self conscious and, therefore, less able to demand obedience to its ideas simply because scientists hold advanced degrees and the respect of society, while for others the postmodern philosophy meant the death of the scientific enterprise.

One of the central notions of this book is that human beings seem to be eternally ambivalent toward authority. On the one hand, we are in perpetual rebellion from demands of obedience to authority and on the other we seek the protection and certainty that authority provides. We simultaneously seek freedom from the control of others and equality with all other human beings while we try to escape from the burdens of responsibility that comes from having choices. We love being human and able to enjoy our lives to the fullest but seek to avoid the slings and arrows of outrageous fortune and the death, disease, and decay which makes us vulnerable. Throughout this book I describe the struggle as we seek to remain human beings and simultaneously attempt to rise above (or sink below) the human condition by creating what I call god-thing stories. It is the goal of the postmodern endeavor, as I understand and use it, to expose these god-thing stories and the dynamic interpersonal consequences that flow from them especially in the intellectual, scientific, and academic arenas. My own professional transformation began as I slowly came to realize that the role I played with my students and patients was often god-like, imperious, arrogant and, in effect, turned my students and patients into things, puppets, and other dehumanized creatures.

My acting as god in the lives of those I was supposed to teach was the result of my own personal needs and was reflective of the attitudes that pervaded both professional fields in which I was a valued member. I was taught that my patients were mentally ill and did not, at that time, realize that the psychiatric nomenclature was nothing but a series of dehumanizing moral judgments. The students that I taught in community college were not the most academically successful and were so-called lazy and unintelligent. I had little insight into the pernicious nature of such moral judgments and the effects it had on them and myself. My growing awareness of the postmodern critique of the manner in which power is used in many institutions that claim to exist for the good of those they seek to serve, while more often than not meeting the needs of the authority of the institutions, began to transform my view. I began to seek new languages to describe my work and new means to carry out my professional operations. During this period of discovery I concluded that my patients were not sick but needed what I called a personal education about their own lives. My students were much like my patients and needed education in much the same in the way.

The content of my courses and the theories that guided my therapeutic work began to fold into one another. I began examining the god-thing stories dominating my clinical work and the narratives that I was expected to teach in my college psychology classes. I began to create my own curriculum along the lines of what some writers were beginning to call a human psychology. I also began to analyze my methods of teaching in terms of activities that I used to think of as therapy but now were firmly entrenched in my own mind as education. Good therapy is educational and good education is therapeutic! As this process of transformation began to unfold I became ever more excited and anxious about what I was teaching and how I was teaching it. I became increasingly bold in taking initiatives and challenging the accepted educational doctrines, psychological theories, and methods that have dominated psychology since I first chose this wonderful field to be my own. The results of my journey, which also form the content of this book, have left me joyful and in awe of what being a teacher and a psychologist can be.

The book is in four parts. The first section, gives an overview of the problems that I faced and the postmodern interpretation of those difficulties that stimulated my intellectual journey. The second section contains three chapters in which I define my educational goals, present my solution to perennial problems such as the mind-body, nature-nurture, and free will-determinism. I also sketch three metatheories that inform my personal psychology: evolutionary psychology, social constructionism and cognitive constructivism. The third section outlines a variety of topics I believe to be essential for any course in human psychology and represents the core curriculum of any course that I teach. The fourth section describes my new teaching techniques and the theoretical justification for these changes. The final chapter is comprised entirely of narratives written by my students and demonstrates the kind of insights that take place when a human psychology is integrated into and directs a humanistic educational procedure.

ACKNOWLEDGMENTS

I wish to express my gratitude for the PSC-CUNY Research Award that was so helpful in the writing and production of this book. I also wish to thank the editors at Praeger and Deborah Whitford of Publishing Support Associates for their professionalism and cooperation with this project.

I

DEFINING AN EDUCATIONAL PROBLEM

1

DISCOVERIES AND INVENTIONS

CONVERSATIONS

"I'm sorry professor, but I didn't read the assignment. I didn't understand very much of it and I'm not very much interested in it. I tried to read after I got home from work but I was too tired. Why do you make us read so much anyway? My other teachers, especially in high school, did not ask us to read this much." I ask my student, a young woman of eighteen, "How many hours do you work a week?" She replies, "Thirty-five" and emits a long sad sigh. I say that I understand why she is so tired and express sympathy that she is caught between the demands of school and work. "Is there anyone at home to help you financially or with your studies?" She stares at me momentarily and then sensing that I am sincere about her predicament and not about to lecture her on her short comings as a student brings forth a torrent of words wrapped in a wail of pain.

> I come from Puerto Rico. My mother died when I was little. I had to take care of my little sister. My father owned a store and my sister and I had to work long hours for my father. We hardly ever went to school. My father didn't pay us because we were his daughters and beat us if we didn't work hard enough. One day he beat my sister with an iron rod so bad that the next day she was the same color of green and black as the shirt you are now wearing. We ran away and came to America to live with my aunt but then she said we couldn't live with her any more. My sister and I live together but we don't really make enough to get by. I am scared all the time. They say financial aid will be cut and then we will have no money for school. I am so scared that I am failing out. Without an education I know things will never get better. I am so lonely in New York. Last night I prayed to God to let me die. I don't know what to do.

We sat together for a while after that, the silence broken occasionally by her sobs or a long sigh (sometimes my own). She became calmer and more composed and finally said, "I feel better now, thank you, I'm going home now and I promise to study harder and try to pass. I like your course when I understand what you are talking about. I do not want to fail." I tell her to do her best and then add that whatever happens she is very brave and I hope that she will be kind to herself. I add, "You can only ask the best of yourself and nothing more. If you ever want to talk to me stop by and we will." She smiles (and to nearly a year later she continues to give me the warmest of smiles whenever I see her although we have not spoken alone since that day) and as she leaves tells me that she will definitely see me tomorrow in class.

THE CLASSROOM

The next day she sits stone faced, like the majority of her classmates, as I introduce them to the basic concepts of evolutionary psychology. There are two students in this section of introductory psychology who seem both eager and able to tackle the material. They are the only two who admit to having heard of Charles Darwin, have any idea of the principles of evolution, or have taken a course in biology with laboratory experience. These same two students are also the only ones who have done any of the assigned reading in preparation for the class. (I would find out later that only about 50 percent of the class purchased the books required for the course.)

The psychological withdrawal that begins to take place in the room is almost palpable. I remember my interaction with the student from the day before and know that she is not alone in living a life in which survival helped shape her skills. She, along with most of her peers, does not possess any way of dealing with this level of academic, verbal, conceptual, abstract, and historically situated material. The vision that guides an increasing number of my students is one of surviving another day or of reducing emotional pain, it is not a vision that motivates the study of ideas for its own sake. It my turn to feel despair. I have been teaching psychology to undergraduates since 1965, thirty-one years, and at this moment I have no idea how to proceed. Anxiety comes over me and I begin to wish I were somewhere else.

At the same moment other emotions well up within me. I feel a sense of freedom and challenge, which on the surface would seem contradictory to the negative emotions that demand I do something even if it is to dismiss the class early. Instead, I close my book, ask my students to close theirs and for several moments sit at my desk in quiet repose. After several moments more, as the class begins to shift nervously in their seats, I ask, "OK. Where do you want to begin, what thoughts do you have on the topic, the assigned readings, or anything?" After several more moments of silence, a male student ventures that, "The guy who wrote the book don't write so good." This is followed by another student's comment, "He writes really boring stuff." The class sits and waits for me to defend either the writer or what he has written. Only several years ago they would not have been disappointed. Instead, I ask, "Does anyone feel differently about the materials assigned and if not where do you all want to go to from here? I, myself, feel rather defeated and frankly I don't actually know how to proceed. I really need your help with this." As I say these words I feel them to be the absolute truth, genuine elation wells up in me; a kind of joy that rarely, if ever, was something I felt while standing in front of a classroom.

The majority of my students continue to stare, but now seem genuinely befuddled. "What do you mean?" asks one, "You are the teacher and you are supposed to teach us." "Yes," I agree, "but you are the students and are supposed to do the learning. I do not know how to get most of you to learn. I take responsibility for only my side of the failure." In my heart I know these words to be true. What I do not say is that my failure is not having tried to both understand and help them develop insight into their motivations and reasons for behaving as they do in class. I am helpless to teach them if they are helpless to learn, and unless we all acknowledge this there is no way to proceed. A problem cannot be solved if you do not understand the problem. I wonder why it took me so long to see this simple truth.

I ask, "Does anyone feel that they are failing in their responsibilities to the class or themselves in any particular way? What can I help you to do that you feel you cannot do for yourselves?" The room is uncomfortably quiet for a moment and then a number of voices begin to respond. "Teacher, you are a nice man but I don't want to be here. I am only here because my father makes me come. He says I either go to school or I can't live at home." Another responds, "Me either, I don't want to work full time at some crappy job so I come here. But this stuff means nothing to me, when I try to read I only fall asleep." Another student adds his opinion, but there is much anger in his voice as he says, "All my high school teachers just put the stuff on the board that would be on the tests and you don't. We have to read it on our own to pass the tests and that's not fair. What you ask is too hard."

I again suppress a desire to argue because I know that it would be useless and counterproductive. These arguments are created in order to avoid dealing with the feelings aroused by questions such as the one I raised today. The students can continue arguing without any resolution until the teacher becomes frustrated or angry and ends the debate by relying on his or her authority and turns to morality to make a final point. The students, it will be argued, are lazy, do not want to learn, and do not appreciate their teachers who struggle to rescue them from the disastrous road their lives are on. Without an education they will be nothing the argument continues and must learn to try harder. I wait again for any students who wish to speak. I hope that someone will begin to go beyond his or her pain and anger and answer the question that I posed which involved examining their responsibility toward the class and themselves as students. Until now all I have heard are their beliefs that they are either victims, especially victims of me, or helpless and blameless about school. However, beneath their defense as victims lies terrible and painful beliefs that they are in some way defective. Today I will wait a bit longer. The next comment disturbs my equilibrium. "Professor," intones a young woman, "why do you even care?" I fumble for words and finally ask, "Shouldn't I?" I get no response. Our class time is over so I close by saying,

"Do your readings and we will pick up our discussion at this point tomorrow, if you wish."

As I leave the room one of the two students who seemed eager to understand how evolutionary psychology might shed light on why men and women seem to be perpetually at war with one another smiles warmly and asks if I have a moment to chat; since I have the time we find a place to sit down. The young women is about thirty, has a child of her own, and has already told me that returning to school is fulfilling her lifelong dream. She is from an orthodox Jewish family and was not expected to seek higher education like her brothers. She had difficulties in her marriage and being a parent had convinced her that she needed to be in the larger world as her own person as well as in the home as mother and wife. She was becoming convinced that it was not God who forbade her to pursue higher education, but those who claimed to speak for God. I was most grateful for her presence in my classroom as students like this make teaching the kind of joy I once dreamed it would be.

We sat down and before she could say a word I apologized for not having covered the scheduled material. "No," she retorted, "that's not what I wanted to talk about. I wanted to apologize for not speaking up when you asked if there where others who felt differently about the readings. I don't need you to cover the readings, that I can do myself. I love them and can not understand anyone feeling as these students do. What's wrong with so many of them? The school is filled with them. I came here because I live nearby and I was beginning to think that coming here is a mistake. I'm not so sure since many of the teachers here are really great. But what I really want to know is how you take what goes on in that room every day and why you don't get angry at them. And what were you trying to do in there?"

DEFINING THE PROBLEM AND SEEKING A SOLUTION

I responded, "Over the last several years I made a number of discoveries that don't allow me to see things as I once did, and won't allow me to teach as I had been teaching. Most basic to my discoveries is that there is nothing wrong with these students other than they think there is something wrong with them. Unless they learn otherwise what you see going on in that classroom will never change. They think there is something wrong with them because they have been told so all their lives, and treated as though there is a terrible flaw in the very essence of their beings by parents, teachers, therapists, clergymen, and other authority figures. These students are the products of relationships in which people have been playing God with one another. Until my realizations I was also playing God in my students lives, although what you saw today was my attempt to not play that role any longer. Today, I was quite successful."

Our conversation continued with my efforts to explain the problems created when people play God in other people's lives and my theory as to why such interactions occur so frequently in the first place. My answers, organized a bit for the purposes of this book are as follows. We human beings have real trouble just being human. We are aware of our existence like no other creature. We are aware that we have a future and have no guarantee that our current actions will produce the desired results. We are aware that we live, as Karl Marx put it, in circumstances not of our own making. We know that we are going to die and have no way to either prevent our deaths or to even control the time, place, or manner of our death. We can not assure that our children will grow up to be happy and successful as human beings or even live past our own deaths. We seem to live in a world in which all manner of awful things can happen to us when we least suspect it. In short, we do not know what we feel we need to know, are lacking in the skills we wish we had, and are vulnerable in ways that most of us find intolerable. As a result, we feel fear, anxiety, powerlessness, and a variety of other painful emotions.

Additionally, human beings seem unable to merely describe the human condition and the events in our lives, we must judge them as well. We continually ask if this or that is good or bad, right or wrong, beautiful or ugly, fair or unfair. We experience ourselves as making decisions and see the consequences of actions based on our own choices. Therefore, we hold ourselves responsible for what we do. We see others as having minds similar to ours and, therefore, hold them responsible for their own actions as well. We are forever asking two simultaneous sets of questions, "What happened and who did what?" and "What's at fault and who is to blame?" We solve problems related to "What is" as well as those related to "what should be." In addition to feeling fear and terror, we can also feel guilty and ashamed. We never seem to be wise enough or strong enough or good enough at the same moment. Our self-awareness or reflective consciousness has created problems for us. Successful solutions seem to forever elude us. We are agents acting upon the world and trying to meet our human desires, wants, and needs, but we are simultaneously moral agents.

In order to deal with the pain of the human condition we have sought to rise above that condition, sink beneath it, or both. We have invented or discovered the gods, (or in our culture God) and think of ourselves as either protected, advised, and (here is where the trouble starts) being God. We deceive ourselves by believing that we are immortal, omniscient, omnipotent, and otherwise more than we actually are. We can also convince ourselves that we are morally perfect. We conceive of ourselves as machines, animals, or some other type of being that is incapable of pain and which cannot be held responsible for its actions in order to avoid the inevitable consequences of human pain. People sometimes interact by playing God while others are cast into roles that make them less than human. While both parties seem to initially escape the problems of being human these interactions usually end in catastrophe.

What happens between people when those with souls, perfect knowledge, and perfect goodness meet others without those qualities? Read the newspapers and pay attention to ethnic cleansing, the slaughter of peoples in the Middle East all justified in the name of God, the bombing and killings between Protestants and Catholics in Northern Ireland justified in the same way, the horrors of life in Afghanistan, Iraq and Rwanda among others. Go back into history and learn about the enslavement of human beings by others, which in American history involved whites buying and selling blacks as if they were animals. Adolf Hitler and his minions were accepted as gods and unleashed the Holocaust in which a modern technological state systematically slaughtered six million Jews and seven million others by claiming that they were ridding the fatherland of vermin and unhealthy germs.

The problems and frustrations that I have experienced in my years as a teacher have in a way been due to the same attitudes that created these larger catastrophes. Several things happen when we enter into a relationship with another in which one feels inherently superior. First, the one playing God tends to overestimate his or her abilities and worth while simultaneously underestimating the abilities and worth of the other. The individuals cast in the inferior role have a distorted, reversed god-like perception. They tend to see themselves as less able and the god-like individual as more able. I have been assuming for many years that I had the capacity to teach even if my students were treated as if they were unable to learn. For example, I would cover material in a text whether or not my students were willing or able to read the texts on their own.

Therefore, my students and I would become enmeshed in a bind in which they were not able to discover what they could or could not do because I did it for them. They would not experience the upper limits of their abilities or struggle to increase skills such as reading, outlining, and interpreting academic materials. They became dependent on me and I became overwhelmed and angered by the very demands that I was, in part, creating. This occurs in hundreds of ways that overwhelm me as the teacher and disempower them as students. But there are other dynamics that become destructive in a hierarchical relationship. Language tends to become moralistic in order to maintain one's inherent superiority to another.

Teachers see themselves as intelligent while their students are unintelligent. Teachers are ambitious and diligent, the students unmotivated, lazy, and unwilling to learn. People, motivated by thoughts and emotions as they struggle to solve problems in a given context get completely lost in this moral discourse. Listen to students discuss mean, hard or nice and interesting teachers as the teachers describe good and bad students and there is nary a human being in sight. What exists are individuals struggling to get a moral leg up on one another and ignoring the educational problems at hand. There are those more than human and those less. In fact, the actual educational difficulties of both the teacher and the students do not get defined or experienced by either.

When I told my students that I was helpless to teach them I meant it. What I have come to realize is that the only power I have is the power to judge them, especially at the end of the term when I hand in their grades. They know that and so our relationship becomes defined by my power to judge them and by their perceived helplessness in the face of those judgments. "What do I need to know?" they ask. "Will this be on the test?" They do not ask, "Can you help explain what I am having trouble understanding?" Sometimes I lecture in a way that becomes a monologue. The majority of my students sit without movement or facial expression and I am rendered helpless and depressed by their passive resistance, a very effective defense against an enemy. This dehumanizing process inflicts more damage to them than it ever can to me. Therefore, nobody wins.

I have learned from my students that while they are pleading, negotiating, and demanding that I do more for them or ask them to do less, while they sit in sullen silence as I lecture on materials to which they feel in no way connected, as they worry about tests they cannot pass but for which they do not study, they are motivated by an unspoken belief. They believe they are defective as learners and as human beings. They call themselves lazy and stupid, learning disabled, crazy, and weird and do so as if these judgments were defining truths. They see themselves as "having a problem," which means "there is something hopelessly wrong with me" rather than "I have a problem to solve which is defined by having something to learn that I experience as difficult." In addition, they see me as their judge and jury rather than an individual who might help them solve these problems.

I am struggling to change both the content of my courses and the process of my teaching. I am seeking ways to restore a greater humanity to my relationship with my students. For some time now I have been developing psychological ideas that explain how and why people play the role of more and less than human and when and how they become more willing to give up the god role. I have been trying to understand how the language people use affects this process. I have developed an ear for the way in which words that reflect moral judgments and values get used as if they were describing and explaining psychological experiences and human motivations. Most importantly, I have been trying to teach these ideas to my students (and colleagues) in order to break the vicious and destructive cycles of interaction.

The following is a story that explains the difference between teaching as a superior moral being and being a teacher and a human being. Last semester I was standing by the open door of a warm classroom while my students were taking a test. Two young women from my class had finished the exam and began a conversation unaware that I was eavesdropping. "Did you pass," asked the first? "Naw," came the answer, "I just can't seem to learn this shit." The first student laughed and said, "Me neither, but boy it is all bullshit." I stepped into the hallway and smiling, motioned them to come over to me. From the look on their faces I thought that the subject of their conversation was about to be all over the hallway.

There was a time I would have judged them harshly and even uttered what I have come to see as one of the worst condemnations one person can use on another, especially an authority figure dealing with youngsters, "What's wrong with you?" But that's not what I did. If they see my teaching as the equivalent of feces then what am I to do as their teacher? I know what to do as their judge, but not as their teacher. Instead, I said, "I feel bad for all of us but if you both feel this way why didn't you let me know? And if you feel this way it must be horrible to sit hour after hour in my class. It is like being locked in an unclean bathroom. Why do you do such a thing to yourselves? Do you feel this way about your other classes? Please talk to me about this because I want to be your teacher not a bathroom attendant who has been locked up with you in the same smelly bathroom." We set up an appointment for one of my office hours, which one of the students kept.

The conversation was wonderful for me, and seemed to be for the student as well. I heard the usual—she felt forced by her parents to go to school (and, therefore, did not see herself as an agent in her own life), she was never very smart in school (and, therefore, did not see that she was judging herself as well as the coursework when she referred to it as "shit." Therefore, she had no idea as to how to understand both), and wanted to work instead of go to college. She also was deeply ashamed of her failures and of not living up to her parents standards. The parents were proud of her sister for achieving entrance to Albany State University, which is a "real" school, not a "Mickey Mouse" one like ours.

The conversation took a full hour but during that time I was her teacher and not her judge. We were just two human beings, with no gods and no one less than human. I did not, as I once would have, admonish her for putting down "the most wonderful community college in the entire universe" (which is how I and many of my colleagues felt compelled to describe my college whenever mentioning its name. We seemed to be without any awareness that it is for ourselves that we need to say it and thus justify being involved in what is, after only a community college, and not a "real" school such as Harvard or Yale where "real" professors work). How much pain I caused myself because I had, for many years made these same judgments and could not see how to be a teacher and rather than a judge. But during that hour I felt I was an educator.

I start every course trying to get my students to understand that a judgment is an opinion that establishes worth or value, and understanding begins by describing that which is experienced while using one's senses therefore the student was able to get her to see the judgments that she was making of me, herself, and the school. I got her to describe how powerless she felt as a student and as a person living her own life. She began to feel the anger, fear, and other emotional pain that she admitted she felt once she crossed the threshold of any place called a school. These feelings have mingled with other emotions (such as shame and guilt) since the third or fourth grade. I excused her nothing in terms of the academic standards of my classroom but on that day I happily helped her learn a lot. Two days later she withdrew from my course and I never saw her again.

I hope that she has found a fulfilling place. In response to my critics who might say that if she withdrew from college, which is what I expect that she did, I aided in her decision, I say perhaps, but it was her choice and her mistake. Perhaps she can learn from it rather than blame me, her mother, her childhood, her conditioning, her programming or of the other explanations that turn her into other than a full human being. I want her to begin to learn and experience herself as a learner, not as a failure in the eyes of authority figures. I want her to understand that she is my equal as a human being and that beliefs that she experiences as truths and guide her actions are no more or less valid than those that guide me. I want her to see her life as a journey in which errors have to be made in order to develop her skills rather than have her struggle to be perfect in some unobtainable and undefinable way. Then I can go on teaching what I love, psychology, not excrement.

These discoveries and their implementation have helped me live in a much happier and more creative fashion. I wish the same for my students. I was trained to be a scientist, an individual who learns by observing, hypothesizing (making educated guesses, not pronouncements) and endlessly experimenting. I'm now helping my students become scientists in their own lives. I want them to feel what any human being feels when they are making discoveries and creating new things—a joy in being alive. Learning the new and giving up the old is very hard to do, and I, and my students will experience a great deal of anxiety as the journey unfolds. But this feels much better than sitting locked in combat with my students and they with me, angry that we are not living up to each others impossible and incorrect expectations of one another, and endlessly judging the other as a consequence. My student wondered where these ideas and techniques came from. Much of my thinking and style of attempting to influence my students derived from my years as a psychotherapist.

EDUCATION AND PSYCHO"THERAPY"

I taught my first class in 1965, the same year I saw my first patient. I was trained as a clinical psychologist and have pursued a double career all of my professional life. I saw people whom I was told were suffering from mental illnesses and I did psychotherapy in order to cure them of these terrible afflictions. For most of my career I worked part-time in clinics and, at the same time saw a few patients in a private office. Until recently I thought of myself as pursuing two parallel careers. When I see a patient it is the patient that does the talking and it I as the therapist who does most of the listening. The potential for learning in therapy is enormous, although unlike school there is no fixed curriculum for the patients to follow.

Patients generally talk about aspects, and people, in their lives who they believe cause their emotional pain. Patients stay in therapy only so long as they feel it is of value. Therapists listen, ask questions and make interpretations based on the patient's descriptions of things that occur in their lives. Therapists also make interpretations that help their patients possibly reinterpret the meaning of the events that the patients describe. The patients are not to be judged by the therapist for what they say or feel. There are no grades given nor diplomas offered. The therapist is paid for his time and the patients are rewarded by learning things that allow them to live a better life. All of the rewards of therapy are to be intrinsic to the process itself. The therapist is forbidden to act in such a way as to interfere in the lives of the patients and create extra therapeutic rewards for being in therapy.

Patients in therapy tell the stories of their lives. Some of these stories are what I now call god-thing stories, that is they are considered sacred and are not to be tampered with. Most of the moral judgments used by individuals, and this includes their attempts to rise above or sink below their human condition, appear in such stories. For a person who does not believe in the truth of these sacred stories, the stories are experienced as myths. Scientists are supposed to call their stories theories and, therefore, avoid making them into sacred stories. As a psychotherapist, I found that listening to a patient's stories allowed them to reflect on the ways in which they judged themselves and others and allowed them to stop playing God in their own lives or in those dear to them. Patients could begin to tell their own stories once they discovered that they were living in the sacred stories of their parents, teachers, and clergymen, and then discovered that many of these stories were myths and could be changed and discarded. (Myths are sacred stories that others consider to be untrue. If a person loses faith in the sacredness of some aspect of their life story then the story becomes a myth to them as well.)

What made therapy so powerful (when it worked as it was supposed to) was the ability of the patient to see that emotional pain was not a moral defect but a response toward others in their lives, or an activity of their own design. The pain, therefore, became a motivation toward changing their lives and skills rather than a condemnation of who they were as human beings. They were able to learn that they had the power to change their lives if they took responsibility for them, rather than live helplessly and dependently on others seen as inherently superior to themselves. They could create and reinvent themselves instead of living in someone's definition of their moral inferiority.

I discovered that I was playing God in the life of my patients and was doing so with my faith in a sacred story. In 1972 I read Thomas Szasz's book, *The Myth of Mental Illness*. Szasz argues that calling people who hear voices, fight with authority, or have problems in living with themselves or others, sick, disordered, or ill was a misapplication of medical terminology. People have medical illnesses or diseases when their bodily organs are affected by pathogens or injury. An illness is something you have. Hearing voices or disobeying a parent or authority is something you do. If we judge what people do then we are making a moral judgment, not a medical judgment. The term mental illness is being used metaphorically and the professional who uses it is simply literalizing the metaphor.

Szasz's ideas behaved like a peanut on its way to my digestive system— it was too low to spit out and too high to be fully digested. It would be another ten years before I would fully realize that calling people mentally sick dehumanized them and placed them below the human condition; placed me as their superior and negated much of what I had been taught were the scientific and moral bases of psychotherapy. People who were labeled as such could be locked up in prisons, euphemistically called mental hospitals, with neither trial nor due process while others could deny their responsibilities in the name of their mental illnesses. (For example, recently a women who owed thousands of dollars on her credit cards had a Psychiatrist declare her mentally ill. The Judge hearing the case agreed that the woman was not responsible for her bills as she suffered from compulsive shopping disorder.)

I discovered it was not easy to understand a person especially if their behaviors did not conform to social norms. But if I asked the right questions, listened to the answers without embarrassing the patient and was quiet long enough for the patient to describe their thoughts and feelings in relation to their descriptions of their parents, friends, community, and physical environment, their behavior almost always began to make sense. I began to realize that calling someone crazy meant that they were displaying thoughts, emotions, actions, or verbal statements that were both unwanted by me, by them, or by both of us and that the motivations for these human expressions were also not being understood by me, by them, or by both of us. When I was able to establish a relationship with an individual based on mutual trust and respect, and when that relationship allowed us both to learn about ourselves (I never learned about a patient without learning more about myself), the relationship become joyful and satisfying and the idea of diagnosing the patient became obscene. I realized that diagnosing another person was done to protect me when I failed to understand that person or they behaved in a way that was threatening to me. Szasz was ultimately correct, my patients were not sick at all, they were only different from me in ways that I found both threatening and incomprehensible.

As the years went by I stopped diagnosing my patients but my field began to increase the use of these moral labels that masqueraded as medical terminology. Not only did the number of diagnoses increase dramatically, but the assumption was made more and more frequently that these people were also brain-damaged or chemically imbalanced and in need of the powerful drugs that the massive drug companies were producing with astonishing frequency. People were not treated as moral agents, instead they were now being treated as defective pieces of neurological machinery. When I saw clients who experienced problems in living and treated them with both support and an expectation that they would take over the responsibilities of their lives I found myself in what the philosopher Martin Buber (1990) called an "I-Thou" relationship. When I saw sick people motivated by their labels and damaged brains, I entered into what Buber called an "I-It" relationship. As I do not want to be an "It" nor do I ever want to treat another human being as an "It" either.

After writing a book on the subject I broke off most contact with mainstream clinical psychotherapy. I joined an organization of professionals who felt the same as I now see patients without any of the trappings of medical jargon or other pseudoscientific nonsense. I renamed my work psycho "therapy" making clear the metaphorical nature of the word therapy, or I called what I do "psychoeducation," or individualized, personal education. At that moment I began to understand as well that what I did at the college and in my office were exactly the same thing only in a different venue. I became aware that my judgments of my students, and the grades that reflected those judgments, obscured my knowledge of who they were as learners, how and why they did or did not learn, and how I might better teach them.

If good therapy is education then good education is therapy. If this is true then what might happen, I wondered, if I applied what I had learned as a therapist to my work as a teacher? Moreover, what might happen if the content of my courses reflected what I had learned as a therapist? What if I discussed with my students, for example, the dynamics of the classroom in the same way I discussed the dynamics of therapy with my patients? In what way could I fuse the two operations and gain the benefits of the therapeutic relationship while maintaining an appropriate student-teacher relationship? More importantly, if I could get my students to tell their stories, especially as they related to topics that have relevance for them as people, would I then be able to understand how they experienced themselves as students? Would that knowledge allow me to help change some of their destructive sacred stories about themselves as students into myths? What might happen if I stopped lecturing so much and delivered fewer monologues or sacred stories of my own? What if I had them tell, and more importantly, write stories as responses to the topics of the course? What you saw earlier in the classroom was an attempt to begin such a process.

The student's next question went something like "Well, are you successful now that you are doing therapy in the classroom?" I responded that every change I make creates as many problems as it solves. It is as if I've entered a strange landscape and there is an infinite set of new skills and ideas to learn. I'm often very tense as I teach especially when I upset a student's sense of the way things are supposed to be. I can't get around the university's demand that I hand in grades and the student's belief that it is the grade and not what they learn that is most important. I can try and make them aware of how destructive grades are to the joy of learning and how they warp every aspect of school, but grades are still recorded and determine much of the student's future. No one knows how to measure real knowledge but everyone knows how to read A or F. One morning a student demanded that I cover the material in the book because she will be tested on it. She asked me to stop wasting her time with stuff not on the exam. It took some real work to defuse her rage but I finally succeeded. I will have to deal with the issue of grades until I retire.

The problem of grades reflects a host of difficulties that are not easy to resolve and are reflected in an ongoing debate concerning standards. How much support should a teacher (or a parent or therapist) offer those with whom they work compared to how much demand should they make of them. There are huge differences in the ways in which these issues are resolved by different people; these differences are often reflected in sacred stories. It is the moral god-like character of these stories that make the topic hard to discuss, let alone resolve.

For a long time I joined with those who saw any erosion of standards as paramount to sabotaging civilization itself. When I was at City College (1958–1962) I saw my teachers as god-like and would never have questioned what I now see was a Darwinian system of sink or swim standards. If you were confused, personally unhappy, or in genuine crisis in your life you neither asked for nor expected mercy—you passed and academically lived, or failed and academically died. The college produced many educated people who went on to medical school, get Ph.D.'s, and achieve other glorious goals but it also produced much arrogance and snobbishness.

Conversely, I see those who work with children and others in need set no expectations at all. Teachers (as well as parents and therapists) see their students as victims of abuse, racism, sexism, poverty, and other oppressive social systems and act as if the victim needs endless amounts of love, understanding, and support. Demands are seen as evidence of continued oppression. Grades are inflated and students are allowed to excuse any level of incompetent work and pass on from grade to grade, class to class without any real growth. One of my favorite oxymorons is high school equivalency diploma. I have youngsters in my classes who believe that attending high school is the same as not attending high school. They may be right. It often seems that the academic preparation of those who attended high school is often the same as those who dropped out in their freshman or sophomore year and took the general equivalency examination years later.

There is no easy way to resolve these conflicts, especially when people feel ideologically committed to them. I do not hold my students to any absolute standards. I believe that a teacher should recognize growth within a student even if it falls short when compared to other students. I believe that high standards must be defined and maintained because to treat children as victims who can not grow is to play god and condemn them in much the same way as those who say flunk the rabble out. I suppose I'll struggle with these questions for the rest of my career.

An old Chinese curse states, "may you live in interesting times." I guess that these times are as interesting as any. The philosopher Friedrich Nietzsche declared at the end of the last century that God was dead. He meant that the basic order of society was no longer based on the sacred stories of God and the Old and New Testaments, our religions had become myths, and authority had lost its right to speak in the name of a higher power. I think this is both a blessing and a curse. We have the freedom to teach and learn as we wish but no one with authority to determine the direction and standards of what we should learn and teach. There can be no authority with the power to say what is true, so we all must determine for ourselves what we believe to be true. There is no longer an authority to tell us the true purpose of the university, or what the curriculum should be or even who we are working for. Do I serve the needs of my students, society, the president of my college, or the many politicians who claim to know what is good for me and my students without setting foot in a classroom? I'll try to answer these questions as well, but not now as it is time for lunch. My student smiled, thanked me for the time, and headed for her next class. I headed off to the cafeteria.

I sat and ate while my mind raced over one of the small triumphs I had experienced in another class earlier in the morning. I had been discussing the difference between play and work. I defined play as any activity done for its own sake and work as any activity done to survive or gain some advantage external to the activity itself. I tried to get my students to see that by introducing grades, test scores, and degrees into the school situation we had turned the learning situation from one of play to one of work. Most students now seek to do well on tests and improve their grades but see this as independent of what they might learn. As proof of this I read the written responses to a narrative I had asked another class to write on the first day of the term. The class had been given the following assignment: "The Klingon invasion of the Earth has been successful. This morning General Dumm, the Klingon commander had issued the following directive concerning higher education. 'Teachers and students are free to read, discuss, and write anything they might wish without any restrictions whatsoever. However, teachers are not permitted to give exams or grade them, and schools are not permitted to issue diplomas.' Write a story as to what you would do as a student on the day after this proclamation was issued."

Over 90 percent of all students (and I have repeated this in many classes) say something similar to, "I would drop out of school and get a job. There would be no reason to stay in school for another day." "Without grades I would have no way to know how I am doing." My students laughed and agreed with the decisions of their peers in the other class but were now not so sure. Some students began to wonder whether I might be right and they might be wrong. One young woman had vehemently told me that I was wrong in not understanding what might happen to her career if she did not get all A's in her classes, and that I had better cover what would be on our first test, now stated that she was confused. Another student ventured that he thought that I was nuts when I said that the only thing the school administration mandates that I do in relation to my teaching is hand in my grades, and that no one seems to know or care what I teach or how I teach as long as the grades are handed in on time, and that the thing I hate most about teaching is giving exams and grading them. Now he wasn't so sure either. But what pleased me the most was the narrative written by the angry female so in need of A's. On the day of the discussion on grades and play I had asked my students to write a narrative about themselves as students. As usual, these assignments would not be collected nor graded but I would seek volunteers to read them aloud in class. The following is the student's response, submitted with her permission to publish in this book:

"The Student in Me"

I'm looking back trying to define the student in me to find out who or what motivated, inspired, or controlled me. I have to admit to find the person behind the mandated function (school) is confusing. This is probably because from day one of our classes together the idea of being a student has taken on new meaning to me. Don't get me wrong, I am no way near to the thank you stage (I haven't learned enough for that just yet), but I clearly recognize the difference of being a student and a participant.

In order to be truthful to you in telling my story I guess its only logical to start with my early memories. I can remember getting up each morning bright eyed and bushy tailed looking forward to my days in nursery school. The whole idea of being with friends and interacting with adults that made my play time even more fun was very exciting. I was always interested and paid close attention, my mom never told me to be this way, I just was. Everyone and everything in this setting was extremely important to me. It gave me so much.

My kindergarten and first grade years were the same, fun filled, pleasurable, and as delightful as a sundae with that ever so important cherry on top. Keeping in mind that I'd like this paper to be honest I feel almost obligated to say that school was actually what I needed to survive; it provided me with so much that I wasn't getting at home. I feel no need to go into a lot of details for enough will be said by saying that school literally provided me with vegetables as part of a meal.

As I begin to tell you my story and my memories flash through my mind I can pinpoint the specific thing that turned my love of learning through play into a competition with the trophy "A" grade.

I was in the second grade and this is the year that I was introduced to the idea of a grading system. This was also the year that I learned how to apply the label "bad" to particular classmates. Everything in this grade became about rules, labels, and grades. None of those weighed that much to me and if they did, not enough to soften my love for school. However hidden within this structure was something pivotal. My teacher had what some people may describe as a positive reinforcement system in place, whereas if you behaved well and did your work each day you would receive a star. This star was then placed on a chart next to your name where everyone could see it. Your tenth star would be a golden one accompanied by a lollipop. After the introduction of this chart all I cared about was getting stars for everyone to see. My every question and action was preceded by the thought would this jeopardize my star for that day. I suffered a lot over those stars in more ways that needed be. Not because my behavior because lord knows I was good, but because of my mother. I had what may be described as a Harper Valley P.T.A.-type mom and that was not a good thing to be so I guess to some extent I was not a good thing. Perhaps my reasoning for getting the stars I rightfully deserved is off, so I'll offer you a couple of other reasons. I wasn't as pretty as my classmates, I wasn't as smart as my classmates, and I didn't have as much as my classmates. Take your pick, it doesn't matter for the end result was the same . . . thereafter third grade and above or at least until eighth (after the stars were gone) it was all about numbers. No one could deny me anything; I was my grade.

Her story went on in a similar vein but the point is made. She has gained insight and opened the door to an infinite number of additional insights. She has begun to see the number of self-judgments that act as if they were self-descriptions. She has written in vibrant, passionate language of an academic topic raised in class and has used it to open a dialogue with me (and with herself) that has no limits. She and I are now co-constructing our course. She is no longer her grade but now has grades. She has begun to establish a vision that will guide and justify her continued struggle to learn. She has become her own intellectual and moral agent and neither my victim nor anyone elses. She can now set her own standards. Her discoveries, best of all, will allow her to reinvent herself. This process will continue for the rest of the semester with me and hopefully with herself for the rest of her life. But for me, at this time, it is very good to be a psychologist, an educator, and a human being.

II

STORIES AND LESSONS FROM PHILOSOPHY

2

GOALS AND DEFINITIONS

INTRODUCTION

The last chapter made clear the need to find a new way of teaching psychology to the undergraduates in my classes at an urban community college. An increasing number of students appear in these classes each year academically unprepared and emotionally unable or unwilling to relate to either the content of the courses or the manner in which the material is presented. They appear detached, disillusioned, depressed, and most of all demoralized. Another growing group represents immigrants from all over the world, many of whom speak English as a second language, if at all. For many of these individuals, the norms and mores of a classroom in a city such as New York represent an environment quite alien from the student's experience. I found that standing in front of the room and delivering a lecture, with passion and love for the material, no matter how well prepared reached fewer and fewer students. I discovered that to use the carrot and stick that grades provide for those who remained in the class (each year a larger proportion of students withdraw prior to the end of the course rather than risk receiving a failing grade) did not motivate the type of response to me or the material that I find meaningful and rewarding for my teaching. I suggested that the problem I was experiencing was my own and my institution's. I theorize that we are part of a system that has helped convince students that they are inherently inferior to their inherently superior professors, therefore we were playing God in our student's lives. I tried to make clear that I had developed these insights while treating patients with psycho "therapy" and that my goal was to improve my teaching by applying the theories and methods gained by my other professional experiences to my classroom endeavors.

There are a number of goals and definitions which must be articulated before the theory and methods that are evolving in my interactions with students can be described and evaluated. I am seeking to reach ends defined by an educational setting with theory and techniques derived from a non-educational setting. I am ignoring a huge body of literature and the traditions that relate to the science and art of pedagogy. As a college teacher, I was not trained in the modern notions of pedagogy had I taught in any grade below the college level. My training was supposed to make me an expert in the content of two related fields of psychology, academic and clinical, and the methods of each of these fields, neither of which specifically involves the traditional notions of schoolhouse pedagogy. Therefore, philosophical justifications have to be made, as well as articulating various definitions and goals. I will not justify my decision not to review the vast literature on educational pedagogy except to say that it is my desire to demonstrate how psychology can be used to create an effective pedagogy and not to begin a new career in a new field of study no matter how worthy that new field might be.

Let me begin with a statement of my educational goals, which are now much broader than having my students understand the various subject areas of psychology. I believe that the methods of science represent the best way to learn about the world in which we live, and psychology, as a science, is the best way to understand how to develop a scientific attitude toward the world and toward significant people in one's life. I believe, therefore, that my courses must do more than help students memorize definitions from science and psychology: It must help them live these methods and help them to grow long after they have left my classroom. I have set as my goals the development of my students as scientists and psychologists. I also believe that the core of the scientific method relates to the creativity of the artist and that art makes life worth living.

I start with the following poem by W. B. Yeats (1920) written at the conclusion of World War I, the second greatest, but unfortunately not the last, man-made catastrophe of this century.

The Second Coming

> Turning and turning in the widening gyre
> The falcon cannot hear the falconer;
> Things fall apart; the center cannot hold;
> Mere anarchy is loosed upon the world,
> The blood-dimmed tide is loosed, and everywhere
> The ceremony of innocence is drowned;
> The best lack all conviction, while the worst
> Are full of passionate intensity.
> Surely some revelation is at hand;
> Surely the Second Coming is at hand.
> The Second Coming! Hardly are those words out
> When a vast image out of *Spiritus Mundi*
> Troubles my sight: somewhere in sand of the desert
> A shape with lion body and the head of a man,
> A gaze blank and pitiless as the sun,
> Is moving its slow thighs, while all about it

Reel shadows of the indignant desert birds.
The darkness drops again; but now I know
That twenty centuries of stony sleep
Were vexed to nightmare by a rocking cradle.

And what rough beast, its hour come at last,
Slouches toward Bethlehem to be born?

Why a poem? Why this poem? There are two reasons. First, I believe that the goals of education must include a vision of students as artists in and of their own lives. Without a sense that whatever a person does should include both his or her unique perceptions as well as the highest standards of quality of which he or she is capable leaves the person in a state of existence rather than in the full bloom of life. I chose this poem as an example of art but also because its content is still relevant both for our age and for the crisis many of us experience as educators. I could have used music, painting or dance. I could have used a scene from a movie such as The Big Night which describes the economic problems of two Italian immigrants who open a restaurant. One of the brothers, the chef, sees food as a gift from God and his responsibility to cook as high art. The other brother is a pragmatic businessman who understands that unless people are served what they like they will not come to the restaurant and if this happens the restaurant cannot stay open. The tension between the loving artist and the practical businessman makes for a wonderful story. The resolution of the tension is the same that I seek in my classroom. I could also have included the stories of one of my students who makes a business of carpentry and floral arrangements and describes with passion the art of his handiwork in such a way that the description itself becomes art. I provide examples in later chapters of students writings that are expressions of their inner beings and how these appear to me as art. It is in their experience of creating and my response to what I judge to be art that the joy of being part of education and life can be found. I think that many individuals in the field of teaching, regardless of subject area might agree. My argument is so mundane and self evident that it should not need even be made.

Little of school experience seems to involve an artistic vision. When I make clear my goals for my students they are rarely moved. Moreover, many become angry that I am trying to waste their time. "I want my degree as soon as possible" says one, "so I can get out of here and get a decent paying job." My students seem to be convinced, perhaps by the poverty and hardships of their life circumstances, and perhaps by the argument of some educators as well as by the pervasive statements by politicians and businessmen that appear in the media, that the goals of education are strictly geared toward commerce, not art. How can I disagree with the importance of earning a living? It is hard to enjoy music with an empty belly. Commerce makes life possible! But it is art that makes it worth living!

I believe that the science of psychology properly applied increases the probability that individuals will learn to see themselves and others as of art as well as able to meet the practical concerns of their lives. The psychotherapist Erving Pollster (1987) suggested that *Every Person's Life Is Worth a Novel*. He meant this both literally and figuratively; both as a judgment of the value of every life and a method in which people can realize their worth (and a better way to live) by writing novels about their lives. There are now hundreds of psychoanalysts such as Roy Schafer (1992) and Donald Spence (1982) who treat their patients stories as texts. I am developing these same notions as a means of teaching, however, I delay describing these methods until I have discussed psychology as a science of narratives and other forms of artistic expression.

The second reason for choosing poetry, or other form of art as a starting point of psychological inquiry into education is that the poem is an artifact of human psychological processes: It was created by a human being for other human beings. A poems creation represents a goal I believe should be shared by all people, though it is in not fact. The psychology of the artist is not one shared by a majority of human beings. The artist represents an individual with various cognitive and motivational differences from others less artistic. (These differences will be discussed in later chapters.) However, the differences that allow an individual artistic expression often create social conditions that marginalize the artist. Any theory of psychology must be able to explain how and why people create art and why others do not. Moreover, any theory of psychology helpful in achieving an educational goal that includes artistic processes must also include an understanding of the "human change processes" (Mahoney 1991) required to enhance the artistic processes in those lacking them. In two previous works (Simon 1986, 1994) I pointed out that the creative efforts of Sigmund Freud and B .F. Skinner are theories that can in no way explain the creativity of their creators. The works of Freud and Skinner dominated psychological thinking for many years and, therefore, represented an impediment to understanding creative science.

If science is inherently creative (as all sciences must be) and psychology is the only science that can deal specifically with the psychology of those who create scientific theories, it follows that psychology would have much to say about these processes. Unlike physics or chemistry, psychology deals with self-reflexive sub-ject matter, that is, itself. Unfortunately, this is not the case. Creativity is a subject within psychology, but it represents a small specialty rather than a place of special concern. How can this be so, and if it is true, how can I use psychology to find ways to increase my student's creative use of their own lives?

To solve the problems created by psychology's inability to explain the psychologist we must first examine psychology as a science, but to understand psychology as a science we must find its place among the other great forms of scientific endeavor from which it evolved. What I consider to be psychology's blind spots concerning creativity were, in part, inherited from assumptions contained in the sciences that psychology has tried to emulate. I discuss the growing critique of science that is emerging from many quarters of the academic and scientific community and trace how this critique helps illuminate the mote in psychology's eye where art and a variety of other crucial human activities are concerned. By placing the arts within the focus of psychology and psychology within the focus of science, I delineate both methods of teaching and the content of my courses so that they help my students become scientists, psycholo-gists, and artists in and of their own lives.

There are still other goals I wish my students to achieve. I hope they become their own moral philosophers as well. No human being can be a scientist and not justify his or her creative efforts morally and ethically. I will wait to spell out my own moral philosophy in the next chapter, but this chapter points out the consequences to science (and the rest of us) when scientists and educators do not ground their activities in a clear set of humanistic rules, but rather take the position that they have no right to make moral judgments of any kind or make such judgments as if they were inherently superior gods. Yeats (1920), summarizes: "The best lack all conviction while the worst are full of passionate intensity."

SCIENCE

There is a revolution going on in the sciences today that has affected the way in which workers in many scientific fields operate, and especially how a growing number of psychologists view their field as a science. Until recently most scientists thought about their work in terms of objects of their interest and methods used to study these objects. Scientists rarely thought about the history of their science except for the work of historical figures and how their work was still relevant to current theory and methodologies, or unless a particular scientist made the history of his or her science the subject of his or her interest. For example, Charles Darwin is a historical figure but his theory of evolution and natural selection still guide much biological research. Most practicing biologists know about Darwin's theory and methodology but they know less about Darwin as a man living in another historical time. If science was studied as history then the scientist would be conducting history and not science. According to the psychologist Kurt Danziger (1990) the historian in most established sciences is an outsider to the science itself. To write a biography of Darwin is a historical, and not a scientific, endeavor. The author would not, strictly speaking, be conducting scientific inquiry. Danziger suggests, however, that the scientist is always embedded in his history.

Danziger is one of many critics of science who have suggested that the scientific enterprise as it has emerged and operated over the last 100 years or so has defined the very era in which we live. This period, known as the modern era, glorifies the scientist and defines progress in terms of scientific discoveries and the technological inventions which flow from scientific laboratories. Moreover, scientists have replaced the clergy as experts in living and morality. The critics of modernism, those in a wide variety of fields, are referred to as postmodernists. Initially it might seem that the postmodern movement is against science itself; while this is sometimes true, it is more often the case that the critics of modern science are against the uncritical attitude that science seems to take toward its own goals and methods. The totality of these criticisms of science might be summarized by the biologist Bonnie Spanier (1993: 3–5) who writes, "Scientists as a group are less apt to embrace the view that scientific knowledge, like all knowledge is socially constructed by, for the most part, a small portion of the population and that it reflects the experiences, beliefs, and biases that serve that tiny but powerful population . . . most scientists disallow that all aspects of science, like any other human endeavor, embody and reflect power relations—the usual inequitable ones." This is the position to be taken in this book.

I should add that I do not see these critics as generally opposed to or disjunctive with the scientific enterprise. I agree instead with the psychologist Louis Sass (1992) that postmodernism is the natural outgrowth of the scientific method as it turns its gaze on itself and therefore is the height of modernism. The sociologist George Herbert Mead claimed that "The scientific method is, after all, only the evolutionary process grown self-conscious" (Mahoney 1991: 118). The postmodern critique is science grown self-conscious. Postmodernism allows scientists to examine the sacred stories of science and determine which stories might be better treated as myths. Important innovators to this now ongoing self examination of the scientific enterprise includes Michael Polanyi (1958, 1966, 1967, 1969); Thomas Kuhn (1970); Richard Rorty (1979, 1991); Kenneth Gergen (1985, 1991a, 1991b); Jacob Bronowski (1963); Robert Merton (1968); and a host of other scholars in a number of disciplines both in and out of the sciences.

There are now scholars studying the sociology, psychology, history, and morality of science and scientists. Science, whose lenses were trained on everything but itself, has become the object of intense scrutiny and criticism. These inquiries into the workings of science are known collectively as science studies and is fast becoming a popular course of university studies. Kuhn (1970), whose work permits me to begin to summarize some of the postmodern critique of modern science, suggested that scientists promote a view of their work and accomplishments in a manner that is more myth than reality. The myths find there way into the elementary textbooks of a science in order that students who are to apprentice in a given science be indoctrinated into the dominant theories and methodologies of the science at any given moment. Kuhn called the dominant theories, methods of study, and technologies of doing research the paradigms of any given science. Since the paradigms of science belong to the human creators who benefit from adherence to them, it is in the interest of these scientists to protect their work by turning them into what I call sacred stories. The sacred stories that appear in textbooks, and are believed by the scientists themselves, are a far cry from what actually happens in the day-to-day work of the scientists. What are the myths of science insofar as we can free them from their sacred armaments and how do these myths affect the work of science, and especially the study of psychology? What sacred stories account for the blind spot in both psychological theory and methodology? If we expose the source of the sacred story, deconstruct (the postmodern term for analyzing a body of human writings for their hidden assumptions) it by locating it in history, social activity, and the human needs of the scientist and ask who benefits by its maintenance, then we find ourselves better able to develop theory and methodology that explains the existence of Yeat's poem, "The Second Coming."

The Myths of Science

Science can be defined as a set of procedures for understanding the nature of the world around, and in, us. The goal of science is to describe phenomena and thereby discover regularities or patterns in the things described. Science then seeks to explain the patterns and relationships between the things observed and the regularities discovered therein; it seeks further to draw hypotheses from the organized body of explanations known as theories and test through further observations the validity of these predictions. Finally, it is the goal of science to control the phenomena under its consideration for, among other reasons, the betterment of humankind. Science claims to be the superior means of achieving the ends of describing, explaining, predicting, and controlling. Science points to the record of its achievements in transforming human existence for the better by extending life, reducing the suffering caused by dread diseases, and by the technologies that have changed the modes of human production and consumption. We are better fed, clothed and sheltered than any people in human history. Moreover, we have achieved this standard of living by removing our need to create wealth by being human beasts of burden. What methods has science employed to achieve these changes? By the use of rationality, specialized means of studying phenomena such as the controlled laboratory experiment, specialized use of language which includes the use of mathematics and perhaps, most important of all, by employing the attitude of *objectivity*.

What is objectivity as it is described by science and in what ways is it a sacred story or myth? Both questions need to be asked since the achievements described above have been accompanied by negative consequences of science. Critics point to the weapons produced by science, the destruction of the natural environment, and for the purposes of this book, the hostility of science to poetry, art, music, and dance. There is no science of the arts and no real recognition of the manner in which art and science have similar goals and methodologies. Objectivity, as it appears in the official pronouncements of science, demands that the scientist be as unbiased and honest as possible in making and reporting his or her observations. Science requires that he or she (many of science's critics suggest that science privileges men over women with the simultaneous result that the language of science is masculinized and women are prevented from entering or achieving status and power within the sciences) report on reality as it is rather than as he or she wishes to see it. Scientists must avoid at all costs being subjective which is the enemy of objectivity. The human needs of the scientist should not influence his or her descriptions of reality however, the scientists must remain rational, intellectual, and logical rather than emotional, intuitive, and sensitive.

In recent years, scientists have also become aware of the importance of language in relating their findings to other scientists. The language of the scientist, it is argued, must also not contain any hidden meanings or expressions of the emotions or other aspects of the subjectivity of the observing reporting scientist. The project to create a perfectly objective language is known as logical positivism and was initiated by, among others, the philosopher Rudolf Carnap (1966). It reached its zenith with the work of R.W. Bridgman, (1927) and the concepts of operationism, which stated that all scientific concepts had to be defined by the operations or means by which they were measured. In psychology, B. F. Skinner (1948) would define the hunger of a rat or a human being in terms of the hours elapsed since their last feeding. Therefore, saying an organism was eight hours food, sleep or liquid deprived avoided the subjectively tainted concepts of hunger, thirst, or feeling tired. The objectivity of the scientific method had to be based not only on observable, but measurable, phenomena. Again Skinner believed that only observed and measured human movements elicited by observed and measured environmental stimuli could be admitted to the body of genuine scientific psychology.

If we examine the notion of objectivity we find a number of problems in the manner in which it is described in the textbooks of science. The scientists in these descriptions seem hardly human, hardly the stuff of which the rest of us, as non-scientists, are made. Not only does the extreme notion of objectivity as described seem impossible to achieve, but a close examination makes it a dubious one as well. What kind of human beings have no human needs as they examine the world around them? What kind of beings are free of all human emotions? Who is free from the pressures and rewards of belonging to a particular university, city, state, national entity, or culture? Who can rise above the historical epoch in which they live? These are biases that can only be experienced as such by actually going back and forth in time and directly experiencing eras other than the present. These other epochs would then have to be experienced through the eyes of a person born and raised in that epoch. What kind of language must be spoken that frees one from the rhetoric inherent in language? Language exists to influence those around us to the same degree that it exists to describe the world. What then are the rhetorical aims of a language that describes human hungers in a way that vitiates and destroys their experiential human qualities? Furthermore, what type of beings develop technologies and experiment on their fellow human beings in a manner that is objective and do not recognize the pain and pleasures inflicted on the subjects of the research or which ignores predicting the moral consequences of the research and technological developments?

The mythical qualities of scientific objectivity describe a god rather than a human being. It is a being that exists as pure, disembodied intellect viewing and manipulating the world around it from a privileged position unobtainable by the non-scientist. I was trained and indoctrinated into such a model both as a teacher and as a therapist. It was the assumption that I was a detached observer, floating above the subjects of my inquiry with manipulations that allowed me to test, diagnose, and treat, mental illnesses without seeing that the psychiatric terms used were degrading moral judgments of those who had sought me out for help. It was these same sacred stories that allowed me to lecture to a sea of unresponsive faces as if the words coming out of my mouth were some form of food from the gods rather than speculations, personal opinions, moral judgments, and often bad entertainment as well as material that might reside in reality and be helpful to those I was teaching. It is this stance of the detached, aloof god that many now see as the enemy of genuine science, especially in the field of psychology, and an attitude that must be countered and replaced by science with a human face. It is the creation of gods, beyond self-criticism and operating with what they consider a perfect view of reality, the Truth, that I see as both universal and problematic for all human relationships but especially dangerous in the sciences and particularly in psychology.

A brief examination of the roots of modernism reveals that the assumptions of extreme objectivity are to be found in premodernistic notions that are to be eschewed by the objective scientist. Most histories of modern science (I. Bernard Cohen 1985) suggest that it was the philosopher René Descartes that established the underpinnings of modernity in science. Ian Hacking (1995) describes those early assumptions. He suggests that Descartes believed that each human being was basically a machine inhabited by a human soul connected to the body-machine at the pineal gland. The machine moved and spoke when the pineal gland was tilted in one direction or another by the soul-stuff to which the gland was somehow connected. It was this soul, not of this earth, that permitted objectivity. The detached, free-floating rational intellect that was the soul was free to observe all the natural phenomena on this planet with complete accuracy as long as it remained uncorrupted by the flesh and animal spirits that made up the machine in which it was a temporary inhabitant. The scientist in this model can understand all that is around him and need not be concerned that his own nature is different and inherently superior to the object of his interest. When scientists play God they do so quite literally with a philosophical history that tells them they are gods, or of the stuff of gods. If we examine the descriptions of science as recorded by the postmodern critique of science we find a very different picture than the one provided by the official sacred story of science as well as the unexamined dark side of the dangers and failings of the scientific enterprise. It is this examination that I now turn.

The first serious consequence of the god myth is to the internal operations of science itself. This is meant in a descriptive sense and not a moral sense because the damage done to humanity when scientists (or any other group) play the god role is catastrophic from my moral point of view. Objectivity is a worthy and necessary goal of any project designed to increase our understanding and control of the world around and inside of us. It is important to know when we are engaging only in wish fulfillment. It makes a difference if a drug is sold as a cure for an illness based solely on the fantasies or greed of its manufacturers and distributors. It is one thing to wish for a cancerous tumor to be gone, and quite another for it to be so. Science does deal with reality, however impossible it is for that reality to be described from a non-human perspective. There is a difference between madness and sanity in my view (even if the difference is one of degree and not an absolute, and even if madness is not a medical condition). Science must belong to the world of the sane however difficult that is to define.

The god-like stance described in the myths of science violate any hope that a human definition of objectivity can ever take place. Like all such sacred stories the very thing that is being avoided is brought about when we can no longer begin with a clear idea of what problem we are seeking to solve. Gods can neither be wrong intellectually nor morally. Human beings are always fallible, which is why we have science in the first place. Scientists call their explanations theories, which is another word for an educated guess. Kuhn points out, however, that scientists more often than not treat their stories like absolute truths. When the average scientist discovers facts which prove his theory vulnerable to a competing theory, he or she, as an objective, fair, and impartial observer is supposed to question, and if necessary abandon his or her own theory. Kuhn believes this rarely happens. More often than not the observed anomaly (the facts which do not fit the theory) is reinterpreted to fit the existing theory and competing theories are disparaged. It is also not uncommon for the competing scientists themselves to be disparaged. Kuhn goes on to suggest that competing theories do not replace mainstream theories without a fight for the loyalties of younger scientists and the newer scientists usually must wait their turn for dominance until older scientists either retire or die. While this essentially conservative process helps screen out many undesirable ideas we can only wonder how many useful and important discoveries have languished or failed to come to fruition in this process.

I have experienced the battles within the sciences that Kuhn describes as commonplace since my undergraduate days as a psychology major. The clinical psychologists disparaged the academic psychologists for being insensitive while the academics claimed to possess methods of study which placed their ideas along side of the hard sciences such as chemistry and physics. The academics warned their students not to go into the clinical side of the field since the clinical methods were either soft or simply unscientific. The clinicians themselves warred over whose theories best represented true science—psychoanalysis or the behavioral therapies derived from the works of B. F. Skinner. Among Psychoanalysts the battle for the hearts and minds of the students raged among the followers of Sigmund Freud, Harry Stack Sullivan, Karen Horney and Alfred Adler. In academia, behaviorists not only collided with the clinicians and with the third force psychologists, such as humanists Abraham Maslow and Carl Rogers.

The struggle of scientists to be above fallibility not only prevents necessary dialogues between individuals with competing ideas in the same field but also has created artificial turf wars between different fields of science. Any necessary cross fertilization between biology and psychology, sociology and psychology, often fail to take place. In addition to these struggles I have seen and experienced the overt hostilities between those who hold ideological commitments to either a primarily biological or sociological explanation of human behavior. Another problem that emerges when scientists fail to examine their own sacred stories involves commitments to methodologies that might be less appropriate than others for the study of any given phenomena. The study of the history of science reveals one battle after another concerning which method of study is the one true method. The insistence of psychologists to mimic the methods of physics, chemistry, and other hard sciences is one of the main reasons why the subjective psychological processes that produce art have never been properly studied. I will delay a fuller discussion of psychology's peculiar and specific difficulties in establishing itself as a science until later, but now I will concentrate on the problems created by scientists for the very people it should be serving.

Playing God in physics, chemistry, and biology has led to the uncritical development and use of technologies that become or were intended to be weaponry. Bronowski (1963: 142) writes "Science has created evil by amplifying the tools of war while scientists have taken no moral stance on their use or production. Scientists did not create or maintain war but they have changed it. They have engaged in acting the mysterious stranger, the powerful voice without emotion, the expert, the god." The discoveries and inventions of the scientist always belong to the human communities of which the scientist is a part. The products of scientific labor should not and cannot be kept from other members of the community, but when other members of that community, people of great power also playing God, use scientific activity in an uncritical manner the results are catastrophic. We have seen the use to which atomic energy, investigations of biological pathogens, and various toxic chemicals have already lead. What horrors might we see when we play God with the results of genetic engineering, the genome project, and the recently announced ability to clone animals.

The dangers of playing God with human subjects are greater still than with non-living systems. We can observe and manipulate atoms, molecules and perhaps even living cells without their awareness or concern about the outcomes of our efforts, but with animals and human beings, the subjects of our studies are the same as us. They are studying and judging us as we are studying and judging them. In psychology, the god-like stance of the psychologist has created warping at every level of science and morality. I have already begun to describe these undesirable activities as I have participated in them both as a teacher and clinical psychologist. An example of the god-like stance of psychologists may be found in many of the theories and activities that psychologists hold dear. For example, psychologists rarely credit their human subjects with the abilities that they hold sacred in themselves. George Kelly (1955) wrote that psychologists see themselves as being motivated by desires to explain human behavior but see the subjects of their studies as being driven by impulses and drives or being pushed and pulled by environmental stimuli. Isidor Chein (1972) similarly chastises behaviorists such as Skinner for casting the image of humanity in such a way as to be unable to choose between right and wrong and therefore to be beyond freedom and dignity. What is being described when Skinner insists that all behavior is either elicited or emitted by the human organism? Can poetry be either elicited or emitted or must it be created? I will return to the pathetic and, I believe, inaccurate image of humanity portrayed in most of psychology in Chapter 5 when I examine a typical introductory textbook of psychology. This critique will be preliminary to what a number of psychologists (Giorgi 1970, 1994; Helme 1992) see as their goal: the creation of a genuinely human psychological theory that does less damage to its subject matter.

SCIENCE WITH A HUMAN FACE

In order for an individual to be objective and follow the methods of science there must be an objective reality. One of the hallmarks of scientific thought is that the focus of science must be directed toward naturalistic phenomena. Science deals with the observable and if something is proposed to exist that is not observable then it is (1) treated as a hypothetical entity and (2) described as potentially observable and as a natural phenomenon. Any proposed entity that helps explain observed events becomes itself the object of technologies and methods that allows it to be directly observable. Science allows no explanations into its corpus that relate to any supernatural phenomena. There can be no gods, angels, devils, spirits, polter-geists, or miracles evoked as entities that explain or cause events to take place. Dualism is purged by scientists from the theories of science. In short, science must categorically avoid sacred stories. Religion and science have been, and still are, in intense competition for the loyalties of those they seek to serve. Any given scientist is free to believe in any spirits that he or she wishes but not in their roles as scientists.

When scientists take the position that only they have a privileged position from which to observe reality, have the methodology by which truth is to be discovered, or do nothing to refute the media's daily claims concerning the latest miracles of modern science, then they have turned themselves into supernatural dualities that deny the rules concerning observable natural phenomena. Everything studied by science is naturalistic but the scientists doing the studying. Scientists are human and every aspect of scientific work must be guided by that awareness. The methods of science represent a morality, a struggle to keep the enterprise as honest and unbiased as it can be but in terms that keep human beings honest and unbiased for much the same reasons—we seek to be honest and truthful so that we do not hurt others and in order to fulfill our ambitions to make the world a better place. We struggle to find moral and ethical rules by which to govern ourselves so that we can live together and prosper socially, economically, spiritually, and in other ways. Polanyi (1958: 30) writes, "Any attempt to rigorously eliminate our human per-spective from this picture of the world must lead to absurdity."

Scientists are as embedded in history and their cultures as any individuals and cannot and should not try to overcome or rise above their place in history. Rather, scientists must be aware of the history of their science and culture and examine these processes from a philosophical and analytical viewpoint. The analysis must help the scientist reject historical texts that merely glorify science, scientists, and scientific achievements and seek to indoctrinate others to the sacred stories of science in favor of historical analyses that are more critical in their focus (Wertsch 1997). The philosopher Imre Lakatos (quoted in Hacking 1981: 107) states, "Philosophy of science without history is empty, history of science without phi-losophy of science is blind."

Scientists are no more rational or emotional than any other group in society even if the organization of their thinking and the direction and expression of their emotions to the world are trained to standards rewarded by the subsociety of scientists. Jean Piaget (1950, 1952, 1954, 1957, 1973, 1975) and Robert Kegan (1982, 1994) point out that human thinking undergoes a number of transformations as biological and psychological development takes place. What science calls rational is in fact what Piaget refers to as formal operations and what Kegan calls Fourth Order Consciousness. Scientists generally utilize these forms of thinking when they study and experiment on the subjects of their interest. However, this hardly substantiates defining their thought processes as rational and those of the nonscientist as irrational or nonrational. In my own work (Simon 1986, 1994) I point out that each adult seems to utilize a wide range of developmental levels of thought and that scientists are as capable of utilizing preoperational thinking as anyone else. An examination of the behavior of scientists, especially when they are employing ideologies and pretending to be above the planet in which they reside will reveal much in the way of magical and childlike thinking.

More importantly, Morris Shanes (1992) and Kaisa Puhakka (1992) point out that much of what is described as scientific behavior is, in reality, those aspects of scientific work in which scientists justify their results to other scientists. What is crucial to science, and mostly overlooked, involves the processes of scientific discovery. The processes of following hunches, experiencing insights and new ways of seeing the commonplace in the world around them involve thought processes that could hardly be called rational. These processes are not even conscious or open to the scrutiny of formal operational analysis

If we continue to focus on the creative processes involved in making new discoveries we find that scientists are hardly unemotional. I would suggest that any scientists who are truly unexcited and lacking in passion about their work and area of interest would not be likely to make discoveries. It is true that in our culture scientists and professionals in general are supposed to appear unemotional but in reality that is hardly the case. David Kohn (1997) points out that Charles Darwin's exploration of the South American rain forests was motivated both by a passionate excitement aroused by the sight of these lush lands and the art and poetry of the romantic era of which he was a part. Let me quote scientist Albert Einstein in relating affect (and rationality) to scientific work: "The most beautiful and profound emotion we can experience is the sensation of the mystical. It is the power of all true science. He to whom the emotion is a stranger, who can no longer wonder and stand rapt in awe, is as good as dead. To know what is impenetrable to us really exists, manifesting itself as the highest wisdom and the most radiant beauty which our dull faculties can comprehend only in their most primitive forms, the feeling is at the center of true religiousness" (Barnett 1957: 105). Is it possible that the reason the works of Newton, Darwin, Freud, and Einstein have excited our imaginations is in part because their work was motivated by and reflects artistic passions as well as some sense that they also expand our knowledge of our world? My answer to this question is emphatically in the affirmative!

Finally we can examine the myth of the single method that will define true science. Science has long recognized that there can be no one method to ensure scientific success. For example, Karl Popper (1961) suggested that any theory called scientific must be falsifiable if it is to belong to true science. Astronomers immediately pointed out that it is unlikely that many hypotheses or theoretical concepts related to their field can ever be either directly tested or falsified. Many psychologists feel that adherence to the demands of logical positivism has strangled the development of any psychological approach trying to utilize human experience a variable in explaining human behavior. The philosopher Paul Feyerabend (1988) has argued that the search for a single method of scientific research has hampered the development of many aspects of the creativity necessary for real scientific work. I argue throughout this book, along with psychologists such as John Greenwood (1989) and J. A. R. Smith, R. Harré and L. Langenhove (1995) and numerous others, that if psychology defines itself as a human science then most of its current methods of research will have to be jettisoned. For now, let me suggest what might be necessary for science to develop and maintain itself as a human activity and not one plagued by adherence to the destructive myth of its belonging to a higher than human realm.

I began this book by suggesting that I require a psychology that can explain why poetry and art exit as products of the consciousness of some and not others. I conclude this chapter by suggesting that when we examine science as a human activity, we find that like art it involves the same creative processes. The theories of scientists are themselves narratives and other acts of creativity that tell a story about things observed by the scientist. Like any good story the theories of science always contain narrative truth not just empirically derived truths. Physicists now speak of mathematical descriptions of the phenomena that they encompass as having to be beautiful as well as accurate. Science has begun to understand what it has long recognized and that is it must always factor in the human being that is doing the observing as well as the thing being observed. In the early part of this century physicists such as Bohr and Heisenberg recognized that when they tried to study the basic particles that make up the universe their observations in part determined their results. Those studying quantum mechanics found that trying to measure atomic particles changed the direction or speed of the particle. They could either know the particles location or its speed, but not both. Scientists who study light have concluded that light is a wave if studied using one method but it is comprised of particles if another method is used. The physicists had discovered that while atoms and light are constructed by the laws of physics they cannot be known to the scientist except as they are reconstructed by the particular methods used to study atoms and light. When physicists turned to psychology for help in understanding the human factors that influence the observations scientists must make they experienced a field using the same methods that they used to study particles and other non-living, non-sentient materials. Physicists had discovered that they were living in the same plane of existence as the phenomena that they were studying but psychologists were not yet ready to admit the same for their own science.

Psychology needs to be a science and emulate the best aspects of the sciences from which it has evolved. It must be empirical and base its methods on firsthand observations. It must concern itself with phenomena that are naturalistic and avoid dualisms in its theoretical formulations. It must make its findings known to both scientific and non-scientific communities in language that is clear and appropriate to its subject matter. Psychology must recognize that its subject matter must be the creative acts of invention that accompany every moment of discovery which in turn reflect the personal, historical, political, and social context of the artist scientist. Psychology can then become a legitimate science as well as become the necessary element in the development of all sciences.

3 _____

THE MORALITY OF GODS
AND HUMAN BEINGS

INTRODUCTION

In the last chapter I discussed some of the problems created by science and psychology when scientists do not accurately portray their subject matter by invoking god-thing stories instead of basic human descriptions. Psychologists studying human beings are, in effect, studying other psychologists. We are all individuals who are aware that we are being studied, for whom being studied matters significantly, and who are studying the scientist as we ourselves are being studied. Unlike molecules and microbes, human behavior is based, in part, on the experiences and choices of the individuals involved in the study. Therefore, human beings can be understood and held responsible for their behaviors. Human beings constantly trying to explain, predict and control the world around them while judging the goodness and badness of that world. The assumptions we make about ourselves and other people that share our environments makes judging both necessary and appropriate. The judgments we make concerning human behaviors can only be expressed by the words "should" and "ought" (Perry London 1986) and taken collectively represent the moral system of those making the judgments. I argue that all human beings must be scientists if they are to survive and flourish, and must be judges if they are to justify how they survive, especially as they relate to their fellow human beings. It is at the nexus of science and morality that psychologists, who, if anyone, should know the difference between a description and a judgment and create the conditions that have warped both the science and morality of their field. Unless we deconstruct and untangle the assumptions created by the god-stance of our science, psychology will continue to be less of a science, of no real use to the other sciences (which we saw in the last chapter) and become dangerous to those it is supposed to benefit.

I am holding those who are scientists and especially psychologists to a higher standard than those who are not trained specifically in the sciences, but I am describing a problem that I believe is universal because of the need of all people to be both scientists and moralists in their lives. I have already begun to describe these problems as they have affected me as a teacher and a clinical psychologist but could also add descriptions as to how this has affected me and everyone I have ever met as we form all sorts of relationships including the political, economic, personal, and public. The problems begin when we confuse our roles as scientists with that of our roles as moral philosophers and begin to use descriptions as if they were judgments and our judgments as if they were descriptions. Most of us are unaware that we are confusing these two critical human activities, however, the confusion is no accident. It develops out of our need to rise above the human condition and assume that we have achieved the intellectual and moral perfection of a god or when we transform ourselves into something less than human by conceiving ourselves to be a machine, a puppet, or some other being incapable of being responsible for our own lives.

THE CONFUSION OF PSYCHOLOGICAL DESCRIPTIONS AND MORAL JUDGMENTS

I begin with the results of a lesson that introduces every course I teach. I place on the blackboard the following incomplete sentence: I am _____. I ask my students to describe themselves with as many words, phrases, and short sentences as they can think of in the time allotted. I walk out of the room for about five minutes and when I return I ask for volunteers read their lists of self-descriptions. I organize their responses on the board separating what I consider to be descriptions from what I consider to be judgments. I have been requiring students do this exercise ten to fifteen times a year for at least five years. What follows is distilled from several classes carrying out the assignment in the spring semester of 1997. It is typical of what my students produce in every class.

I am _____

Male	Teacher	Anxious	Intelligent	Honest
Female	Student	Confused	Hard working	Lazy
Black	Mother	Tired	Ambitious Shy	Tall
5'10"	Sister	Trying to understand	Short Weird	Loyal
160 lbs.	Brother	Sitting in class	Friendly	Outgoing
Blond haired	Musician	Depressed	Bitchy	Stubborn
Blue eyes	Christian	Reading the board	Sensitive	Crazy
	Jew	Wishing I was in bed	Interesting	Boring
	Muslim		Optimistic	Loveable

The lists are divided on the board forming columns. I've shortened the lists which, with an exuberant group, can get quite large.

I ask the reader, as I ask my students, if he or she agrees that the two sides of the board represent two distinct categories of words. If they do, I point out that I had requested only descriptions. If there are two separate categories only one can be descriptions. The other must belong to another set of definitions but is being treated as if it belongs to the category of descriptions. Since it is impossible and unnecessary to recreate the process by which my students redefine the wrongly categorized set of words I will present the results as I understand them. The words on the left are descriptions and represent all that can be known about human beings. The words on the right are moral judgments that pose as descriptions. The confusion with descriptive facts has profound meanings and produces equally profound consequences.

Why do I insist that the words on the left side of the board are descriptive and factual? First, they are all, in one way or another, capable of being experienced through the human senses and each carries no inherent value either positively or negatively. The first column contains descriptions of the physical appearance of an individual although male and female can also imply social roles connected with gender. Male and female could also have been placed in the second column as well. The second column contains things people do (and, therefore, are observable) but expressed in sociological terms. I would have to agree with those who object that the roles themselves are social constructions and are not directly observable, however, for the purposes of making a discrimination between judgments and descriptions these terms are better placed among the descriptions. The final column contains descriptions of observable actions carried out overtly by individuals or mental operations observable only to the individual performing the action, that is, wishing to be elsewhere. Finally, the last column contains a number of affective responses, such as feeling anxious, which are observable but only to the individual. I ignore the objections of behaviorists that internal cognitive and affective events cannot be consensually validated and therefore be must removed from any list of facts because to do so invalidates any phenomenological descriptions that I find essential in understanding human beings. I insist that we now have all of the elements that can exist to explain human behavior. I would have to add certain elements such as breathing to the first column to demonstrate that the body being described is a living, active biological structure without which there can be no psychological activity. Everything else that can be known about any human being comes from observations of overt and covert operations or actions and the affective consequences of those actions within the contexts in which they take place. These represent the conscious experience of any individual. If we can know the thoughts, memories, anticipations, wishes, and other psychological actions directed at the individual's past, present, and imagined future situations, as well as the emotions, drives, and other affective elements of response to those situations, we have all the necessary elements of an effective descriptive psychology. The development of such a psychology will be presented later in this book.

It is important to point out that the vast majority of what makes us psychological beings are overt motor actions or covert psychological processes that are also actions, which can only be described with the use of verbs. The judging of those behaviors would, therefore, have to take the form of adverbs as in "He played the piano beautifully." The only adjectives to be properly used would be applied to the physical characteristics of the individual which exist as nouns. Therefore, it is appropriate to say, "She has beautiful blond hair and blue eyes." It is not appropriate from this perspective to say, "He is a beautiful piano player." unless we are speaking of the player's physical characteristics. To use an adverb as if it were an adjective should sound as incorrect as saying, "She has blond hair beautifully."

If we return to the words produced by my students and placed on the right side of the board we find that they are not descriptions but judgments. Each term is an opinion concerning the value or worth of something. Unlike the facts just discussed which contain no essential value (there is no implied worth in having dark hair or blond hair, being a student or an aunt, wishing to be asleep or feeling anxious, or reading a book or a blackboard), being referred to as intelligent, weird, sensitive, crazy, or loyal usually invoke deep emotional responses that are either painful or pleasant. They are clearly establishing the value or worth of something.

But what are these judgments judging? If they were judging behavior, which is all that can be known experientially about an individual, then these words would be adverbs and since they are about what is being done by someone they would be moral judgments of that behavior. But these words are not adverbs, they are adjectives. They are directed toward a noun but a noun that does not refer to the physical corporeality of any individual. We must, therefore, conclude that they are judgments of some non-physical aspect of the individual, some thing that is perhaps described as mind stuff. I suggest that they are moral judgments of the essences that human beings seem to need to create and which are reflected by words such as soul, mind, self, ego, character, personality, and other terms that construct an agency or permanence capable of directing the actions or processes that make up our psychology.

The next chapter attempts to explain and resolve the paradox created by the fact that we experience our mental activities, which are always actions described by verbs as if they were substances described with nouns. For now I will merely assume that we transform our selves from verbs to noun out of necessity and deal with some of the consequences of creating this illusion of self, ego, soul, and kindred concepts. I suggest that we create and construct our selves into more substantial fare than can be described with a verb for many reasons, the most basic being our experience that we have the ability to choose to behave as we do. We also create a vision of ourselves as substance so that we may conceive of ourselves as agents capable of making choices and holding people responsible for the consequences of their actions. Without a belief that we are something we have neither a basis for our humanity nor our morality. Suffice it to say that there are other reasons that we create ourselves as we do including evolutionary and social forces.

It is the consequences of turning descriptions into moral judgments that requires attention. When we use moral judgments as if they were descriptions we render invisible the whole of what can be known psychologically. We automatically change differences between people into moral hierarchies, creating an illusion that we understand why people behave as they do, and justifying almost any actions taken by those assigned a higher moral worth against those judged to be of lower moral worth. We damage our science and warp the moral underpinnings of our social relationships. How do we achieve all of these negative consequences and what must be done to reverse the process?

I will first describe the process of rendering our psychological processes invisible. All that can be known about us psychologically are the actions we perform and the thoughts and emotions which make up the reasons for those actions. It is difficult to fathom the motives of our own behavior, and far more difficult to understand the reasons others behave as they do. By substituting a moral judgment for descriptions of the actual psychological processes the difficult struggle to understand the psychological processes becomes suddenly moot. For example, let us begin with the observation that when John finished his dinner in a restaurant he paid his bill but left without leaving a tip for the waitress. This is an action that requires an explanation but which in our culture might also lead to moral disapproval. If we begin with the sentence, "John left no tip for the waitress," we have an observed behavior with no explanation. Did John disapprove of the waitress's performance and is he expressing his disapproval, did he order more than he could afford to pay for and still leave a tip, or is the waitress John's sister who insisted that her brother not leave her a gratuity? We have no answer to these questions but we can still disapprove of John's morality in this circumstance and probably will since we hold John responsible for his actions. We might then say, "John behaved in a stingy manner toward the waitress."

If we left the process at this point we might be accused of prejudging poor John since it is clear that we do not know John's motives for stiffing the waitress. But that is not what will happen in most instances. What will usually follow is the statement, "John is stingy." (The sentence, "John behaved stingily." will never even be uttered.) If an hour later we are asked, "Why do you think John did not tip the waitress?" we might answer, "Because John is a stingy person." By turning the adverb "stingily" into the adjective "stingy" and by judging the constructed essence (soul, self, ego) that is John rather than his behavior we have simultaneously made a moral judgment and created the illusion that we have explained John's behavior. What is now invisible are John's thoughts and feelings concerning the restaurant, the waitress, his relationship with the waitress, the history of John and waitresses, the nature of the situation in which John found himself in this restaurant, and a countless number of other variables that might have aided John's decision not to tip the waitress. We have achieved a deal in which any semblance of a scientific understanding of John's behavior has been lost. (Later that night John awoke with a headache and a hangover from having had too much to drink earlier that evening and realized that he had left the restaurant without tipping that very fine waitress. He returned the next evening, made his apologies, and left a tip twice his normal amount. The waitress explained his behavior by saying, "He is a very nice, generous, and well-brought up gentleman.")

The second consequence of using moral labels as if they were explanations of behavior has now come into view. John has moved from being "cheap" and "stingy" to being "nice" and "generous." His social status has also improved; he is now much better positioned in the vertical hierarchy of social relationships. The third consequence of our two-for-one deal has also made its appearance as well—we are now justified in seeking out such a fine fellow rather than avoiding or shunning a scoundrel. John has been judged and categorized and we have an explanation of his present and even future behavior as well as a justified set of automatic actions to be taken toward him. There are literally tens of thousands of terms similar to "stingy" and "generous" in the English language that are used in precisely the same way as these words were used about John. This same process pervades the so-called science of psychology with terrible consequences for the field and those it purports to help. I will again redescribe the process and the consequences of using judgments as descriptions in clinician and college professor.

I begin with the sentence, "Mary claims to hear voices that no one else can hear." We do not know why Mary hears voices speaking to her, and in our modern culture we assume that there are no external voices speaking to her. Mary is somehow constructing these voices by herself. We do not know her motives or her means of carrying out this feat but we can judge Mary for her actions if we say, "Mary is behaving psychotically." What I was trained to say, however, that "Mary is psychotic because she is hearing voices." What begins as a judgment of Mary's behavior is now an explanation for the behavior being judged and the psychological processes that inform Mary's actions are now rendered invisible. In the case of the clinical psychology model in which I was trained, another step was added when it stated that "Mary has a psychosis." The adjective is now constructed into a noun and psychologists and psychiatrists can now hunt down, measure, and excise the psychosis as if it has corporeal reality. Psychologists with ink blots and other projective techniques make manifestly real, at least to themselves, the nature and dimensions of the incurable psychosis now afflicting poor Mary. (If Mary is crazy for constructing voices and treating them as real why aren't the psychologists, psychiatrists, and other mental health workers who construct psychoses, literalize them, and treat them as real, equally crazy?) Once diagnosed with a psychosis or as a psychotic Mary has been cast into the lowest strata of the social hierarchy (Farber 1993; Goffman 1961; Szasz 1970, 1987; Sarbin and Mancuso 1980; Simon 1994), justifications are in place to deprive Mary of her liberties, dignity, and other human qualities. Based on a narrow series of observations in a hospital setting, with an often unwilling patient, the professionals believe that they can explain and predict her behavior in all situations.

Finally, let us examine one of the terms most loved by psychologists and educators that has done more damage to children and adults than perhaps any other moral label: intelligence. I begin with the descriptive sentence: "Tommy solves 25 math problems in an hour while Sally solves 1 math problem in an hour." Do we have any idea why this fact is so? Not only do we not know how the children feel about doing math problems, or why they feel as they do, but we have no idea how either of them, or anyone else, is able to solve math problems. All we know is that human beings solve such problems and that wide variations in individual differences exist for how they are solved. If we were honest about our ignorance we could begin to seek the cognitive bases of mathematical achievement and begin to assess their motivational differences as well. But instead we label the children involved and use the label as if it were the explanation of both the child's success in solving the computations and the differences between the successes of the two. "Tommy behaves more intelligently than Sally." This is transformed into, "Tommy is more intelligent than Sally." or conversely "Sally is less intelligent than Tommy." The adverb "intelligently" has been changed to the adjective "intelligent." As with "psychosis" the final transformation involves turning the adjective into a noun. "Tommy has more intelligence than Sally." Intelligence is now a concrete reality to the educator and psychologists who actually create intelligence tests measure both children's intelligence. Intelligence is now given as the reason we can compute; the amount of intelligence allows us to explain the differences between the number of problems computed correctly or in a given amount of time.

Not only do we now believe we can explain how learning takes place but (as with psychosis) we now have an intellectual and moral basis for treating Tommy and Sally differently in school. New judgments may even be added to the old to create very different perceptions and treatments of Tommy and Sally. Tommy may be labeled gifted and Sally diagnosed learning disabled or perhaps even borderline retarded. Teachers, school psychologists, counselors and administrators regularly differentiate children on the bases of how much intelligence and how many mental handicaps a child possesses and to what degree or amount they are owned by the child.

Based on a series of observations in a test situation in which the child did not even volunteer, and which taps into only those behaviors valued in school situations, professionals now make all manner of predictions as to how these children learn in all types of situations. The psychological test is used to make a moral judgment and the judgment is constructed into a non-existent thing called intelligence. Even with the efforts of psychologists such as Howard Gardner (1983) and Robert Sternberg (1985) to broaden the types of behaviors to be included as representative of intelligence, psychologists and educators are measuring a product of their own fantasies because intelligence does not exist as a noun.

Robyn Dawes (1994) refers to the whole so-called process of diagnosis as "a house of cards" while R. D. Laing (1967, 1969) calls it a degredation ceremony. I am regularly overwhelmed with a sense of shame when I think of the thousands of children and adults I labeled as morally and intellectually deficient while unable or unwilling to see the dishonesty and danger involved in my use of psychological tests as I diagnosed children struggling to solve problems related to school and home. Instead of recognizing my ignorance I utilized a set of socially created constructs to explain how the problems belonged in the children instead of between them and the more powerful authorities in their lives. Both the psychological processes that motivated these youngsters and the social contexts in which these thoughts and emotions were appropriate remained unknowable to me and to those who now tried to fix or cure these children. I will never again play God in the same way again!

Any child or parent of a child so constructed can attest to the enormous consequences that flow from the transformation of moral labels into descriptive concepts. In poorer school districts meager resources are often shifted from the less intelligent to the more intelligent creating a warehousing of inferior learners and an enriched education for the superior learners. Even where financial hierarchies are not created the attitude of teachers can be quite different when it comes to setting standards or goals for the more and less intelligent. I have spent the latter part of my professional career teaching students who do not see that it is possible and morally correct to take a year longer to learn a course of study but rather believe that little or no effort is warranted because "I am not as smart as my sister." or "I am not as intelligent as I am supposed to be." or "I am the dumbest kid in this school."

MORALITY

By the time I have finished trying to get my students to comprehend the difference between a moral judgment and a psychosocial description, I must deal with the many students who believe that I am arguing that it is morally wrong to make any judgments. While it is an incorrect interpretation of my position, it is one reflected everywhere in our society. For example, as a student tries to write an essay on why mental illness is a myth, she proclaims, "Since we are all individuals then our meaning to the same situation will obviously vary . . . that does not mean that one response is either right or wrong it is simply . . . just different there is no right or wrong, there is only what that particular person sees as being right or is comfortable with for that situation . . . since we are all human we must all be entitled to this freedom, so why would anyone want to judge it? If society could only remember this and reflect on their humanism then they would know that judging these responses as right or wrong is immoral. It is immoral because all of us have our own value system and no one is better than anyone else . . . the mere fact of judging another person is immoral." Another student, this one older and an honors graduate, argues just as forcefully that it is immoral to make moral judgments and in great passion questions, "Who has the right to judge a person's behavior? Who determines what is correct or incorrect?"

My students require answers to their questions concerning the legitimacy of making moral judgments. What are morals and what is the relationship between descriptive science and moral philosophy and religion? On what authority do we make moral judgments? On what authority should we accept the judgments of those making judgments? I believe that the position my students have taken, and which is expressed by many in university systems including faculty and administrators, leaves all of us in an untenable position. If we understand all and judge nothing might we be saying that to understand all is to forgive all? Do we agree with Dostoevsky when he states, "Without God all things become lawful"? I believe that it is impossible to take a stand on any issue without that stand being moral and there can be no stands unless one has a moral position from which to take it.

A description involves a person's experience of the descriminanda and manipulanda (Chein 1972) of the objects and events in his or her life. Desciminanda involve those aspects of experience by which we can tell objects and events one from another. Shape, color, size, hardness, position, weight, movement, speed, and temperature are descriminanda. Manipulanda are those experiences of actions permitted by objects and events as we interact with them. Things may be pick-upable and put-downable, liftable, throwable, sit-down-uponable, lay-down-uponable, driveable, rideable, flyable, readable, typeable, throw-ourselves-offable, loveable, hateable, understandable, incomprehensible, or any of a very large set of psychological and physical act-uponables. In short, that which can be described refers us back to that which can be known about people, namely that which comprises their experiences of things and those behaviors which express their experiences. When we describe, we shift the emphasis from the experiencing agency to the things and events being experienced.

Our judgments follow our experiences: they express the value of that which has been experienced. The descriptive basis of judgments are to be found in the affective consequences for an individual as a result of some experience. In general, those experiences that produce pain, diminish or end life, liberty, and the pursuit of happiness will be judged as bad, while those that decrease pain, increase pleasure or happiness, and add to life and liberty will be judged as good. In general, these judgments will be made by the individual to whom the experience is taking place, or to those with whom the experiencing individual shares a common set of interests. One individual's pleasure may be the cause of another's pain. Under these circumstances we may predict that these two individuals will have opposite and irreconcilable judgments. One individual may judge an experience as good because of its immediate consequences while another might see it as bad because they believe they can predict long-term consequences not foreseen by the other. Such is often the case in disagreements between parents and their children, teachers and their students.

When we make judgments and hold ourselves or others as responsible for the consequences that cause pleasure and pain, happiness and unhappiness, life and death, our judgments are moral in nature. Moral judgments are directed toward the agency that created the conditions of experience, especially when we assume that that agency had intent, and then capacity to create such experience. It is the function of moral judgments to decrease those actions causing painful experiences and reward those actions that increase life and pleasure. When pain is inflicted on those agencies whose actions are judged to be bad such infliction will be judged as good not bad since the assumption underlying such punishment is that in the long run there will be a net increase in pleasure, life, liberty, and the pursuit of happiness. Morals can also be conceptualized as social rules which embody judgments that increase pleasure and decrease pain. Morality, conceived in social terms, has as its function a shaping action on the various agencies in that social system so that they will choose to create more good consequences and fewer bad consequences. Morals as rules also underlay the human search for justice and fairness, which grow directly from our awareness that what is judged good for one may be the cause of what is bad for another.

Judgments are always opinions as they have no existence independently of the person(s) creating them. Once placed into language judgments exist as words which may be spoken, or otherwise recorded. But a judgment can never be given an objective empirical existence as those things and events that provide the basis of sensory and motor experience. Therefore, to accept a judgment as true is to commit an act of faith no matter how many individuals agree that some thing, event, action, or person is good or bad, worthy or unworthy, beautiful or ugly. The acceptance of the truth of any judgment is an act of faith. When we accept the judgments of another person we are investing our faith in that individual. Since acts of faith can have significant consequences, it behooves us to know and understand those moral authorities in whom we invest our faith. Moreover, it is also in our interests to understand the manner in which the authorities create their moral stances.

It would seem to be in our interest to demand those who make moral judgments or create moral rules to make clear the descriptions of experience that preceded those judgments. Who was hurt or helped by a given action, how was their pain or pleasure created, what was the nature of their pain or pleasure, and by what means and capacities did the various agencies carry their intentions out. In the case of those authorities predicting long-term consequences that differ from those experienced in the short term, just how are such predictions arrived at and with what confidence might we all agree that such predictions will be borne out. If a judgment is made as to the justice of a decision it would be necessary to describe just who got what as a consequence of the decision. It would, therefore, seem to be in our interests to demand those making moral judgments that the empirical science upon which such judgments are made be made explicit and kept separate from the judgments based upon them. In this way the morality of the authority making and carrying out judgments could be justified by all who are involved with the decisions of the authority. Such an arrangement of description and judgment is the exception and not the rule. The functioning of authority and authority's justification of its own actions operates in a different manner.

We, as a species, have a need to rise above our human condition that includes so much pain, unhappiness, death, and limitations on our liberties and freedom of action. We require the experience of being agencies but often experience unbearable guilt created by the negative consequences of our own actions or the helplessness experienced when our abilities do not permit us to reach our goals. We find unbearable the experience of ambiguities created by our endless ignorance where the future is concerned (especially the future that extends beyond our own predicted and certain death). We wish for the feeling of certainty rather than the anxiety and dread that fills our consciousness when we cast our imagination forward in time. We require a sense that we are permanent rather than some momentary flash of existence that flowers and disappears in the blink of a cosmic eye. We yearn for justice and fairness, at least where we and our loved ones are concerned, and find the moral outrage that follows our perceptions of injustice as hard to live with as the anxiety that pervades the moment to moment ambiguity inherent in our awareness. For all of these reasons and more we create a transcendent level of existence and then try to become or find someone to be a member of that omnipotent, omniscient, and morally pure level of existence.

By confusing our judgments with descriptions, by transferring the judgment qua description into an assessment of the essence of the individual performing the action rather than the action itself, and by creating nouns out of verbs we create a hierarchy in which some have more wisdom and morals (notice that morals also have gone from actions of judging or socially maintained rules to things that are carried around by people in measurable amounts) and others have less of these essential qualities. The conscious experience that people have of each other changes from one human being interacting with another to a being of greater inherent worth interacting with a being of lesser inherent worth. We have, therefore, taken a step in creating beings that rise above and others sink beneath the human condition. Not only do the beings above no longer have any need to justify their actions descriptively but the dehumanized things beneath the human condition have no right or even conscious need to demand the justification.

Science dies in these situations with psychology dying first and most grievously. Without descriptions of the thoughts and affects that are basic to human motivation, science, and morality there can be no psychology. But worse are the moral crises created when beings of superior substances deal with those of inferior substances. We find ourselves in trouble when we cannot see that the moral rules of the authority benefit only the authority and are noxious to our selves. When some individuals see themselves as morally superior to others we find ourselves dealing with the worst acts of human degradation that include war, slavery, and in our own century, the mass extermination of whole groupings of human beings in the holocaust and other mini-holocausts that dot the temporal landscape. Under these circumstances we can literally define what kind of evil species we can be in the name of morality.

We need a moral compass if we are to avoid the kind of consequences that emerge when human beings degrade and destroy themselves and others in the name of morality. But we need a morality that leaves intact the very processes that define human activity and agency. We, therefore, need a morality that is based on the descriptions found in science, particularly those revealed by a psychological science of human beings. If we need a human psychology then we need a morality of human beings as well, one that coordinates itself by judging the activities of human beings as human beings and not creatures resembling gods or things. I demand that we need a morality that judges as immoral the processes that creates gods and things out of human beings even as it demands that we understand these processes as scientists.

It is at this juncture that I introduce my students to the concepts of moral humanism and begin the long and arduous process of helping the students who have been treated as if they were things both understand the psychology of their thingness and their need of moral humanism to restore themselves and their relationships to the joys and sorrows of being just human. It is my goal to help them achieve the status of both psychological scientist and humanistic moral philosopher.

HUMANISM

There are many forms of humanism in many contexts, in many societies, and at various times throughout history. Humanism appears in sacred, and secular contexts. Historically, humanism begins to appear in written form with the emergence of the great organized religions, although the principles of humanism remained subtexts to other more dominant themes. Humanism has historically appeared in religious texts, however, explicit forms of secular humanism emerged with the enlightenment and have become increasingly dominant with the emergence of modernity. The practice of humanistic principles has been equally difficult to realize in religious contexts as in secular ones, in our present era as in the distant past. Humanism can be stated as follows:

> All human life is to be treated as precious, with no life to be treated as more or less precious. (The religious justification of humanism involves the notion that we have a soul given by God that demands we be treated as precious. The secular justification demands that we treat ourselves and others as if we all have a soul even if we recognize the soul as metaphorical rather than as actual.) All human beings are to be treated in ways that maximize the development of those qualities that best define their being human. The qualities that best define what it is to be human involve the unique form of human conscious experience which permits us to make choices and therefore be responsible for our own actions. Our humanity is maximized to the degree to which we develop our capacity to exercise our freedoms and liberties by making informed choices and the degree to which we accept responsibility for the consequences of the choices we make. The unique form of human consciousness creates unique needs that also define the human being—a need to see ourselves as substantive, to believe that we are agencies capable of acting upon our world, dignity, social justice and fairness, forgiveness, compassion, redemption, and creativity.

There are many philosophical and psychological problems raised by the definition of humanism that must be explicated and discussed if we are to hope for a realization of life lived according to humanistic principles. There seems to a very widespread belief in the value of humanism (and many hold themselves forth as humanists),but there are few instances in which humanism is widely practiced. I am not only talking about governments and religions that proclaim their humanism and then actively subvert their own stated values, but practices such as modern psychotherapy and education where teachers and therapists become horrified and enraged when it is suggested that they do not practice what they preach. It has been the theme of this book, the very reason for its existence, to point out how labeling of patients mentally ill, or students lazy and unintelligent, violates the fundamental tenets of moral humanism. If the reader accepts that such a discrepancy exists in his or her own life then certain fundamental questions become immediately apparent. The first set of questions might ask whether it is possible that we consciously wish for a humanistic world but on a less conscious level wish the world to be otherwise? Are we fundamentally ambivalent or even hypocritical on this issue? Or is our ambivalence or sheer ignorance responsible for our not having found the means to put humanistic values into daily practice? The second question, which if answered in the affirmative would render the first set moot, asks if it is possible that humanism exists only in principle but is not possible in actuality? In principle we can build a ladder to the moon, in actuality we cannot. I discuss the second question first since my answer determines if there is any reason to try and answer the first.

Is the human experience of having choices an illusion or does it describe a scientifically acceptable set of causes in much the same way as gravity is seen as making events happen? This question has been debated down through the centuries in terms of the free will of human beings. The debate has a long history with many of its chapters written with rancor, confusion, and urgency. It is impossible, therefore, for a book of modest size to describe in any detail the history of this debate or a psychologist of modest intellect to find a resolution. However, it is impossible to ignore the debate or not express one's own personal solution, however inadequate that solution may be to anyone else. How we conceive of ourselves as human beings determines how we treat ourselves as human beings. Without some notion that we are indeed agencies and have some degree of free will, that is, our choices matter, we cannot treat ourselves as human as the definition of humanism demands. Without a description of ourselves as capable of at least some degree of freedom we cannot hold ourselves responsible or worthy of dignity or genuine creativity. Without a humanistic underpinning we become things and hence the questions of morality become moot. Therefore, I feel compelled to treat myself and others as having free will regardless of how elegant and forceful some arguments may be to the contrary, or how inadequately I make my case for my beliefs. I have to believe that free will is either a reality or a possibility even when as a scientist I believe otherwise or else I cannot see myself or others as human.

The arguments concerning free will lie along a continuum that ends in two extreme sets of contentions, both of which I reject. On one side are those for whom the idea of human choice seems to be inconsistent with what might be called materialistic determinism. There are two interrelated assumptions, implicit or explicit, to this viewpoint. The first is that legitimate causation can only come from material substances and be expressed through the laws of physics, chemistry, and biology. The second is that at any given moment the events of the present were caused by the events that preceded them. Both assumptions can be seen in many psychological theories, for example the assumptions concerning mental illness as expressed in modern psychiatric theory. The real causes of psychiatric disorders can be found in anomalies or as yet undiagnosed diseases of the brain and the causes of these diseases are either in prior assaults on the brain or psychological traumas that occurred in childhood.

My arguments against the determinists derives from my understanding of the ideas of the psychologist, Isidor Chein (1972) and Brent Slife (1993, 1994), whose seminal works are required reading for anyone wrestling with these issues. While it is true that psychological variables derive from the physical, chemical, and biological (they are technically caused by these factors) once they come into existence they are as real and determining as any other set of forces. A problem exists when scientists do not define the term determinism and implicitly assume that only physical and biological variables can be determinate. The changes we human beings set in motion are as potent as any other set of determining forces that exist. Our desires, wishes, and reasons for behaving are both naturalistic and materialistic even if our experience of them is not. I shall return to the issue of subjectivity and materialism in subsequent chapters. Therefore, the idea of free will does not argue with a deterministic view of the world, it broadens it.

A second solution to the problem of free will involves reinterpreting the Western version of time. Time is considered from a linear point of view in which there is a past, present, and future. The cause of things are in the past and therefore it is the past that causes the present. There are serious logical and empirical problems in conceiving time in this way, however intuitively correct it might appear. (Isn't it true that the past is behind us, the present is now, and the future has yet to happen?) To argue this way is to argue that all events that have ever occurred, as well as all future events, were determined at some distant historical point that might be considered the prime causation. If one sees the big bang as the first event then all subsequent events are merely subsidiary to that event. Under this argument not only can we rid ourselves of psychology as a legitimate science but, we can also dispense with chemistry and biology (and if psychology goes why not sociology and all the other sciences as well). If the first event is physical, and the only cause, then only physics has a right to exist and only a very limited version of physics at that. History becomes the only legitimate science!

Slife points out that the linear view of time destroys the concept of time itself. If the past no longer exists, and the future has not yet happened, then there is only the present. But how long is the present? Is it an hour, a day, a year or any other arbitrary amount of time we wish it to be? Or is time the point between that which no longer exists and that which has not yet happened? That might make the present a nanosecond or some other point too small to measure. Time under this conception simply disappears and for most of us that is counterintuitive and nonsensical.

How then do we escape this quagmire? I suggest that we stop abstracting and separating time from the actual events whose changes in space and transformations in quality are the actual measurement of time. Time is change and nothing more or less than change! If we stop separating time from actual events, just as we stop separating the soul or mind stuff from the body we restore time to its naturalistic and nondualistic status. The past can then be considered not causative but as providing the antecedent conditions for the present. If time is change then the past is in the present to the degree that all past changes and transformations can account for present observations. It satisfies our view of the past as past, but also allows us to connect the past to the present. Most of us feel as if the past pervades the present. However, to say that there have been changes in the past is not to say that either change or time has ceased happening in the present. There is still change taking place but the changes we undergo at the moment represent a real present. The causes of present change are those happening together in the moment that exists even though this moment's causes will be the next moment's antecedent conditions, and if we agree that human motives cause change then the decisions each of us makes at the moment must be seen as causes and, therefore, we must have free will.

Not only have we rescued some notion of free will but we have rescued psychology as a science. In the beginning all change was physical. At a given level of complexity brought about by transformative rules of which we are not clear, chemical reactions emerged with new sets of properties and new potentials for transformation as time continued to evolve. The emergence of biological phenomena, in turn, gave rise to new properties which were psychological and bore the qualities of consciousness and self-consciousness. There are legitimate bases for physics, chemistry, biology, and psychology to exist as natural sciences. They are all related and therefore reducible one to the other, although the reductionism here means understanding the developmental relationship of these sciences not obliterating younger sciences in favor of older ones (Weinberg 1992).

I also reject arguments on the other end of the continuum that suggest human beings have an infinite free will and that none of our behavior is determined by the various antecedent events of our individual and collective histories. Such a position suggests that we are gods, as it is only in sacred stories I interpret to be myths that god-like consciousness both precedes and determines the material world. Instead, I take an intermediary position that suggests that human consciousness is an emergent and developmental concept that has its history in materialistic processes, is part of the naturalistic world, and as it develops, it widens, deepens, and plays an increasingly deterministic and causative role in the situations in which it exists. In the final analysis, however, I realize that my adherence to this position is based on faith, and is a sacred story that to others may well be a myth. In the end, however, I find I must hold on to my belief that my students possess free will which may provide the only hope that they will eventually come to believe and behave as if they have a free will.

I now return to the second set of questions that ask why we do not put into practice our faith in moral humanism and how we might achieve such a practice were we to understand the impediments to our motivation. I will bring this chapter to a close by providing my answers in general philosophical terms. We will return to these questions, however, when I discuss them using specific psychological and sociological descriptions. Ultimately, morality involves the judgments of psychological and sociological phenomena. Eventually all moral discussions refer back to the descriptive psychological and social phenomena upon which they are based. This brings me to the basic reason why I believe that we do not want to or know how to implement our stated desires for moral humanism: We are so desirous of rising above and sinking below our human condition that we refuse to accept humanism. To do so places us squarely in the human condition with all of the psychological and social experiences that we find so unbearably painful. Because our psychology is often based on the moral judgments that we confuse with descriptions, we lack even the basic language to begin discussing how to reach our goals.

We cannot hold others as precious unless we also hold precious those psychological processes that permit human beings to make choices. I believe these processes to be our cognitive and motor skills as well as the emotions aroused whenever we interact with and act upon our environments. We cannot maximize the development of thought and other motor skills unless we question the specific means by which human beings develop such skills. I believe that these ultimately take the form of firm loving adults where love is defined as unconditional acceptance Carl Rogers (1961) and Robert Kegan (1982) implicitly expresses it as taking delight in the conscious developments of others.

We must also recognize that to hold ourselves as precious does not mean that we are all the same or that we will desire the same things at the same time: it is to recognize that conflict is inevitable and that we will inevitably be drawn into conflict with one another. The manner in which some individuals satisfy their desires will be hurtful to others and will, therefore, be judged as immoral. We must recognize our need for mechanisms of conflict resolution and for authority whose responsibilities will include both determinations of right and wrong and enforcement of our shared rules of behavior. Perhaps our greatest challenge to maintain humanism will involve demanding that authority describe the empirical details that go into their judgments. Who did what wrong to whom, who was hurt, and how specifically were they hurt? Who lost what and who gained what? And finally, can we continue to see as human those who have failed to develop psychological qualities that define our sacred souls and those who have transgressed against others and violated our humanistic norms? I believe this only begins to be achieved in political democracies where people live as equals under voluntarily created laws. I further believe that the philosopher John Dewey (1929) was correct in noting that science and democracy flourish best in the presence of the other.

If we are to develop the capacity for humanistic practices we must develop the human capacity for making informed choices and what is expected of human beings morally. Responsibilities must also be described and made explicit. There must be clearly defined standards that represent our version of good and bad, higher and lower, quality and trash. These must be stated in specific descriptive terms. To impose standards on individuals and not help achieve them is to enslave and oppress by the use of authority; to allow freedom without guiding the moral directions of those freedoms is to invite chaos and enslave individuals with their own impulses and desires.

The reason for imposing standards on children, students, and all those we seek to help lies in my middle of the road position on free will and my view that free will depends on an individual knowing that choices can be made. I often see children whose lives contained nothing but rejection, cruelty, and hurt. How can I hold them to the same standards as those whose lives have been more fortunate? How can I expect a person who has no knowledge of a particular thing to be familiar with it and choose it over other things? Isn't it the height of cruelty, hypocrisy, and oppression to do so? At such moments I do believe that person's choices are determined but it is at that same moment when it is most important that we, as authority, take our stand and hold such youngsters responsible. We do not hold them responsible or blame them for their present actions but as expectations for their future choices! How can children be directed toward what we believe is right unless they experience what it is we believe is right? How can they experience the events or behaviors we define as right unless we insist that the events and behaviors be experienced! Only by taking a moral stand can we have authority and present experiences for children that create the conditions that make free will possible. Gertrude Himmelfarb (1994: 43) quotes the philosopher Tocqueville describing the necessity of maintaining the idea of free will: "It is important not to let this idea [free will] grow dim, for we need to raise men's souls, not to complete their prostration."

If I have now provided a justification for why there must be morality and why I believe moral humanism represents the best of many possible moralities, then I must also answer my students demand to know by what authority I make these moral claims. The answer is simple, but perhaps not very satisfying. I make these claims on my own authority, as there is according to my beliefs no higher authority upon which I can depend. God is dead, suggested Nietzsche, and this is the very place where his death is most missed. If, as I have argued, all judgments are merely the opinions of human beings, then there is no higher authority for human beings to turn to when establishing moral judgments and the rules and laws that derive from them. It is both the curse and blessing of democracy that we have the freedom to create our own laws but then must live with what we know benefits some and not others. Only a benevolent and just God can create totally fair moral rules. Only an all-knowing God has the wisdom to always choose correctly. Therefore, each of us must develop those skills that permit us to be an informed moral authority ready to engage the moral opinions of their fellow human beings.

The death of God has engendered crises throughout society and affects every social endeavor including religion, law, education, and in this instance science. What are we to do without authority or a privileged position from which to make statements of truth or morality? The postmodern crisis in science and education is expressed by the statements and positions of extreme moral relativism that my students regularly demonstrate. Who has the right to judge or say what is true? I agree with the philosopher Richard Rorty (1991: 29) when he states, "I have been arguing that we pragmatists should grasp the ethnocentric horns of the dilemma. We should say that we must, in practice, privilege our own group, even though there can be no noncircular justification for doing so. We must insist that the fact that nothing is immune from criticism does not mean that we have to justify everything."

I state the values I try to live by and then as I work with children and those in distress try to find a humanistic way to enforce those rules. I rely on the hope, in terms of enforcement, that when individuals experience themselves being treated humanistically, (that is, with love and respect, with appeals to their better selves, with arguments that make explicit the psychological theory that precedes my morality) will convince these individuals to join me in a common developmental task.

I describe the developmental psychology that may explain how people learn to make choices and how and why they develop into moral beings with such different notions of morality. I also describe why some individuals become scientists and poets, and others fail to achieve these humanistically important modes of being in the world. We need to understand why some live in god stories that seem to benefit everyone but themselves and others live as puppets, slaves and as other types of things when it appears that they could choose to live as full human beings. Finally,

I begin the task of explaining what it takes to help others achieve human status as a scientist or poet, avoiding the traps that lead them to seek godhood or thingness as their way of being in the world.

4 _____

PSYCHOLOGY, BIOLOGY, AND SOCIOLOGY

INTRODUCTION

In this chapter I define the proper domain of scientific human psychology. I have already stated that for psychology to be scientific it must be naturalistic, non-dualistic, amenable to empirical study, and capable of describing beings that attempt to explain their own behavior as scientists and as creatures that might write and love poetry. At the same time, my human psychology must conform to my moral beliefs in humanism. The demands of moral humanism involve painting a picture of beings that can evaluate both their own behavior and that of others, and make choices based on those evaluations. My theory must be able to describe beings capable of responsibility, worthy of dignity and creativity, be judged for their success in living up to their responsibilities. In addition, I believe a theory of human psychology must also meet a number of other criteria which flow from the demands that we be scientific, artistic, and moral. My theory must be able to state in descriptive terms the psychological processes that make science, poetry, and moral judgments possible and how they achieve these ends. Since science, poetry, and morality are all products that reflect meaning, we must be able to describe beings that seek and create meaning as basic to their way of life.

Moreover, since many individuals do not reveal much in the way of science, poetry, or humanistic morality we must be able to answer two additional sets of questions. First, we must ask why individual differences exist in these areas. Are we dealing with discrete processes that are to be found in some and not others, or are we dealing with processes that undergo development making it vital that we understand not only how human beings differ but how development plays a role in the emergence of these differences? Second, we must ask how such differences in development come into existence and as teachers, therapists, and most importantly parents, how can we influence these individual differences in development to make sure that science, poetry, and moral humanism that define our lives (and which we hold so dear) has the best chance of emerging in those individuals who also define our existence and the reasons for our being. We must understand what the psychologist Michael Mahoney (1991: 3) refers to as our collective "human change processes."

Finally, I believe that once the domain of the psychological is established, we must define the relationship between psychological processes and those of the biological on the one hand and the social and cultural on the other. We are biological beings; the result of a long evolutionary process. We need to understand our psychological processes from two developmental perspectives: (1) our own individual development, and (2) our development as a member of a species which is itself the end result of a very long developmental set of processes. Perhaps most importantly we must be able to describe the relationship between our biological form and function and our psychological state of being without disconnecting the latter from the former or reducing the latter to the former.

At the same time, we must be aware that from the moment of conception our development takes place within a context comprised of other human beings. We are, until birth, biologically enfolded within another being whose behavior is determined in part by both her psychology and the demands placed on her as a pregnant woman by her culture. From the moment of our births our psychological processes are enfolded within the psychological awareness of our mothers, fathers, siblings, close and distant relatives, the communities, and the larger cultural institutions that make up our society. We must be aware of how our individuality is shaped by sociocultural forces without detaching our psychology from these forces or reducing our psychology to them.

In the last chapter my solution to problems relating psychology to morality involved taking a position on the free will controversy. In order to establish the relationship of psychology to biology and sociology two perennial problems affecting psychology will also be discussed and solved. These are the nature-nurture controversy and the mind-body problem. My solution to these problems, which will not agree with some, allows me to create some coherence to my theoretical musings. But whatever solutions I have been able to come up with have come into existence, in part, because of my growing familiarity with three newly emerging, often contradictory perspectives on the human condition: cognitive-affective constructivism, evolutionary psychology, and social constructionism. I see these three developing fields of inquiry as metatheories with the potential of establishing a single paradigm for the field of psychology that can replace the multiple perspectives and cult of personality and hero worship which have defined the field for many decades.

Cognitive constructivism takes the position that was explicated earlier when I suggested that every scientist is a human being that is incapable of seeing the world from anything other than a human perspective. The way in which human beings discover meaning in the world is reflected by the manner in which meaning is constructed. We see a world organized by us according to a wide variety of developmental characteristics, needs, technologies and languages employed to describe it. I present a more detailed picture of constructivsm when I present a theory of psychology in the next chapter, but for now I merely suggest that it is constructivist theory that permits us to analyze the psychological processes that define consciousness as the central concern of psychology and consciousness as comprised of the meaning-seeking and meaning-making processes that define human beings. The interested reader is referred to seminal works in cognitive constructionism by George Kelly (1955); Jean Piaget (1950, 1952, 1954, 1957, 1973, 1975); and Michael Mahoney (1985, 1991) as well as works which extended the constructivist ideas to include affective processes, Jean Piaget (1981); Richard Lazarus (1991) and Laurence Simon (1986, 1994).

Evolutionary psychology and social constructionism have, in effect, collapsed the walls between biology and psychology on the one hand and psychology and sociology on the other. The insights provided by these emerging fields create new perspectives and demand whole new languages with which to discuss and study human beings and their constructivist psychological processes. Social constructionism is often associated with postmodern theorizing and has provided much of the basis for my earlier discussions concerning scientific studies and the growing self-consciousness of the scientific enterprise. I also consider evolutionary psychology to be no less potent in disturbing our modernist Cartesian outlook and hence part of the postmodern revolution. These two sets of ideas create both a mandate that demands that scientists to see human consciousness as the legitimate object of the psychologist's interest and an insistence that we understand human consciousness as embedded in, and shaped by, evolutionary and biological processes as well as being inexorably shaped by their embeddedness in historical, cultural processes.

The demands of space preclude a detailed description of each field separately but the interested reader can be introduced to the ideas of social constructionism and its related fields of hermeneutics and narrative psychology with seminal works by Kenneth Gergen (1985, 1991a); Philip Cushman (1995); Rom Harré (1986, 1992); John Shotter (1991); George Howard (1991); Donald Spence (1982); James Mancuso (1986, 1996); Theodore Sarbin (1986); and Dan McAdams (1993). The reader is also urged to attend to much of the growing feminist literature as it is steeped in social constructionist theory that has as its goal countering the simplistic views that the psychology of women can be derived from biological sources without simultaneous consideration of the role played by culture in shaping women's psychological processes. The works of Nancy Chodorow (1978); Jessica Benjamin (1988); Carol Gilligan (1982); and Hannah Lerman (1986) are recommended as starting points in a fast growing oeuvre. The works of Jerome H. Barkow, Leda Cosmides, and John Tooby (1992); and David Buss (1994) provide excellent entry points into the new science of evolutionary psychology, while Robert Wright's (1994) book *The Moral Animal* provides a fine, less technical description of the emerging field.

The rest of this chapter defines consciousness, which is composed of the processes by which human beings seek and make meaning, and which I hold to be the legitimate central topic of the psychological sciences. I define psychology as the scientific study of human consciousness. Then, I develop a highly conjectural description of the roles of evolution in the changing structure and function of consciousness that finally made the social embeddedness of human beings a necessity. Finally, I introduce and provide my solutions for the nature-nurture controversy and the mind-body problem.

CONSCIOUSNESS

I define consciousness as an *organism's purposeful response to a meaningful event*. While this definition is unusual, a discussion of some of the elements contained within the definition might bring it into focus and place it in a more familiar context. Consciousness as a topic until recently was missing from psychology. As the philosopher Daniel Dennett (1991: 66) suggests in one of the works that aroused interest in this topic and remains indispensable for those interested, everyone assumed that their personal, unstated definition of consciousness agreed with everyone else's unstated definition. He refers to this as "the error of the first person plural." Other indispensable works defining the new interest in consciousness include those of Julian Jaynes (1976); John Searles (1995); Antonio Damasio (1994); Robert Orenstein (1991); David Chalmers (1996); and Joseph Rychlak (1997). A large and growing list of books and articles continue to emerge attesting to the importance this topic is assuming as psychologists struggle to create a human psychology and restore to psychology the philosophical underpinnings of the field, which for so long were ignored with many negative consequences.

The first term to be highlighted is organism. I take the position that consciousness is an evolutionary phenomenon and that all creatures in the kingdom known as animal have consciousness. A student pointed out to me some time ago that my definition of consciousness might also define life itself; after some thought I agree with him. Life shown by the plant kingdom might also be called consciousness, although I would call this vegetative consciousness. The next term to be considered is meaningful event. I assume that an event involves some transfer of energy or matter from one place or state to another, but not all events are meaningful for any given organism. An event becomes meaningful when an organism is affected by the event in such a way that the event becomes known to the organism through its cognitive and affective processes. All conscious animals have some psychological means of gaining information concerning events that make up situations in which they seek to survive and maintain their life processes. The cognitive processes are those that allow the organism to experience the discriminanda and manipulanda of a situation and the events that comprise it, while the affective processes inform the organism as to what the situation means to its survival and life processes. Pleasure and pain, broadly defined, represent the affective information utilized by an organism. Organisms might be said to experience the meaning of a situation or event through its collective cognitive-affective experience of that situation or event. Finally, a purposeful action is defined as motivated by the organism's experienced meaning of the event.

Let me provide an example of consciousness in a single-celled animal such as a paramecium. An individual touches the paramecium with an electric probe that provides a charge of electricity but does not exert enough pressure to move the animal. The animal moves in a direction away from the electric probe. I maintain that the animal felt the presence of the probe on its outer skin and felt whatever is pain to a paramecium. The actions taken by the creature were purposeful in that they had as their immediate goal the cessation of the pain induced by the electric current. Therefore, a paramecium has consciousness and it is fair to say that describing the behavior of such an animal is to describe its psychology. The consciousness of a paramecium is not the same as the consciousness of a human being because a human being would not only be conscious of the probe but also would be aware that is was a probe and was called a probe. The human being would also be aware that he is a human being who was touched by an electric device. He would be aware that he is aware of the probe supplying the experience with many additional levels of meaning. The person being shocked might also be conscious of the reasons for his being probed and might also be aware that the electricity might be turned higher, turned off, or reapplied at a future time. However, the fact that the human being is conscious of more than the paramecium does not mean that the paramecium is not conscious in the way paramecia can be conscious.

I also suggest that consciousness carries with it a specific quality of subjectivity and that every animal has its own particular mode of consciousness. The philosopher Thomas Nagel (1980: 159–160) writes,

> Conscious experience is a widespread phenomenon. It occurs at many levels of animal life, though we cannot be sure of its presence in the simpler organisms, and it is very difficult in general what provides evidence of it. No doubt it occurs in countless forms unimaginable to us, on other planets in other solar systems throughout the universe. But no matter how the form may vary, the fact that an organism has conscious experience at all means, basically, that there is something like to be that organism . . . an organism has conscious mental states if and only if there is something that it is like to be that organism—something it is like for the organism.

He later wonders what it would like be to be a bat with its perceptual system based on sonar and concludes that while it is impossible to know what it feels like to be a bat it must feel like something that is real and detailed for the bat.

In most unstated definitions of consciousness it is the full adult human kind of consciousness that is offered as the only legitimate definition of the word. I theorize that it is the sacred god story that says we are special and unique among all creatures and that our conscious minds are the creation and gifts of the gods that create the perception that other animals do not have a conscious organization that is peculiar and appropriate for those animals. I argue below that the god stories (such as those stating that we have souls and are agents with choice) are the direct result of how human conscious experience is organized. Animals are often seen as automatons, behaving according to impulses, instincts, and innate stimulus-response connections. After living with my pet cat for many years I am convinced that he perceives the world around him and feels emotions as a result of his appraisals. It feels like something for him to be a cat. While the range of his appraisals emotions do not equal the human beings with whom he shares his life and depends on for his survival, he clearly has consciousness that is significantly greater than a paramecium.

PSYCHOPHYLOGENESIS OR EVOLUTIONARY PSYCHOLOGY

I employ a concept coined by Klaus Holzkamp (1992) to describe the evolution of consciousness in such a way as to resolve the nature-nurture and mind-body problems. Psycholphylogenesis describes the development of psychological phenomena in relation to Charles Darwin's theory of evolution: it studies the manner in which consciousness affects and is affected by the evolutionary process. I will assume that the reader has some working knowledge of evolution, of the notion of natural selection, and its role in the processes of speciation. I assume, too, that the reader has some, although not necessarily a technical knowledge of genes and deoxyribonucleic acid, or DNA, which contains the information that directs the construction and duplication of the cells that make up the paramecium and, in collections of billions, human beings as well. One of my great frustrations as a teacher is that the evolutionary psychology makes no sense to individuals who have no idea of the biological developments which underpin the psychological events which emerge from them. Biology can be studied concurrently with psychology but it developed first as a science and is usually presented earlier than psychology in the developmental sequence of our educational curriculum. Few of my students have studied any biology prior to their study of psychology.

The theory of evolution sets forth that the goal of all living things is to replicate themselves. This struggle is known as adaptation. For those concerned with psychophylogenesis, evolution involves studying how consciousness is involved in self-replication. Any organism, suggests the biologist Richard Dawkins (1976) exists as a vehicle to transmit the genetic material of which it is composed into the future. Biologists believe that all life began as organic matter that had a capacity to self-replicate, and through processes still (and perhaps forever) unknown to us began to evolve into the organized creatures that we call plants and animals. The offspring of these living creatures were composed of the same materials as their parents but contained variations in the genetic material that made their size, shape, and elements of their functioning different. As the offspring struggle to maintain their lives long enough to replicate themselves they are forced to compete with other organisms in their environment for often limited resources and in changing environments. The genetic combinations that construct the most effective organisms become the dominant or most frequent type of genetic material. The ability of an organism to survive and replicate is known as its fitness; the process whereby a set of genes become dominant is called natural selection. All of the diversity of life on this planet biologists such as Edward O. Wilson (1992) believe are the product of natural selection and the forces that create genetic and environmental variations.

The idea that random forces could have lead to the exquisite variety of purposeful life on this planet has not, and still does not, sit well with those whose beliefs are embedded in god stories. If the structure of living things have designed within them purpose then they must be the work of a designer. Daniel Dennett (1995: 63) documents the struggle between those who favor and those who deplore Darwin's "dangerous ideas." He suggests that Darwinian theory has acted as a type of "universal acid" eating its way through whatever ideas have been set up to contain or defeat it. I suggest that at present we are seeing this acid work its way through the social sciences, it is often resisted with much the same energy as it is fought by the major religions with whom the theory of evolution has already clashed. At present, the work of psychologists who refer to themselves as advocating and promoting evolutionary psychology is infiltrating every aspect of the social sciences with often stunning breakthrough concepts.

As evolutionists chart the changes in species over time, they note that there has been a tendency for successful species to grow in size and complexity. The means by which animals are successful in achieving their adaptive aims is represented by the consciousness of that animal. Therefore, as animals became more complex the nature of their consciousness also became more complex. The process of evolution has been one in which more complex animals have evolved from less complex animals by both adding and developing cells that became specialized in function. The process in a paramecium responsible for its knowledge of the electric probe involves chemical changes in its cell wall. It is the evolutionary development of specialized nerve cells responsible for the transmission of information and collections of such nerve cells called ganglia, and ultimately brains, that have much to do with the changes in consciousness that marked the success of the larger, more complex species on this planet. In addition to the development of nerve tissue, changes in the organs that open onto the world also evolved transforming the nature of consciousness. A single cell animal makes contact with its environment with its cell membrane, evolution created specialized cells and eventually organs for sight, sound, smell, taste, and touch. Finally, the growth of specialized organs that permitted an organism to act on its environment to achieve survival and reproductive ends also defined the new forms of emerging consciousness.

Changes in size and complexity have been marked by changes in both the structure and function of species. The growth of the sense organs and the highly complex organs of nerve tissues have been organized together in a process of increased encephalization. The organs of movement have also evolved in terms of arms, legs, paws, digits, and finally hands and feet. The organs that sustained the life of complex creatures also evolved with specializations taking place in respiration, digestion, elimination of waste, reproduction, etc. For every improvement in adaptive ability brought about by the growth in size and complexity there were increased demands placed on the creatures who benefitted in terms of what it took to maintain its life and mode of consciousness. Every improvement in the ability to survive for longer periods of time, more effectively compete for resources, and find appropriate mates and reproduce came at a cost in the time it took to maintain the specialized organs of adaptation and the vulnerabilities produced by having to

perform such specialized act of adaptation. Changes in consciousness were, therefore, also required to maintain the coordination and integration of the emerging new
organs of specialization. It was the increases in consciousness needed to maintain,
coordinate, and integrate these large complex species that began to give the
consciousness of these animals their special characteristics and determined how it
would feel to be that animal.

How might we conceptualize the changes in consciousness brought about by the
evolutionary increase in size and complexity of species? As each cell has its own
consciousness there must now be cells that are aware of the consciousness of the
cells in cooperation with one another. It is clear to us now that nerves and collections
of nerves supply the higher levels of coordination required to maintain the organization and integration of millions of specialized cells. As cells became organized
and specialized they became grouped according to similar functions as organs. The
organs had to maintain coordination among the cells that comprised them and seek
coordination between organs. The growth in neurological tissue increased enormously and eventually required neurological systems to organize and coordinate
the various subsystems that direct information among other organ systems. The
human brain exists not only to collect and disseminate information to coordinate
the extraordinary number of disparate systems that comprise the living human
being, but to coordinate and direct activities between the human being and its
environment and provide integration between all of these other systems of neurological integration. I have no idea how many levels of consciousness this requires
but two things are clear: first, the cost to maintain such a system is enormous and
equal to the adaptive advantage of having such a brain; and second, it is in the
peculiarities of this organization that the human qualities of consciousness arise.

Arthur Koestler (1967) has coined the term *holon* to help describe this
phenomenon. A holon is a structure with its own ongoing function, which in this
case is described in terms of its consciousness, that is a part of a larger structure
or holon, which in turn is part of a holon still larger than that. Each holon must
operate Janus-faced, that is looking at how it functions and simultaneously
looking at what is required to be a part of a larger organization. Holons that have
a purely coordinating and integrating function must be able to achieve two goals
if the holons they help to maintain are to operate smoothly both within and
between themselves. First, they must transmit information where it is needed;
and second, they must suppress information from going where it might be
harmful. If I consider human beings holons and a social organization such as an
army a larger holon with which individual human beings both comprise and
belong we can see that certain types of information must flow between individuals at the same level and different levels and certain types of information must
not. The larger the holon under consideration, the more coordination and suppression must be accomplished both within that holon and within the smaller
operating units that comprise it.

The human form of consciousness, the only one we have direct access to,
demonstrates some of the effects of transmission and suppression of information
between various levels of organization. Depletions of food, water, and oxygen that

threaten life are presented to our awareness at an organismic level through the experience of hunger, thirst, and fatigue, but the neurological systems which organize such awareness are never available for scrutiny at the organismic level. I submit that our brains are comprised of very complex holons that operate at complex levels of consciousness, but the nature of consciousness at these levels of holonic operation are suppressed at the organismic level. We know from neurological studies of the brain that if the conscious activities of the brain are made organismically available, they cannot be distinguished from information originating outside the brain. In order for perceptions to be distinguished from internal forms of consciousness, the internal forms are prevented from making themselves known beyond a given holonic level of activity. Part of the mind-body problem is that we cannot feel our brain forming conscious experience. We are left with the product detached from its mode of production.

What are some other advantages accrued and prices paid when an organism gains in increased complexity and integration? First, more complex animals become capable of learning in more efficient ways about their environments. This means that they have improved means to become aware of sources of life and death in the larger holons with which they interact and they become capable of remembering that information and utilizing it when necessary. They also become capable of predicting with increased certainty the reappearance of those events which determine success and failure at achieving their reproductive goals. Finally, the more complex creatures become increasingly capable of altering these environments to improve their chances of adaptive success and questioning and altering the very adaptive processes by which they master these environments. The motor skills of such animals develop in ways that allow for the use of tools to amplify adaptive abilities. Perhaps the most dramatic increase in adaptive success comes when similar animals become conscious of one another and form cooperative elements or holons to improve their chances of success. At the human level these cooperative organizations include families, tribes, clans, nations, societies and a host of other organizations which exist to increase human adaptation. It is at this moment that a science of sociology is required, especially one that describes the interaction between the holon that is the separate biological individual and the larger holons that are collections of individuals.

Dennett (1995: 374–375) suggests that differences in learning between species can be described in three levels of skills sophistication. The first level is occupied by what Dennett calls "Darwinian" creatures. These are creatures whose whole behavioral repertoire is determined by their biology and who, like paramecia, survive by blindly meeting up with food and avoiding dangerous enemies. The skills they are born with are the skills that they die with. The next consists of "Skinnerian" creatures whose skills are modified when they are reinforced by randomly coming upon a situation in which they are successful in some adaptive act. Skinnerian creatures have the advantage of modifying and adding to their repertoire of skills or increasing their consciousness, but only if they are lucky enough to avoid danger long enough to do so. The third order is referred to as "Popperian" creatures, represented by an animal (such as the human being) which in the course of its development constructs an inner environment that represents the outer, and as a result learns to preselect its behaviors before it deals with the outer environment. The Popperian creature is able to make costly mistakes internally and in advance of engaging its outer environment and therefore avoid the fate of those creatures whose mistakes end their lives before they can reproduce or be successful in their adaptive ends.

The higher the order of development in terms of complexity, the greater the level of cooperation to be found in that species. Any animal that must learn about its environment must have two things: (1) tutors and (2) a time to learn before having to engage in survival. The periods we call infancy and childhood represents this phase in human beings. Cooperation among members of the same species has, in general, shown itself to be a potent adaptive force. This cooperation reveals its power among human beings—large groups of human beings sharing solutions to adaptive problems, amplifying the Popperian nature of the individual, shows prodigious adaptive results. Cooperation among members of a species also allows for a division of labor in which the individual differences in skills and talents to be found in all individuals can be pooled. One might argue that sexual reproduction divided the labor required to both protect and instruct the young in any species and that the nature of the sexual urges in the higher species, especially human beings, provides a reward system to keep the parents in the relationship that allows such a division of labor in raising children to take place. In any event, the evolution of parental involvement in the early lives of their offspring seems to be necessary for the fullest development of Popperian consciousness.

However, in complex systems there are always prices to be paid, and in the human being the costs of achieving human consciousness are enormous. Biologists make clear that in the evolutionary process all organisms were designed to pass on their individual genes. Dawkins's book entitled *The Selfish Gene*, suggests that the behavior of any organism (including the behavior of human beings) can best be understood from a gene's eye perspective. Behavior is motivated in such a way as to maximize the chances that the organism's genes will continue to exist. Therefore, any organism will be most concerned with the survival of its own genes lending the adaptive process a selfish or self-interested quality. The biologists William Hamilton (1964) and Robert Trivers (1985) pointed out that altruistic behavior and cooperation between members of a species exists to the degree that they are kin and share the same genetic material. Sexual reproduction means joining in a cooperative effort with a mate not comprised of one's own genes and the protracted childhood of our species demands that both parents give up long periods of their lives to offspring who are made up of only 50 percent of their genetic material.

Moreover, as David Buss (1994) points out, the cost of impregnation is very low for a male but very high for a female who can, in the case of human beings, only become pregnant one time a year and must carry the offspring for nine months before risking her own life in the delivery. Therefore, while male involvement is required in the human family much of the developed consciousness of the male is in conflict with those evolved desires to help in the care of his offspring. The desire to mate, which is experienced at an organismic level as lust, is experienced quite differently between male and female especially when she is pregnant or caring for young. The affection for the young is also experienced quite differently by mothers and the males who lust for these women and other available females.

The conflicts between males and females over the raising of offspring and the conflicts within individuals whether or not to respond to more immediate self-interests or by delaying self-interest in order to benefit by participating with other members of a group (particularly one made up of non-kin) affect every individual and every relationship. The nature and resolution of these conflicts creates risks for all concerned but makes the long childhood of the human particularly risky, especially if it takes cooperative effort to help a child develop the full potential of his inherited Popperian consciousness. This vulnerability is currently a contentious topic in human affairs and in discussions of morality as large numbers of children are living in situations which impede the development of what is currently called intelligence. In Western culture the protection and tutoring of the young is deemed so complex that a cooperative effort is required by a whole host of adults not at all related to the child or even of his kin. The final issue to be discussed in this context is the vulnerability of entering into relationships with members of a species that have become proficient at deception. Before I discuss the nature of human deception, I must discuss some other peculiarities that are related to Popperian consciousness.

The Emergence of Self

The evolutionary development of an inner-world representative of an outer world in which actual adaptive struggles take place brought with it forms of conscious experience that were disjunctive with those appearing earlier in evolution. First, it involves a need for sets of symbols that can stand for the external events being portrayed in the inner world. In human beings these symbols can take the form of pictures, gestures, or words, the latter being unique to our species. Once in place these symbols require various internal actions to simulate the overt behavioral actions to take place during the adaptive struggles to come. What is commonly called thought or cognitive behavior has been termed operations by the biologist-psychologist Jean Piaget to reflect the action-oriented nature of the inner human attempts at adaptation. The development of cognitive operations leads to the development of a conscious experience that there is an inner actor or agency involved with these symbols. The agent is in control of the operations performed on the symbols as well as an observer of inner psychological life. Further developments could lead to the symbolic representation of an inner actor-observer, not only in control of inner operations but of the overt actions performed in real acts of adaptation. Finally, the actor-observer would also be able to experience events as happening to this emerging set of inner experiences and the symbols that represent them. The actor would then simultaneously be an object as well. This set of actor-observer-object experiences becomes an essential part of consciousness and over human history has been called many things. Today we refer to this constellation as the self.

The development of the symbolic world did not take place within the isolated individual. Noam Chomsky (1972, 1975, 1980); Steven Pinker (1994); John Locke (1993) and others have postulated that language developed through evolutionary processes and that each undamaged human being is born with an inborn neurological language acquisition device that matures after birth and becomes ready to permit the individual child to learn language after signaling the caretakers in his life to begin speaking to him or her. It is clear that the development of linguistic symbols added enormously to the value of shared cooperative efforts at adaptation in human beings but it also defined one of the most important aspects of the infant and caretaker relationship. The immature human being is developing an inner life which contains symbolic experiences of being an actor-observer, the nature of the symbols which will represent the actor are derived from those whose responsibilities involve teaching the child to speak. Therefore, in addition to the development of a self, human beings have a self that is in part the product of symbols used by others. The self is, in part, an interpersonal invention. The self is, therefore, both an evolutionary achievement aiding in the adaptation of the species and a product of social construction. At the moment the self was created and required the cooperation of others for its emergence, human beings created and were influenced by what might be called social evolution as well as biological evolution. It is at this moment that I ask my students and the reader to consider that psychology, biology, and sociology are three simultaneous perspectives of the same phenomenon.

The emergence of the self as an essential and unique aspect of human consciousness and the interpersonal nature of the self as shared experience were fueled by organisms seeking adaptive advantages over competing animals of other species and between competing groups of non-kin of the same species. Adaptations include those involved in mating, and the protection-tutoring of offspring, as well as maintaining the complex functions that maintain the life of the adult individual during the reproductive years. These functions include eating, sleeping, drinking, breathing, eliminating wastes, and fighting and escaping from others also involved in the competition for potentially dear resources. Every adaptive struggle may end in success or failure. Some failures end in death, but others in the affective experience which defines for the animal in question that there has been an adaptive failure and for which renewed struggle is demanded. Adaptive failure is defined by hunger, fatigue, thirst, and suffocation, as well as fear, anger, and pain. For many animals failed adaptations and the inner demand for renewed struggle is represented by these affects, but for human beings the picture is far more complicated.

The emergence of the self also includes an awareness of failure that goes beyond the affects that define unmet biological needs. There is also an actor-object who has failed and is responsible for failure and to whom the suffering is happening. For the first time we see the act of judging and the emergence of affects that represent failures of the self. We also see affects such as guilt and shame. If we can act we can have symbols for freedom and if we fail to achieve success with our actions we can be held responsible as well. Michael Polanyi (1967) has written that success and failure in adaptation are necessarily critical. Since most of our human adaptations take place in cooperation with others, the judging of failure is a shared experience. We may blame ourselves or others, we may be blamed by others, we may also blame ourselves or others for faults in observable actions or faults in our internal operations of adaptation. It is clear, however, that human beings have a whole set of adaptations not shared with less complex animals. Avoiding the emotions that represent judgments of failure and achieve the affects that represent judgments of success such as pride and esteem become central to the human adaptive effort.

There are a host of additional differences that begin to separate animals and humans because of the development of the self and self-consciousness. At this juncture I will deal with only the emerging human need to protect, enhance, extend, and redesign the very consciousness that comprises the self. With the emergence of these needs, and the judgments which accompany them, we enter a realm that cannot be reduced to biological needs, including the need for replication. Dawkins (1976) considers the consequences of Popperian consciousness when he speaks of the human creation of memes, the intellectual product of human beings that behave like genes. Memes are ideas, inventions, and discoveries of all kind which are the products of Popperian consciousness that work their way into the consciousness of large numbers of people because they add to the adaptive fitness of the human beings who encounter them. The wheel, psychoanalysis, the bow and arrow, and Beethoven's nine symphonies are examples of memes. There are literally millions more and every author who writes a book hopes that it becomes an important meme. However, I do not think that Dawkins appreciated the needs that motivate the production of many memes. Many memes are motivated by those who choose not to have children because it will interfere with their desire to become famous and have their very consciousness be recognized as a meme.

The need for human beings to achieve immortality is not reducible to a desire to pass on one's genetic inheritance particularly when celibacy is demanded as the price to receive everlasting consciousness. The whole basis of Western theology involves not only the separation of mind and body but the denial of the body, particularly the sexual desires which represent our reproductive needs. I argue that in human beings the need to reproduce the self is so great that those who control the symbols that stand for fame, immortality, and enhancement of the self may have even more power than those who control food and water. Many of the dynamics described later will be predicated on the theory that parents will be willing, under certain circumstances, to destroy their children when they refuse to imitate and identify with their parents form of conscious expression. Being labeled good or bad depends on how well the child accedes to the moral demands that they see the world like their parents, teachers, and other caretakers such as psychotherapists want them to.

I close the discussion of psychophylogenesis by returning briefly to the topic of deception. All animals have evolved methods to deceive their enemies, however, human beings have developed self-awareness and with it a need to justify their actions morally. The human conflicts between kin are particularly painful when it comes to conflicts between the needs of the self and mate or the self and offspring. Deceptions are easy where children are concerned or wherever more powerful figures are dealing with less powerful or less developed beings. However, moral pain may be especially high in these conditions as well. Evolutionists suggest that human beings have simultaneously developed the capacity to deceive the self in order to be better deceivers of others and avoid the moral condemnations which attend harmful practices to those one is committed to helping. Psychoanalysis has long held that human beings may block from organismic consciousness those emotions that represent failure in biological and moral failure. With human beings we will have to consider as well those self-deceptions that exist in order for one individual to gain biological or moral dominance over another. We must consider that many of the dynamics that mark the conflict between parent and child, teacher and student, and all other important social relationships are marked by deceptions and self-deceptions that occur as one individual seeks to replace the self of another with his or her self or prevent the development of forms of self different from his or her own.

NATURE-NURTURE, MIND, AND BODY

Thomas Nagel (1980: 159) writes, "Consciousness is what makes the mind-body problem really intractable." Why is this so? The manner in which our subjective experience of ourselves is shaped by the consequences of our biological evolution, our social embeddedness, and our self-deceptions creates a subjectivity or experience of self that has no connection to either its biological or social roots. Moreover, the nature of human subjectivity also creates an inescapable experience that the "I" that refers to me and the "we" is actually substance no matter how many arguments are produced to demonstrate the fallacy of our subjective experience (Robinson 1991). The disconnection of experience from the biological and the social also makes it difficult to create newer and perhaps more useful perspectives how nature and nurture interrelate as we struggle to adapt to the world in which we all live. Since I am as much a product of evolutionary and social forces as anyone, I must write of these other perspectives without the full capacity to experience them. These perspectives are, therefore, nonempirical in that my knowledge of how it would feel to experience the world differently than I do is as impossible to achieve as experiencing the subjectivity of what it would be like to be a bat, my cat or the simple paramecium. But I will not let such ignorance stop me any more than it stopped Copernicus from ignoring the fact that he experienced the world as both flat and in the center of the universe as he wondered how the heavens might appear if viewed from the perspective of the sun and not the earth.

Consciousness is shaped because of its evolutionary history as both the cause and effect of adaptation: it is what makes adaptation possible and it exists because adaptation is possible. If consciousness is experienced subjectively, then subjectivity must be necessary to the adaptive process. How people experience themselves and the world must also be the cause and effect of the evolutionary struggle to adapt. It must make adaptive sense that it feels like it does for us to be who we are, and how it feels to be who we are must be the product of our adaptive struggles up to the moment that we feel ourselves to be whatever it is we feel ourselves to be.

Therefore, as I seek other perspectives to help illuminate the nature of consciousness, I am not seeking an alternative to subjectivity. I am not, as so many others seem desperate to do, trying to explain subjective consciousness as a function of the neurological events upon which, among other things, consciousness depends for its existence. I accept that neurological understanding is one of the necessary perspectives in understanding consciousness. However, I reject the kind of reductionism which state that consciousness is nothing but the activity of sense organs and the operations of the brain. Without sensory input and neurological processing there would be no consciousness. But our adaptation depends upon our subjective experience of the world, and therefore while our awareness of the world depends upon sensation and neurological activity it cannot be reduced to these activities.

The nature of our subjective experience creates what Dennett (1991: 101) refers to as the Cartesian Theater. We experience ourselves as either watching a show going on around us or, in the case of introspection, going on inside of us. Moreover, we experience ourselves as both an agent of action and a unitary one at that. We also experience the paradox that our unitary self is unchanging over time no matter how much evidence forces us to recognize that as time passes we are not the same as we used to be. We must, therefore, add to our nonsubjective perspectives the fact that a massive amount of conscious activity is going on to create the theater, and that these levels of consciousness are not objects of the spectacle itself. Much of the time our adaptations go on without ever becoming the objects of our experience and remain what Polanyi (1958) calls tacit experience. Robert Orenstein (1991) suggests that much of the conscious activity that goes on outside of subjectivity is accomplished by stupid decision makers. Dennett (1991) concludes that events only enter the theater after much lower level conscious activity makes it possible. Mahoney (1991) refers to those aspects of consciousness which support full subjectivity as superconsciousness. I would suggest that it is when adaptive actions are required on an organismic level that full subjectivity comes into play. We experience ourselves as unitary creatures but from this perspective we are in fact comprised of multiple consciousness or holons. Our minds are modular but we experience ourselves as unitary.

Subjectivity allows us to experience ourselves as the passive observer of events, even events that are happening to us. Another perspective is required that suggests that every act of consciousness is an intentional act whether we experience the intention or not. Consciousness, suggests philosophers such as Edmund Husserl (1962) and I. N. Mohanty (1974) is inherently intentional. It is always directed toward an object other than itself even if at times the object is itself. This is what gives consciousness its subjective experience of "aboutness" and why it can never be reduced to its neurological underpinnings. Consciousness is a directed activity that cannot be understood without reference to the objects of its intentions. If this book is now the object of my conscious activities the book is not inside my brain. My consciousness is what exists in my subjectivity as between me and this book.

If all acts of consciousness are intentional and directed toward some object, then all consciousness is motoric in nature and can only be described with verbs. We can change our perspective on ourselves and our conscious experiences by avoiding nouns wherever possible when describing ourselves and others. We do not have minds, but rather we mind. Even the "I" and "we" that seem so necessary for our existence as adult human beings can be understood to be the process of the physical body. Mind is to the brain what turning is to a wheel—one is the process of the other. While even the most ardent reductionist says, "I have a brain," we can still intellectually understand that the "I" is created by the motor activity of the nervous system. It is experienced as a noun but it is the result of a verb. Similarly, from this perspective that can not be experienced we have no such thing as an imagination, rather we imagine things; we have no personalities but rather we behave in consistent and unique ways across many situations. With these perspectives and others we can see that mental activity is of the body but not reducible to it and that no matter how hard we wish for ourselves or souls (or whatever we call the experience of our essences to be) they are not things in themselves but result from the activities of fully naturalistic phenomena.

I close this chapter with a brief tour through the so-called nature-nurture controversy. Psychologists like to say that our behavior is the product of both heredity (the source of nature) and the environment (the source of nurture). It makes them happy to suggest that both are always involved but the real question to be asked is, "How much is heredity and how much is environment." Students also glow with warmth and a sense of justice if it can be concluded that our behavior is 50 percent nature and 50 percent nurture. However, from the current perspective what makes us so happy is neither logically nor empirically sustainable. All behavior is a function of an organism with consciousness making the behavior 100 percent a function of psychology. From the moment of conception our heredity works to shape the biology of the organism with consciousness. We remain biological creatures until death ends the existence of our consciousness, which is the process of the biology that has been shaped by our heredity. We are, therefore, 100 percent a function of our nature. Since we cannot exist without an environment, our consciousness requires environmental objects for it to exist, and since from the moment we are born our consciousness is shaped by the social and cultural forces which enfold us we are also 100 percent the product of nature. There is no nature-nurture controversy once we define our terms and analyze another sacred scientistic story. We require an integrated science of biology, sociology, and psychology to begin to understand the creature we human beings happen to be.

III

STORIES AND LESSONS FROM PSYCHOLOGY

5

TOWARD A THEORY OF HUMAN ADAPTATION

INTRODUCTION

In this chapter I begin to present a theory of human psychology that focuses on the development of human consciousness and its role in human adaptation. I discuss the elements of human conscious experience which include the cognitive and affective processes, their development, and their interactions in a variety of social settings that define the main context of adaptation. But before I discuss the psychological processes that are needed for a theory of human adaptation I will briefly discuss why I need to undertake such an endeavor in the first place. If I am to help my students understand their own behavior in the context of our classroom and begin to convince them to examine and change those aspects of their conscious-ness that prevent them from achieving a scientific and artistic mode of experience I must have materials that are capable of explaining who we are, where we come from, and how we are to get where we want to go.

Much of the content of psychology is useless in portraying human beings as I believe they should be pictured; the textbooks which summarize psychology for the beginning students are actually harmful in producing the kinds of under-standings that represent my educational goal. While some of the materials I require are certainly available and many of those works were mentioned in earlier chapters, I find that I am increasingly forced to summarize and integrate the works of others to produce writings to achieve my own specific educational ends. If, and until, our field develops a consistent paradigm of human psychology I will be burdened and challenged to produce my own reading material for my students. This chapter, and the four chapters that follow, are in effect a summary of the curriculum of the human psychology that I present my students.

If we examine any of the current textbooks that introduce psychology to students we see similar patterns and conceptual problems in all of them. (They are, in fact, mostly clones of one another.) The first chapter always reveals these major problems. The author(s) always establish the methods used by psychologists to study the subject matter. Charles Morris's (1996: 4), book is a popular text used by a majority of the full and part-time faculty at my college for many years; it defines psychology's subject matter as "the science of behavior and mental processes." Morris never makes clear the relationship of behavior to mental processes nor does he define what these processes are or to what ends they exist. Instead, he describes how psychologists study behavior and mental life through the use of observations, correlations, experiments, and the like. Dodge Fernald's 1996 textbook, sent to me by the publisher begins the description of the methods of psychology without even bothering to define psychology's subject matter. How can either of these two scientists demonstrate the efficacy of their methods without an extended discussion of how the methods relate to that which they are supposed to describe and explain? Both texts demonstrate the contention of Brent Slife and Richard Williams (1997:119) as they write, "Psychology, however was born of a determination to apply the positivistic science to human beings. Only those questions that could be cast in ways amenable to scientific study were taken up by the discipline." The subject matter of psychology was dependent on predetermined methods rather than the methods chosen to fit the subject matter. Human beings were constructed by the science to fit the methods resulting in disastrous consequences for what was termed by Isidor Chein (1972) the image of humanity.

For example, in the first chapter of virtually any introductory textbook in psychology we are told that psychologists learn about the world through the application of the scientific method and that they are bound by various ethics and morals as they pursue knowledge which is to be used to enhance the dignity and quality of human life. But how do the subjects of scientific investigation learn? Morris deals with learning in Chapter 5, Fernald in Chapter 7. According to both authors, the main authority on learning is B.F. Skinner who described learning as operant and classical conditioning, two interrelated processes conducted on experiments on rats and pigeons. Don't all people learn in the same manner as psychologists? Isn't George Kelly (1955) correct when he states that we are all scientists trying to understand the world around us? If not, then why don't these authors explain how psychologists create their sciences as the result of their rat-like conditioning? The answer is that you cannot explain the creativity of human beings through the processes of conditioning (the theory does not even do justice to the rats and pigeons used in the experiments).

Moreover, the subjects of Skinner's theory can not be held to the ethical or moral standards by which Morris, Fernald, and Skinner obviously hold themselves with much pride and expectation of reward. A science of rats modeled on physics and chemistry is of little use in the study of human beings. Skinner constructs his human subjects as emitting behaviors in much the same way as flashlights emit light. This is not an unbiased description of human beings but a nightmare version of what most human beings, including Morris and Fernald, consider themselves to be. (If a patient went to a psychiatrist and claimed that he emits behaviors rather than acts according to his own volitions he would be diagnosed schizophrenic and placed on psychotropic medicines. When psychologists say the same things they are hailed as making scientific breakthroughs.) These books violate their subject matter in a profound way and, therefore, represent scientism rather than science.

We can go through chapter after chapter of these books and find example after example of human beings cast in ways that both violate human experience as well as violating the authors as creative scientists. The chapters on personality theories contain descriptions of Freud's version of psychoanalysis that conceives of human beings as driven by sexual and aggressive urges as if they were some form of energy transformation creatures whose behaviors mimic a wolf or some other type of hunting animal. While Freud's theory might be criticized in these texts for his failure to conform to positivist methodology, I have never seen it said that his theory, as with Skinner's, cannot even begin to explain the creative processes that Freud used to develop his masterworks in the first place. I have never seen a discussion as to why theories such as those of Skinner and Freud achieve the success they do and why other theories languish and disappear. Why do theories that cast human beings as less than human, and especially less than the scientists that create them, become so popular to other scientists and the public? While the metatheories of evolutionary psychology and social constructionism have begun the attempt to answer these questions their ideas still seem far removed from the introductory undergraduate textbooks that dominate the field.

There is still another dehumanization of humanity that is beginning to dominate psychology and, therefore, is reflected in basic textbooks. Our modernist society has long been in love with its technology and the field of psychology reflects that love. Lately it appears that love has turned to worship especially where the computer is concerned. Psychology is now convincing students and the public alike that the best way to understand human behavior is to think of people as complex mobile computers. The basic texts all have chapters that suggest the best way to understand human cognition is through the concretized metaphor of information processing. The thought processes of the human beings who created the computers have not yet been properly studied, indeed according to the behaviorists they could not and should not be studied since they do not exist. Yet, the products of our intelligence are to be studied as if they created our intelligence and not the other way around. I recently described a problem I was having with my computer to a friend and colleague who is quite expert on these machines. He suggested that to understand the problem I must think of the computer as a brain having a spasm in one of its arteries. I laughed and suggested we had now gone complete circle, the human being is to be understood in terms of the machine and the machine is to be understood in terms of the human being.

The awe in which our culture holds these new computers and the artificial intelligence which supposedly can teach us about our own cognitive processes is staggering and wholly pervasive both inside and outside the field of psychology. The myths of our society are beginning to reveal sacred stories about machines as gods. Consider the two movies starring Arnold Schwarzenegger as "The Terminator." The first is a low budget and gritty cautionary tale about a future society being destroyed by the very machines that had been invented to serve humanity.

Schwartzenegger plays a nearly indestructible cyborg (part machine, part flesh and blood) who is finally overcome by the two human heroes of the story. In the second film, a splashy, big budget, colorful Hollywood extravaganza, Schartzenneger now plays a good terminator trying to save the human protagonists, as well as all of humanity, from an even more advanced killing machine that appears in human form. Not only does the good terminator destroy the evil machine and those he represents, but he becomes a father figure to the boy whose hero father is killed in the first film. After saving humankind the terminator commits suicide to save humankind from any more killer machines. I have discussed this film many times with students and colleagues alike and all agree that what we are witnessing in the second terminator tale is a retelling of the Christ story in which the son of God is replaced with the son of machine as humanity's savior.

It is true that animals can be used as metaphors for human beings and that the manner in which they learn can shed light on human learning. It is equally true that computers can be used as metaphors for human beings and that the step-by-step processing of the computer can shed light on the processes by which human beings solve problems. But in both cases it is wholly illogical to then assume that rats and computers are human beings. Animals feel like something as they interact with the world but they feel nothing like a human being; and machines feel nothing as they compute because they are not conscious, do not react to meaningful stimulation, are not purposeful nor possessed of intentionality like the human beings who designed them. "Cognition," writes Elizabeth Wilson (1996: 590) "is not the product of a binary and restrictive logic, it is a process that is active, reconstructive, cultural, embodied, affective, non-conscious, non-unitary, and over determined. Cognition is a process which of *necessity* is embodied as the active interpretation of sensory information through pre-existing internal states and pre-existing external systems. These processes are not peripheral or secondary to an essentially logic-driven process, *they are the very mechanisms of cognition itself.*" Wilson's remarks are clearly directed toward restoring cognitive processes to their human context but they can find no place in the introductory textbooks mentioned. As a result of being driven by methodology, the introductory textbook lack coherence in its organization of what is ultimately selected as subject matter. Wilson's work is not only hostile to positivist methodology but places cognition as subordinate to the human beings whose process this is.

The subjects as described by psychologists in their texts and research are not human beings as I believe they should be described. Human beings live lives dominated by meaningful purposes pursued in a variety of social and natural contexts. The human processes studied by psychologists are presented as divorced from both their place and function in the human beings who should be psychology's subject matter. Postmodern theorists frequently call for psychology to be a study of persons rather than disembodied processes that are constructed by the method-ologies of the particular scientist who happens to be interested in that particular function. Therefore, we have chapters on learning, perception, thinking, emotions, and memory that have nothing to do with one another except for what we learn about them as a function of some experiment divorced from the actual arenas where these processes operate, interact, and function as adaptive devices for human beings. It is almost as if psychology, having inherited the Cartesian view of mind divorced from body, then continued to divide up the human being into smaller and smaller pieces for an ever more detailed investigation. Learning could be studied in terms of rats, thinking in terms of computers and memory in terms of studies using nonsense syllables. Rollo May (1991), after discussing the study of memory with the use of nonsense syllables, wondered if all of psychology was the study of nonsense.

I could continue at length discussing one disconnected, incoherent chapter after another. Social psychology, developmental psychology, and so-called abnormal psychology all discuss human beings from different vantage points, unrelated to one another. Does not abnormal behavior have something to do with both social psychology and human development? Does not human development have some-thing to do with social processes? Do not all of these topics involve thinking, perception, memory, and the emotions? Not in the introductory textbook! How then do we begin to develop a coherent view of human beings that can be studied with methods other than those formulated by an outmoded view of physics? What is the data of psychology to be and how can we approach it with a genuine science rather than the scientism that all too often represents our field in the introductory textbooks?

The methods of psychology vary but the highest and most respected type of study is the experiment based on the type of work that physicists might employ and which demands distortions, simplifications, and reductionism, as well as others. In a typical experiment the researcher tries to isolate a psychological process and brings it into the laboratory setting. Psychology laboratories were, in my experi-ence, invariably in dungeons or attics tucked far away from the rest of school life and usually found after walking down long, narrow, and dark hallways. They were often cubicles, starkly and simply appointed. There seems to be no awareness on the part of the experimenters that, "When removed from their usual social and personal contexts, human experiences and actions are altered." Martin and Thompson (1997: 632).

The experiments themselves usually involve measuring some aspect of the individuals psychological profile with a pencil and paper test and assigning the differences on this test to the status of an Independent or experimenters variable. The independent variable is defined as the cause variable. Changes in this variable would account for changes in the outcome or effect variable known as the dependent variable. The dependent variable usually involves counting some form of behav-ioral activity and noting changes in the activity or behavioral response as different levels of the independent variable were applied to the behaving organism as people and animals are so often called in these procedures.

Variables thought to interact with the independent variable or believed to create changes in the dependent variable are controlled by being held as constant across test subjects. The variables to be controlled were themselves scores on paper and pencil tests or were garnered by questionnaires in which the examiners were trained to ask all subjects the same questions in an identical manner. In order to keep the subjects focused on the task at hand each experiment is carefully planned to keep the subject from knowing the real goal of the study while hopefully controlling their attention while the experimental manipulation does its magic. What is implied in these pieces of research is that all motivations for behavior are to be found in the independent variable, the stimulus as measured by the experimenters paper and pencil test, or other set of observations made independently of the perceptions of the subject. In a real sense there is no subject because there is no living embodied person in the study except for the scientist performing the research. The person is gone and replaced by a collection of variables, some left free to vary and others supposedly controlled. This collection of variables is frozen in time and completely passive except for changes in observable behavior induced by the stimulus independent variable.

The full range of conscious beliefs of the subjects are now thought to be controlled and irrelevant to the experimental outcomes. Consciousness had been bypassed and replaced by simple, isolated pieces of motor behavior. For example, I remember in my graduate school days young women looking quite frightened and upset being brought into experimental cubicles after following young men who were strangers down long dark hallways. But the reactions to the strange surroundings were not part of the research protocol and would not play any role in the assessment of the outcomes. In fact the idea that several pencil and paper tests could account for the wealth of detail and motivations in any person's human consciousness is rarely examined in the ongoing production of tens of thousands of these studies year after year. In all my years attending research meetings, I never encountered any study that could withstand the scrutiny of its critics. Researchers evaluating a study would suggest that hundreds of variables other than those under consideration could account for the reported results. What was clear to me was that many of these studies might have demonstrated what they intended or they might not have, they were unable to be replicated, and outside of the research program of the experimenter whose tenure and promotion rested on the publication of these dubious works of science, they had little or no relevance at all. It is for these reasons and more that I turn my efforts to create a scientific study of human beings that does not violate its subject matter.

PHENOMENOLOGY AND HETEROPHENOMENOLOGY

In order to begin our discussion we need an example that represents the products of human consciousness or, in effect, human consciousness itself. I refer back to the story in Chapter 1, or to any of the stories in Chapter 11, where we are presented with examples of various individual's subjective experience. These narratives are the data of psychological inquiry. Whatever theories we develop must flow from this kind of data making it mandatory that we have methods that do justice to our scientific endeavors without violating the subject matter that is the source of our science. If we examine the data we see that it contains thousands, if not an infinite number of potential variables, many of which are not amenable to statistical evaluation. We observe an agency representing perhaps millions of potential variables, not a collection of static variables. We see complex beings in the process of change and we can reflect on the possible nature of that change. We are privy to an emergent process becoming aware of some of the antecedent activities from which the process itself emerged and in doing so causing change to itself and the present manifestations of the antecedent conditions. From this perspective we are encountering a system of unimaginable complexity and since we as emergent systems ourselves are enfolded in the same antecedent and concurrent conditions we must feel awe at the thought of making sense out of this data. In the Jewish religion we learn that to save another person is to save the world in its entirety. This is because all human beings are worlds unto themselves. I believe that to try and comprehend my student's experience is to try and understand a world in its entirety. But we must try to understand and remain fallible and humble when we begin.

The study of human consciousness has been advanced by philosophers such as Edmund Husserl (1962); I. N. Mohanty (1974); and, more recently by Don Idhe (1986) and Neil Rossman (1991) among others. Implicit in my definition of consciousness (an organisms purposeful response to meaningful stimulation) is that which exists independent of human beings but which does not become meaningful in a psychological sense until it is made so by an intentional human action. Idhe (1986: 43) writes,

> Every experience has its reference or direction toward what is experienced, and contrarily, every experienced phenomenon refers to, or reflects a mode of experiencing to which it is present. This is the intentional or correlative a priori of experience taken phenomenologically. Husserl gave the two sides of this correlation names. For what is experienced, he used the term noema or noematic correlate, and for the mode of experiencing, which is detected reflexively, he used the term noesis or noetic correlate.

There are, therefore, no stimuli producing behavioral responses but stimuli as experienced leading to purposeful behaviors. The world is not created by our consciousness of it but it is our consciousness which gives the world any meaning in human terms. We do not create the world but we do create meaning that the world might have for us. If we accept reality as that which is created through an act of noesis then we must conclude that there is no reality other than that which is experienced phenomenologically by the experiencing individual.

Husserl was not advancing an antiscientific position when he discussed reality as a function of phenomenology. His goal was to help us reach to the objects themselves. However, there is no way to discuss the nature of objects independently of some living person's experience of those objects. Phenomenologists, constructivists, and constructionists, all of whom rely on phenomenology to a certain extent, are often accused of suggesting that the world is nothing but a figment of human imagination, fantasy, or perception itself. This is not the case, although the writings of some who identify themselves as part of these fields suggest that they do take such a position. But, I hold that the construction of reality is not the fabrication of reality. Those who take the position that there is nothing independent of our individual or social perceptions are unable to differentiate between madness and sanity a distinction that I feel it is important to make even if making the distinction is very difficult and even if madness is not in any way a medical condition. Moreover, they place themselves in the position of defending Bishop Berkely's thesis of radical subjectivism from the withering attacks of David Hume who was able to logically demonstrate that any such belief must reduce itself to an absurdity. Science does try and understand a real world, real events, and real people although no reality exists without an act of noesis to make it so.

The psychological and scientific consequences of accepting a phenomenologically based view of human functioning are fraught with complications and difficulties. First, we must be able to understand how subjective experience is organized and how it operates as the motivating force of human behavior. Scientists must give up the hope expressed by W. F. Lawless (1996: 141) that they can ever achieve a "theory of the dynamics of social objects comparable to Newton's dynamics of physical objects" wherein scientists alone can observe people from their own subjective third person stance and explain and predict the behavior of the observed.

Moreover, psychologists must also give up the comforting methodologies that permit the measurement and quantification of various forces and instead rely on the subjective reports of the observed as to the reasons they did this or that. Even scientists such as the psychoanalyst Roy Schafer (1980, 1992), who is committed to understanding the subjective experiences of the people with whom he works has argued that reasons cannot be causes. Instead Schafer opts for explanations of behavior in terms of drives which are more in accordance with projects that attempt to keep his field in good stead with the hard sciences of physics and chemistry. Carlo Strenger (1991) makes clear, however, that if one accepts human beings as operating in their world based on the perceived meaning of that world then one has no choice but to accept that reasons can be fully responsible as the causes of behavior.

A second problem that rears its head once we accept that people behave according to their subjective experience of the world involves the questions, "Why does subjectivity change." and "How is subjectivity influenced?" Simply understanding how subjectivity provides motivation is not enough (as if such a task is simple!). The study of human experience demonstrates that human beings undergo profound changes between birth and death, in predictable and unpredictable patterns. Parents, teachers, psychotherapists, and all those who work with children and try and influence the development and behavior of anyone suddenly see their work as dependent on not answering the question, "How can I make Johnny do this or that?" but instead answering the more difficult question, "How can I make Johnny see the world as I wish him to see it?" In addition to asking the purely scientific questions as to how to influence human subjectivity, we are confronted with inevitable moral questions as well. If we are to have a predictive science we must have theories that allow us to explain, predict, and control human consciousness and to do so in ways that fulfill the dictates of humanistic morality. We must, therefore, go beyond pure phenomenology without going all the way to positivist formulations that are appropriate to physics. I believe the concept of heterophenomenology, coined by Daniel Dennett (1991), allows us to bridge this methodological gap.

Heterophenomenology questions those conditions experienced in a third person account of an event that lead to changes in what is experienced in a first person account of the same event. It creates the conditions for a much more complex analysis of independent and dependent variables. We ask in a heterophenomenological analysis not how the independent variable affected the dependent but rather, how did the human subject construe, experience, or interpret the events happening to him and how did his subsequent construal, experiences, and interpretations change as a result. We can then ask in what way overt, observable behaviors changed as well.

For example, if I observe an adult strike a child after the child spoke to the adult then as a heterophenomenologist I should try and conjecture what the child's words meant to the adult, how they changed his experience of the child, and how that shift in meaning made the striking of the child a meaningful and logical act to the adult. I can simultaneously ask how it felt to the child when he was struck in the context of saying what he said to the adult and how his tearful response is meaningful in relation to how it felt to be struck. I can make these conjectures based on my own experiences of being both a child and an adult, my reading and discussions of adult child interactions, as well as asking each of the participants in the interaction for their individual descriptions and judgments of the incident. I can also ask questions about the long-term consequences of this event on the conscious experiences of both the adult and the child with each other and with other people as well. In this way I can learn about patterns of development as they relate to various types of human interactions without losing sight of the fact that what is being affected by these events is the organization of human consciousness, which is ultimately needed to explain the events themselves.

I can integrate the three metatheories suggested above into my conjecturing. I can describe the biological development of an individual and include gross changes in the structure and functioning of the body as well as the microscopic events occurring in the nervous system of the individual and ask how all of these influence the individual's conscious experience of the self and others. I can chart and describe various types of human interactions and ask questions about how consciousness changes as a function of short and long term relationships on a variety of social levels. Finally, and in many ways most importantly, I can ask how the emerging activities of consciousness itself contribute to changes in how individuals experience themselves and their worlds. I believe that psychology has just begun to ask questions concerning how human beings invent themselves and are responsible for some of the profound shifts in phenomenological experience that human beings regularly demonstrate. If I don't yet have enough questions to ask I can begin to question the interaction of these three sets of variables on each other in every combination and permutation possible.

But as we begin the development of our theory it must be clear that the power needed for such analysis is not yet available. In recent years chaos theory, systems theory, and other conceptual techniques that the writer John Horgan (1996) refers to collectively as chaoplexity have been shown to be helpful in understanding complex phenomena in areas such as weather prediction, heating and cooling systems, and other physical and chemical systems. In these systems it becomes impossible to separate cause and effect in neat, linear models as one variable changes as a result of interaction with another and in turn alters the variable which is thought to initiate the original effects. In human beings we find incredibly complex systems even at the biological level and to my knowledge there have been no applications of advanced nonlinear systems of analysis. We lack a language and adequate methods with which to begin to describe and analyze consciousness, perhaps the most complex system in the universe. Isidor Chein, remarked to a group of students that we lack a language of "simultaneity." I am trapped by the languages of the disparate fields in which I was trained and have operated these many years as a member of one discipline and academic department in competition with other disciplines organized as other academic departments.

Not only do we not have a language of simultaneity but we possess a babel of languages that seem to exist to the degree that they obfuscate and hide our disciplines one from the other. For example, in a recent discussion with two colleagues from the biology department it became clear that what I refer to as a paramecium's consciousness is referred to by them as irritability. We had great difficulty in ironing out the differences in perception on this topic because all of us were unable to agree on a common language with which to describe the phenomenon at hand. With all these difficulties, however, there is still a need for a theory that begins to do justice to human beings as they live and experience their lives, especially if as educators we wish to affect the nature of those lives and experiences. What is needed, especially in psychology, is a set of concepts that will allow students to see themselves reflected within them and be able to use those concepts for their own adaptive purposes.

The proper level of analysis would contain a language that would permit description of consciousness as being simultaneously comprised of neurobiological activities and environmental events including social interactions with others possessing consciousness as well as emergent psychological processes. A language as this would allow us to recognize that when we speak of biological events we are speaking of consciousness just as when we speak of environment we are also speaking of consciousness. We would see that a change at one level of analysis involves a simultaneous change at all others because while words imply differences the differences are created only by our language. We would be free to see that a change in any component of consciousness, at any point in its development, would mean an alteration in the subsequent emergence of that system of conscious experience. We are our history and any difference in the genetic-biological or social events shaping our consciousness changes all aspects of consciousness from that point forward. We would recognize that all causes occur at the same moment in time and the multiplicity of causes become a multiplicity of effects, which turn on themselves and all the other variables in the ongoing development and changes in any given system. But such an analysis is not yet available and we must be content with poorer fare than we might someday enjoy.

THE STRUCTURE AND FUNCTION OF HUMAN CONSCIOUSNESS

I begin my analysis of consciousness by framing my student's story in terms of its structure and function. I use the term structure metaphorically to denote a set of ongoing processes that are involved in systematic relationships and therefore can be spoken of as a structure. Psychological structures are composed purely of functions. We experience ourselves as a literal structure but in fact can find no actual objects or things when we search for the self. Instead we find a variety of cognitive and affective processes that seem consistently related over time. The self seems to be the psychological position or perspective from which various events are viewed and interpreted. Moreover, the cognitive and affective processes that comprise conscious experience are related to a set of social interactions with other beings whose consciousness are comprised of cognitive and affective processes. Our personal consciousness is given meaning through consistent interactions with other people and other forms of consciousness.

We can also speak of social structures recognizing that such structures are also metaphorical. Anthony Giddens (1984: 26) states that social structures are created by the process of structuration. He goes on to suggest that, "A structuration begins with the human agencies that knowingly participate in all interpersonal practices. Structuration is the continuous reproduction of relationships across time and space." We can therefore speak of intrapsychic structures as well as interpersonal structures if we recognize that all structures are composed of sets of relationships that depend on all other sets for their existence.

For too long now biologists, psychologists, and sociologists have acted as if the processes of their fields concerns had nothing to do with the concerns of the other two fields. Biologists, especially neurobiologists, have studied the functioning of the brain as if these neurological processes had nothing to do with the subjective experiences and psychological processes that were being created and shaped in the adaptive interchanges with the physical and social environment. Psychologists studied intrapsychic processes as if they had nothing to do with other events in their subjects lives. All of our cognitive and affective processes relate to the objects that comprise the contexts in which we seek to adapt. Without these contexts there are no psychological or intrapsychic processes to study or be concerned about. The very distinction between inner and outer, subject and object is rendered meaningless by this framework. What is inner and separate from outer is a product of the god story that separates mind (or soul) from the body and from the material world. No matter how compelling that aspect of subjectivity is it will not be the perspective taken here. Similarly, sociologists have conceived of social structures as existing prior to the human beings who enter into them. Giddens explains that social structure is a duality not a dualism. They do not exist independently or prior to the actions taken by human agencies that are necessary to create the structures. From this point of view all such distinctions between fields must somehow disappear when we speak of the structure of adaptive consciousness.

What then can we impose on my student's story that will be found with regularity in the descriptions of human experience by any who allow us entry into their personal worlds? Given the regularities noted, what can we glean about those activities that will allow us to change those modes of experience in the directions dictated by our educational-therapeutic and moral goals? I will focus on the following: (1) My student presents her description to us in the form of a story or narrative. (2) Her narrative, told from a first person point of view, is an intentional act demonstrating an effort to create the narrative. (3) The narrative interrelates events which occur in time and space some, of which my student experiences as existing outside of herself, and others that she experiences as occurring internally. (4) The narrative is comprised of both cognitive and affective processes and is directed toward these processes. The narrative would not exist were it not for the language, the perceptions, memories, and anticipations utilized by my student. The existence of the narrative seems motivated by a series of emotions and other affective processes as well.

If cognition and affects are the tools of the narrative they are also the objects of these processes as well. (5) The statements in "4" make us aware that my student's conscious experience exists in various levels of reflexivity. Some of her cognitive processes are tools that allow her to experience only the events on which her cognition are focused while in other places in the narrative she is focused only on her own cognitive or affective processes. In still other places she seems to be simultaneously aware of external events and the fact that she is aware that she is aware. This leads me to the observation that she knows more than she can say (Polanyi 1958) and that she is saying more than she knows she is saying. (6) The narrative reveals a wide variety of change inside and outside the frame of the narrative. Relationships are in transition, cognitive and affective processes are varying and changing, and the student is aware of changes taking place in the very nature of her narrative as they are taking place. (7) Finally, her narrative and all the events that are described within it, are directed toward some stated or unstated goal, that is, the narrative and all its processes have some adaptive purpose.

The concepts with which I frame my narrative of consciousness and its development will begin with the work of Jean Piaget who began his career as a biologist with research into the adaptive behaviors of mollusks. He saw adaptation as defining the goals of all living things and when he turned his attention to human adaptation he focused on the cognitive processes as the main tool of achieving adaptation. It was the manner in which human beings learned to construct an understanding of their world as they sought to adapt to that world that determined their success and failure both as individuals and as a species. Piaget ties human development and the development of lower species together with the same concepts and describes adaptation as a universal set of processes. Moreover, the process of adaptation that generates the changes in the cognitive structures that form our construction of the world and that are the ultimate vehicles of success and failure in adaptation.

All animals must adapt. In biological terms, successful adaptation is defined by achieving the goals of continued life by having viable offspring who in turn could produce viable offspring of their own. All animals must have adaptive devices to permit them to achieve their adaptive goals. The manner in which such devices operated and changed during the struggle to stay alive and have offspring were of one or another subprocesses that defined the overall process of adaptation. While an organism is seeking adaptive ends it is either engaged in acts of assimilation or acts of accommodation. In the act of assimilation the organism attempts to reach the goals representing successful adaptation with its existing skills. Kegan (1982: 43) defines assimilation as "fitting one's experience to one's present means of organizing reality." When the demands of adaptation outstrip the capacity of the organisms existing skills then the organism must seek ways to modify or add to its existing repertoire of adaptive behaviors which include its mode of making sense of its external and internal environments. The struggle to modify existing skills and abilities is described as the process of accommodation or to again quote Kegan (1982: 44), "accommodation is the reorganizing one's present way of making meaning to take account of experience."

In human beings the predominate skills of adaptation are cognitive. Piaget focused most of his conceptual energies in describing how the initial schema or primitive cognitive organizations with which the infant constructs and frames his view of the world changes as a result of the demands of accommodation over the long course of human development. In the language of the phenomenologist, Piaget is describing how the interaction of noesis and noema leads to changes in the noetic side of the correlate and hence new subjective readings of the self and the environment. The heterophenomenologist would be concerned with the biological and social events surrounding these adaptive struggles and how they contribute to these changes in the modes and manners with which the developing child constructs and reconstructs his understanding of his world and his place in it.

COGNITION

The development of an individual's cognitive abilities in Piagetian terms will be delayed until the next chapter, however, the concepts of George Kelly (1955) provide a useful metaphor in our understanding of the function and purposes of the cognitive processes. Kelly considered all human beings scientists in that they sought to describe, explain, predict, and control the events that enfolded them and in which they must survive and develop. We might say that in order to adapt an individual must learn to change their scientific understanding and skills from those judged naive to those judged more sophisticated. The noetic constructions of noema are most effective in relation to meeting and achieving adaptive goals when they take the shape of the activities of science when these are at their best. The infant is born with Darwinian intelligence and hopefully proceeds through Skinnerian to Popperian modes of being in the world. As we discuss these developments we try and answer the riddle as to why some become adept at scientifically observing their environment and others do all that they can to avoid direct observation of their environment. We wonder why some ask critical questions about commonly held beliefs, believe that their own conclusions are theoretical, probabilistic, and in need of revision no matter how compelling they are felt to be absolute truth, and why others believe what authority tells them is true no matter how compellingly their own eyes tell them otherwise. Perhaps most importantly we need to understand why some individuals experience new events as anomalous to their existing ideas and accommodate their ideas in the face of the anomaly, and others assimilate the anomaly into their existing constructions no matter how torturous the demands of such assimilation become.

The idea that human beings can accommodate their existing modes of perceiving the world, thinking about it, or maintain existing modes despite adaptive pressures not to do so, demonstrates the constructive nature of human cognitive processes. Our ideas about the world around us are not merely a function of information passively accumulated about external events but are the product of motoric and what Mahoney (1991) refers to as feed forward activities. From the moment of our births we are prepared to search for human faces and spend the most time evaluating these objects. Our basic perceptual processes automatically select a figure from the environment while holding all others to be the ground or contextual framework. The work of the Gestalt psychologists (Max Wertheimer, Wolfgang Kohler, and Kurt Koffka) demonstrated that there was often no one-to-one correspondence between a physicist's description of an object and our phenomenological experience of it. For example, a series of still pictures flashed in sequence appear to be moving smoothly and continuously rather than discontinuously. It is clear that from a physicists perception there is no actual movement but from the constructed experience of the individual there is movement.

Our basic perceptual processes are constructive and feed forward but the mechanisms of construction are most often prereflective and not open to conscious scrutiny. We cannot explain how we create figure and ground, or see the series of still pictures as moving. These nonconscious processes seemed to have emerged during the long period of human evolution and have as their goal our ability to negotiate our way through a world of objects and events, some of which could be our lunch while others would make us their lunch. Our constructions begin with processes that make the world around us appear solid, colorful, endowed with sound, smell, taste, and a host of experiences involving touch. We construct our experiences, but experience the world and its contents as if they were external to us and immediately given. It is the immediacy and certainty of much of perceptual experience that makes constructivism a somewhat counterintuitive concept. It is also the immediacy, vividness, and certainty of perceptual experience that leads us to be harshly judgmental when individuals disagree with us, particularly when we as a group agree that our beliefs are enhancing our adaptive success. Our strongest judgments of so-called mental illness are reserved for those who do not perceptually experience the world as we do.

Establishing that our cognitive processes allow us to describe, explain, predict, and control ourselves and the world in which we struggle to live and survive; that we define our adaptive goals with our cognitive processes and use these processes to assimilate necessary information into them in order to improve the manner in which we adapt, have we now explained the entire process of adaptation? I believe not, for we still do not know when we, or any organism, knows when accommodations are necessary. We need information other than cognitive to know when our adaptations are successful or are failing. It is clear to many of us studying psychology that our cognitive processes alone do not create the full experience of meaning and cannot by themselves provide the motivations to either change our own adaptive processes or seek help from others to help us assimilate necessary adaptive goals. Meanings require perception, thought, memory, and anticipations but they also require an accompanying and integrated affective process as well.

AFFECTIVE PROCESSES

Until recently the affective processes, the drives, and the emotions were the poor stepchild of psychology. The biological drives such as hunger and the need to sleep were respectable topics for research. Psychoanalysts concerned themselves with sex and the emotions of anxiety, and to a lesser extent guilt, but the wide range of human emotions went largely unnoticed or found their way into psychological discussions implicitly but not as the center of research. This should not be surprising since many of the god stories of Western culture reveal that logic and thought are the functions of the soul and emotions, and the drives are seated in our weak and easily corrupted bodies. In many Western cultures the overt display of emotion is regarded as uncouth and lacking in civility, especially if displayed by the gentlemen of that society. However, in recent years emotions have become of central concern for an ever larger number of psychologists in fields across the discipline. The work of Caroll Izard (1977, 1979, Jerome Kagan (1984, 1994), Robert Zajonc (1980, 1984), Nico Frijda (1986, 1988), George Mandler (1984), Michael Mahoney (1991), Robert Plutchik (1977, 1980), Laurence Simon (1986, 1994), and especially Richard Lazarus (1982, 1984, 1991) have been in the forefront of this revolution.

Let me begin with a definition of the affective processes, whose most important subcategories are the drives and the emotions. Affect provides the felt qualities of meaning. There is no motivation provided by the cognitive processes by themselves; it is not until the organismic, felt qualities of affect are infused and joined with the perceptions and thoughts of an event that meanings exist capable of stimulating action. All cognitive actions are motoric in nature. As with all physical activity that involves a movement in relation to an object there is a resultant feeling. Kegan writes (1982: 8), "Affect is essentially phenomenological, the felt experience of a motion (hence, 'e-motion')." Affect, as with cognition, is evolutionarily based and vital to the adaptive process. It is affect that most fully determines adaptive meaning because it provides both the demands of adaptation and signals success and failure in adaptation. Drives are the phenomenological representatives of homoeostatic imbalances. They tell us which tissue needs demand adaptive action. They focus attention on those goals or aspects of the environment that reduce the homoeostatic imbalances that threaten our continued biological functioning. Their removal, or satiation, represents the phenomenology of success in these endeavors. Emotions are the phenomenological representatives of success and failure with our adaptive struggles with the physical and social environments. If we return momentarily to Piaget, I would say that emotions represent the motivation for the processes of accommodation to take place.

There are no cognitive processes that can be assessed without an understanding of the emotional processes with which they are integrated. For example, psychologists will measure a child's intelligence by giving him a series of cognitive tasks. The child's emotional responses to the tests are seen as interfering with or benefitting his achievements but they are not seen as part of actual intelligence. When I tested children I saw many who so feared failure and the judgments that these inadequate performances produced from teachers and parents that they often made little or no effort to engage the tests. I defy any investigator to tease apart the cognitive from the emotional while evaluating a child's cognitive capacities.

One of the weaknesses in Piaget's framework was the scant attention he payed to anything other than cognitive development. When an imbalance existed between the existing skills of an individual and the demands made by some environmental event, Piaget suggested that the individual existed in a state of disequilibrium. Disequilibrium was the closest thing to a motivational concept that Piaget developed until the end of his career (Piaget 1981). Brian Rotman (1977) and Jerome Bruner (1966) were among others who criticized Piaget for his failures to integrate affect into his descriptions of cognitive development as well as integrating the developing child into his social surroundings. Bruner felt that Piaget's work was, in fact, a developmental epistemology rather than a true psychology because of its weak motivational constructions. I suggest that what Piaget called disequilibrium is better represented by the wide range of human emotions with the various emotions defining success and failure in adaptation. For example, fear defines a perception that the organism is in danger and therefore in need of taking action and if necessary, developing skills that deal with that source of danger. A feeling of safety will define for the organism that it has successfully adapted to the requirements of having done something to remove itself from dangerous events in one way or another.

Carroll Izard (1977: 48–49) defines emotions as "complex processes with neurophysiological, neuromuscular and phenomenological aspects. There is in each emotion a pattern of electrochemical activity in the nervous system, particularly in the cortex, the hypothalamus, the basal ganglia, the limbic system and the facial and trigeminal nerves. At the neuromuscular level is primarily facial patterning and secondarily it is bodily [postural, gestural, visceral, glandular, and sometimes vocal] response. At the phenomenological level emotion is essentially motivating experience or experience that has immediate meaning and significance for the person." (I would add that this is true for a wide range of animals as well.) We see that emotions are organismic responses and that newer evidence exists to suggest that even an individual's immune system responds to the demands of emotions such as anger and fear. While emotions energize behavior the fact that emotions are felt and seen on our faces, the one body part that cannot be observed by the self without a mirror or similar device, suggests that a wide range of emotions exist simultaneously as social signals of our responses and intentions to others.

It is out of our cognitive and affective responses that consciousness is constructed. Cognition and affect develop as a result of the attempts to assimilate and accommodate to the adaptive demands made by the physical and social environments. With development, consciousness becomes more reflective, and with increased reflection, the perception emerges that we are capable of creating change in our own internal processes and external events. With development, there comes the need to justify and judge as well as describe and explain. Simultaneously, we begin to join and create the narratives that hold the patterns of our experiences together. With continued interactions with others, our narratives begin to reveal just what and how we describe and judge, and how we experience being described and judged by those with whom we share our lives. I continue to create an adaptive theory that includes some of the intra- and interpersonal dynamics that affect the development of conscious experience.

6

ADAPTATION AND THE DYNAMICS OF CHANGE

INTRODUCTION

We must now consider the different ways that people invent meaning systems, including those that preclude any significant new adaptations from taking place. Not all people become scientists and artists, some try to become gods capable of assimilating all new experiences into their existing forms of mental organization, while others attempt to become things for whom the adaptive process and the reorganization of consciousness are seen as taking place in people other than themselves. We must also consider how people influence the adaptive development of others and how they seek to resolve the inevitable conflicts that exist as people struggle to adapt and make sure that their offspring are capable of surviving and adapting on their own. A major focus of this book concerns not only how one generation shapes the consciousness of another in the processes of parenting, teaching, and psychotherapy but how these conflict-ridden processes create scientists and artists rather than gods and things. Finally, we must consider those forms of development, which may be universal, and those we judge to be desirable, which will form the basis of the standards and morality that will guide our efforts as we work with others.

Having set forth the goals of this Chapter and the remaining chapters of Part III, I now warn the reader that I do not provide a satisfying narrative to achieve my stated ends. The first reason I fail has to do with the fact that I am simply too ignorant to do anything but ask questions and occasionally describe some of the theories and processes I believe are relevant. The second problem is created by my efforts to cover so much material in a short space. There is much material available that is relevant to help explain the human adaptive process which includes how human awareness is affected by the social, biological, and personal constructive processes that make up the adaptive struggle.

I try to balance two approaches to this material. The first approach involves discussing general psychological processes that cut across development. The second approach is to broadly discuss development as it cuts across a variety of general psychological topics. For example, I will discuss the role of play and work in the adaptive process. I could describe all of development from the lens of play and work. I discuss the self as a general topic of concern, as well as topics such as the internal-external locus of control. Both of these topics have broad implications for development.

I present a discussion of Piaget's stages of cognitive development, as well as Kegan's theory of the development of the self-concept that is based on Piagetian theory. Other important contributions to this theory which attempt to integrate Piagetian concepts and dynamic psychology are based on the writings of Stanley Greenspan (1979) and Hugh Rosen (1985). These discussions of development are so broadly based that they can be used to illuminate a nearly infinite number of general topics such as the self and its organization, the relationship of cognition and emotions, play and work, and the internal-external locus of control. My complaint about many textbooks is exactly the complaint I will be forced to levy at myself. Developmental theories are presented in the early chapters only to be ignored as the physical, cognitive, emotional, and social aspects of childhood are discussed in term of the chronology of children's birthdays. Each chapter of these texts includes general topics such as discipline or morality creating the illusion that discipline belongs in early childhood more than at any other age or that it is somehow more logical to discuss morality in the chapter on adolescence rather than later in childhood. With these caveats in mind, I forge ahead and hope to provide a meaningful framework about the adaptive process.

FROM DEVELOPMENTAL EPISTEMOLOGY TO DYNAMIC PSYCHOLOGY

The first problem to be tackled involves tying together the developmental epistemology of Piaget with theories of the emotions and social constructionism. If this can be achieved then we can utilize developmental constructionism in a framework that does justice to the emergence of the self, the wide range of human motivations, and the intra- and interpersonal dynamics that mark the human species as unique.

Figure 1 suggests that the nomenclature used by the biologist Piaget has its parallels in both heterophenomenological and phenomenological language. When individuals seek to assimilate an experience into their psychological organization that experience is of an event or object needed or wanted by those individuals. The object may serve to satisfy a drive or resolve an emotion, but in either case the event or object of their attention will either increase the possibilities of gene transmission, maintain the life of the adult or the offspring, or in some way serve the development of the selves and the memes that are the expression of selves. When needs cannot be satisfied organisms, or in this case the persons, must accommodate their experiences to the demands of the situation in which the events and objects are to

Figure 1
Adaptation

Biological: Assimilation————————————Accommodation

(Natural Sciences)

Psychological: Needs————————————Problems to be solved

(Psychology as a Natural Science)

Phenomenological: Cognitive-Affective Experience

(Postmodern, Human Sciences)

---

be found. From a psychological point of view we can also say that the individuals have a problem requiring a solution. The degree to which the individuals solve the problem is the degree to which the necessary accommodations have been made that allow assimilation or need satisfaction to take place. Growth and change are engendered by what takes place in the act of accommodation or problem solving.

Finally, we can move to the third line of the figure and recognize that people tend to define both their needs and their problems with statements that reflect what they experience in or about a situation in terms of their cognitive appraisals and felt emotional responses to the situation. The statement "I am hungry and I am going to make myself something to eat." reflects both a need and a potential problem, especially if the individual cannot find something to eat in the usual and expected manner. "I am afraid of X and I don't know where to hide." expresses both a need and the adaptive problem to be solved by the individual.

From this point of view every cognitive-affective evaluation of any situation and the objects and events that comprise the situation represents (1) an assimilative act with the potential for the necessity of accommodation; (2) a need to be satisfied with the potential that a problem exists requiring a solution; and (3) a statement that describes the subjective experience of how it feels for that person at that time and that place to be experiencing that situation. The meaning of the situation is reflected by the cognitive-affective processes which now provide the motive for the individuals to behave in relation to the situation being construed. The patterns of emerging action are chosen by the individuals with the aim of either reducing, maintaining, or increasing the affective component of the situation's meaning to the individuals. Drives are satisfied when the objects of adaptation are assimilated, the hunger need is reduced as tissue imbalances are restored, or when emotions are resolved as when, for example, the individual perceives that the sources of danger are no longer threatening. Success or failure in adaptation is based on the ongoing cognitive-affective experiences of the situation.

I now describe a dynamic model of adaptation. This model is derived from the work of Richard Lazarus (1982, 1984, 1991) although I have taken liberties with the model. Each adaptive act takes place in a situation comprised of objects and events which have possible consequences for an individual. The situation has no meaning until it has been given meaning by a primary cognitive appraisal (PCA) of the participating individuals. It is this evaluative act of noesis that defines for the individuals the needs and possible problems associated with the situation. The PCA is accompanied by an emotional response to the situation, which along with the cognitive act defines the full felt meaning of the situation for the individuals. It is the meaning of the situation as construed by the individuals that defines the nature of the adaptive task for the individuals. It should be noted that the primary appraisal is made by individuals with their knowledge of just which skills they believe they have or do not have to meet the adaptive demands of the situation. The nature and degree of a perceived problem is not merely a function of the situation itself but how the situation is seen in relation to how individuals believe they are capable of responding to the events comprising the situation. Actions are carried out in order to satisfy needs or solve problems in terms of the secondary cognitive appraisals (SCA) which also play the role of assessing how effective these efforts were in achieving relevant adaptive ends thereby setting in motion a new adaptive set of efforts. It must always be kept in mind that our verbal or diagrammatic descriptions of adaptation tend to freeze the action and change.

As we perceive the present, our perceptions are embedded in our past and our memories of the past. The emotions aroused by memories of the past may deeply color the perceptions of the present and needs and problems that have gone unsatisfied or unsolved may have much to do with how we define our present needs and problems. But as we live in the moment we also rewrite the past. The past lives in the present and is always remembered as a function of present needs and problems. The typical textbook description of memory as being comprised of specific traces stored in the long-term memory and accessed as exact replicas of past events is being replaced by a view of memory as a series of reconstructions designed to meet current adaptive needs. The work of John Kotré (1995), Elizabeth Loftus and Kenneth Ketcham (1994) and Donald Spence (1982), among others stresses the constantly restructured nature of our historical remembrances. The past is also our guide to the future as our anticipations and predictions grow out of past conclusions and present modes of cognitive-affective experiencing.

Any discussion of adaptation must include the satisfaction of needs and the solving of problems as they relate to the conscious processes of others. Modern psychoanalysts such as Steven Mitchell (1992), Donna Orange (1995), George Atwood and Robert Stolorow (1984) refer to the interactions of human conscious-ness as intersubjective spaces or the intersubjective field. R. D. Laing (1967) describes how words can never capture the subtleties of interactions as individuals are aware of each other, as they are aware that they are aware of each other, as they are aware that they are aware that they are aware of each other, etc. This book will deal with the dynamics that arise in intersubjective space when individuals of equal and or unequal cognitive development describe and/or judge one another, love and/or hate one another, help one another adapt or try and prevent adaptations, struggle to be honest or attempt to deceive, delight in their individual differences, or battle to replace those difference with a mirror image of their own selves. We will pay particular attention to the uses of power within the intersubjective space because power marks, in one way or another, all human relationships. It is the dynamics that occur within intersubjectivity that define the work of parent, teacher, and psychotherapist and it is the means and modes of cognitive affective interactions that define success and failure in those endeavors.

I turn next to the emergence of reflective thinking wherein individuals can appraise their own behaviors as well as their own cognitive-affective processes. With development, human beings demonstrate a wide variety of states of consciousness based in part on how able individuals are in reflecting on their own states of consciousness. Neil Rossman (1991) suggests that when we are aware of our environments, but not aware that we are aware, we are demonstrating prereflective consciousness. When we are aware that we are aware we demonstrate reflective consciousness. A discussion of those states of consciousness that we wish not to be in our awareness which psychotherapists refer to as unconsciousness and as being the result of defense mechanisms and which Rossman calls nonconsciousness will be in the next chapter. I close this section as I turn to Piaget's descriptions of the development of our appraisal system as a function of the adaptive processes.

THE DEVELOPMENT OF THE COGNITIVE APPRAISALS

It is clear from the previous discussion that human beings are not born with full complement of needs to be satisfied and problems to be solved. Needs and problems emerge and present themselves as a function of both development and the nature of the events confronting the developing individual. In this model emotions are not aroused without a cognitive appraisal of a situation, and since the objects and events that comprise the situation must be constructed by the cognitive processes that inform the person of these objects and events, the nature of human needs and problems are constantly changing as a function of the changing organization and transformations of the cognitive processes as they are used by the individual to attempt to satisfy needs and solve problems. It is at this juncture that I briefly introduce the reader, as I do my students, to the stages of cognitive development outlined by Piaget.

It has been one of my ongoing missions as a psychologist to introduce these developmental concepts to all of my colleagues, especially those in the field of so-called clinical psychology. Psychoanalysts refer to the collection of human adaptive skills as the ego. It is the ego that assumes responsibility for human adaptation. It has long seemed to me that it is Piaget, more than any other scientist, who has provided clinicians with their most detailed descriptions of the ego. Moreover, it is Piaget's developmental descriptions that provide insights into the nature of what is called psychopathology if we recognize that the moral judgments that are referred to as diagnoses are in fact better described as the adaptive efforts of individuals utilizing cognitive organizations judged more appropriate to younger age groups.

Piaget (1952, 1954) describes four stages of cognitive or intellectual development, each of which has both qualitative and quantitative differences from the others. The first stage is the sensory-motor stage. When children are born, suggests Piaget, they are equipped to respond purposefully to the world by reflexes alone.

The children initially engage in a series of motor actions that produce sensations or respond motorically to the sensations impinging on their sensorium. There are no coordinated activities nor are any of the behaviors purposeful means to selected ends. However, as the months unfold children discover that some activities inevitably lead to pleasurable feelings in their bodies. These behaviors are repeated to produce the pleasurable sensations producing the first differentiation of means and ends. Piaget refers to these as the first acquired adaptations or the primary circular reactions. Sucking, grasping, looking and rocking are some of the activities that begin to be repeated by the infant. From the infants point of view the sole purpose of the movements is to enhance pleasurable sensations but from the developmentalist's perspective the baby is not only assimilating the objects sensory qualities but is constantly accommodating his motor responses to the "affordances" (a term used by the psychologist James Gibson (De Jong 1995: 253), for the action possibilities the environment affords) or manipulanda of the objects and events with which he is interacting. The baby is, in effect, being stimulated to develop the skills required for further adaptations.

The primary circular reactions give way to the secondary circular reactions as babies becomes aware that some of their actions not only produce pleasant sensations but also make interesting things happen. Any consequence of an action that does not lead to pain is repeated leading to an explosion of new and more coordinated motor skills. These new skills allow still more sophisticated explorations of the environment to take place. Around eight months infants make one of the critical leaps in the organization of their intellectual understanding of the world. Children discover that objects continue to exist even when they are not in sensory contact with them. If a younger infant is looking at an object and the object is covered up the infant loses immediate interest in the object, however, with the achievement of object constancy the child will push aside the cover to retrieve the lost object. In a very real sense, Piaget notes, for the first time children have constructed real objects with which they can relate and with which they can have a relationship. The enormous implications for the discovery and constructions of psychological objects, especially human ones, will be discussed. With the creation of objects children begin to discover themselves as objects as well and begin to separate time into past, present, and future. The objects independent of children may cease to exist (past) or be anticipated to return or be found again (future).

Infancy comes to its psychological end when, in the last of the six substages Piaget created to account for the sensory-motor stage, children achieve still another monumental act of creativity and discovery. Children begin to represent the objects and events with which they have been interacting with images experienced internally, or in the Cartesian theater as it were. In turn these images are expressed symbolically by means of delayed imitations and other motor actions through drawn pictures, and most importantly, by means of language. Children now enter the preoperational or second stage of cognitive development. To understand the Piagetian meaning of preoperation we must define the term: *an operation is a mental act with reversibility.* Children who until now have been performing a variety of motor actions on objects have internalized the objects and now begin to internalize the actions as well. The goal of these actions is the same as the earlier motor actions—they seek adaptive ends and are subject to the same assimilative and accommodatory processes which lead to changes in the organization and content of the inner world that we call the mind. Thus, the beginnings of Popperian intelligence are born.

I ask my students (and the reader as well) to imagine an apple in their mind's eye. I now ask them to cut the apple in half. This action defines the achievement of the preoperational stage. I ask the reader to reassemble the apple in their mind's eye. This second action, reversibilty, represents the achievement of a true operation and simultaneously defines the limitations of the preoperational stage. Preoperational children can cut mental apples in half but not put them back together. Preoperational children begin the work of organizing the objects and events into meaningful categories called concepts. By organizing objects and events in this way we reduce the time necessary to choose adaptive responses to the elements that make up the situations to which we must adapt. Once stable categories are formed and the categories themselves organized not only does the individual have a feed forward or anticipatory set of responses waiting should a member of the category appear but an emotional response that will provide the basis for action toward the object or event will be ready as well.

We observe in the preoperational stage children beginning the process of putting the objects and events they have by now constructed into conceptual relationships. But this process, as with all human learning, contains much error and requires not only putting things together but taking them apart and placing them elsewhere. The early concepts reflect the putting together but are marked by the inability to reverse a decision and separate what is now conceptually joined. Children will center their perceptions on one aspect of similarity between two objects, and because they cannot decenter or reverse their percepts they will ignore what adults or older children consider essential differences and form a category based solely on the perceived similarity. For example learning that his pet is called a cat, a child will center on the four-leggedness, or the fur as the basis of catness and call a dog, or virtually any other animal, a cat. The concepts of young children reveal the tendency to overextend or be overinclusive. Similarly children may center on a trivial difference between two objects and refuse to include them in the same category giving the preoperational children's concepts their quality of narrowness or under-inclusivity. Finally, the bases of categories can change if children center on some other aspect of an object's sensory or motor characteristics making their concepts fluid and highly unstable.

The tendency to center and the inability to reverse or decenter has still other important consequences for children's understanding of their world. They lack an identity element that permits an appreciation of one-to-one correspondence or that the amount of something does not change if its shape or surface appearance does. Children lack an identity element such as $1 + 0 = 1$ or $1 \times 1 = 1$. Four ounces of water poured into a tall, thin glass is said to be more water than four ounces of water poured into a wide, short glass. Children, therefore, can not seriate or place objects according to their sizes or respective weights. Children can judge, however, making any comparisons the most versus the least, or the worst versus the best. Finally, time cannot be well-differentiated by preoperational youngsters and, while there is a past and a future as compared to the timelessness of infancy, the experience of the preoperational child is that of now or not now.

One of Piaget's most usable concepts was that of egocentrism, defined as children's inability to take the viewpoint of another. While egocentrism is usually discussed in relation to preoperational children (ages two through seven) one can see all of psychological development as a reduction in egocentrism. The infant who has not yet achieved object constancy and closes his eyes making the world cease to exist is demonstrating perhaps the highest degree of egocentrism. Preoperational children now know that the world exists independently of them but are still embedded in the objects of their perceptions. Therefore, their perceptions of objects contain elements of their own feelings creating a world that can change with their moods or the arousal of their drives and other shifts in their state of consciousness. The experience of an object, even a human being, can be perceived as being changed in essence if it is described or judged, or creates pleasure rather than pain in the child. Therefore, there can be mean mommies or nice mommies depending on how the very same mommy is construed. Not only are objects changed by the feelings of the child but inanimate objects are alive and have human motives. A cup on its side may be sleepy, thunder and lightening are monsters in the night sky, oceans are literally angry and both the monsters of the sky and the ocean are trying to hurt the child. The night terrors of childhood seem predicated on the egocentrism and animisms of the epoch of development.

To preoperational children, thoughts are real and wishes can make things happen with no other efforts required (magical omnipotence). Therefore, children's defenses against the things that go bump in the night are often their own thoughts. Thoughts that are real, however, can hurt others if they are filled with anger or visible to parents, Santa Claus, and a variety of other kindly and malevolent mythical figures. The child's sense of causality is dominated by beliefs that events occur because people or objects wish them to. All events are puposivistic: "It rained today because I wanted to go to the park." Children at this stage also believe that if they are bad then they must be punished, but if they are punished they must be bad (immanent justice). Morality structured in this way can lead to beliefs that one is permanently bad and irredeemable if enough painful events occur in a child's life that are interpreted as punishments.

By the age of seven children undergo another transformation and find themselves in the stage of concrete operations. True operations are achieved when children can reverse their mental operations, decenter from specific and often trivial aspects of the perceptual field, and become capable of simultaneously attending to and coordinating a number of perceptual elements. The same children that insisted the tall, thin glass had more water than the short, fat one now decenter their perceptions from the height alone and make judgments based on width and circumference. Children are now capable of understanding, at least implicitly, that their comparisons are those of volume and not height, width, or circumference. In addition, if children watched us pour water from a four ounce tumbler into the two disparately shaped but larger glasses then they are also able to mentally reverse the process recognizing the common origins of the water in each glass. This new integration of cognitive skills leads to what Piaget called the conservations of quantities, time, distance, and many other aspects of the world in which the children are embedded. No longer can a parent split a cookie in two and have a contented child who now believes she has two cookies. No longer can the child push unwanted vegetables together to make less of them while spreading out his favorite foods all over the plate to have more of them. Concrete operations allow children to live in a world that appears more stable and consistently organized into categories whose affordances are more predictably functional and related to successful adaptation.

The stage of concrete operations represents a further reduction in egocentricity as children now become involved in the activities of creating more complex concepts into which the world can be made to make sense and trying to understand how the objects and events that comprise the categories relate and are made to work. Children begin to understand the difference between the animate and the inanimate and therefore begin to understand the difference between the physical and psychological sciences. Piaget, who often refers to children as scientists exploring their world, described this stage as one in which the scientific endeavor became more focused and systematic. But the explorations of children whose logical system is now more in keeping with those expected by adults are still rooted in the concrete objects and processes that can be experienced through the five senses. The next leap forward involves the progressive replacement of actual objects with symbols such as words and numbers and the continued interiorization of operations that mark the stage of formal operations.

The stage of formal operations is marked by the developing capacity of children to turn their attention on their own thought and life processes and those of others. In the concrete stage children could utilize reversibilities to create concepts but they now can create concepts out of their reversibilities. They now ask, "Why did I think that?" or "What was so and so's motives for doing this or that?" The ability to ask such questions marks the presence of what therapists have long called insight. Whereas concrete youngsters can memorize the dates of history, with formal operations the same individuals can study the history of history. The concrete child learns to tell and conserve time, with formal operations it is time itself that becomes the focus of study. The understanding of long time frames combines with a newly discovered ability to make predictions, hypotheses, and inferences and allows the developing individuals to evaluate their lives in powerful new ways that create hithertofore unimagined needs and problems. It is because of formal operations that we conclude inescapably that we are mortal and that all life is finite.

The knowledge that life is finite changes both an individual's organization of goals and the time frames in which to achieve those goals. With formal operations we see the emergence of what Alfred Adler (1968) called fictional finalisms, long-range goals, usually of a moral nature and defined by changes in the definition of the self that force individuals to subordinate all other goals toward their realization. I have suggested (Simon 1986, 1994) that the emergence of these long range goals, which to the individual are experienced as making life meaningful and purposeful, allow us to describe the behavior of the individual as guided by the future principle rather than merely by the pleasure principle or the reality principle, concepts long utilized by psychoanalysis. I am also suggesting that the emergence of consciousness dominated by a future principle simultaneously creates consciousness dominated by what the philosopher Sydney Hook (1987) called a historical principle. Individuals guided by long-range, future goals understand that the key to understanding the future is to understand the past.

The stable concepts that enclosed and differentiated between classes and types of concrete objects are also now organized in turn by the emergence of abstract categories of categories. Abstract categories such as democracy, freedom, liberty, tyranny, justice, and morality have a profound impact on the adaptive behaviors of those possessing them. But these are categories that can include a multitude of concrete examples and exist by reason of words rather than any specific object or event capable of being experienced. Human beings can now create concepts that organize and overlay any aspects of their lives, including relationships human or otherwise. Concepts can be created which run counter to fact; debates can be engaged in for their own sake. Individuals think about the infinite, and about all possibilities, and in short develop all of the arts and sciences which depend on abstract, propositional, and theoretical ideas. I will now return to a description of the adaptive processes by discussing the needs that human beings must satisfy which emerge and change as a function of the individual's cognitive development.

NEEDS

I have been using the word need without a definition. A corrective demands that we recognize that need is just a word that provides us a means of discussing an aspect of subjective experience. However, it is another example of a process or set of activities being described by a noun rather than a verb. It is only when we restore the concept to its phenomenological language that the motor, action qualities of experience are restored: "I feel hungry, the meal I ate this morning no longer sustains me and I plan to have something to eat soon." or "I am frightened and I am looking for a place to hide." However, an abstract language is necessary if we are to apply the heterophenomenological method of analysis and move as simultaneously as we can between a third person and first person account of behavior. What then is a need? I define a need as a cognitive-affective experience that will not be satisfied or resolved until successful adaptations are achieved. Needs represent those subjective states of experience that become intense, unremitting, and preemptive of other psychological states. Needs, however, are but one form of human desiring.

Human beings also want things. Wants are also motivating and defined by cognitive-affective states of consciousness. However, wants do not preempt other patterns of behavior in the same way as those desires experienced as needs. Wants are defined as desires that can be put aside if more important demands are experienced by the individual as requiring adaptive attention. It is interesting to note that one person's needs may be another's wants and vice versa. If needs and wants can vary from person to person then can we speak of any needs as being universal or as being discussed from any point of view except from each individual's first person experience? Jerome Kagan (1984) believes that there are as many needs as there are emotional reactions to situations making it difficult, if not impossible, to organize our emotions into groupings that can then be abstracted from the situations in which the emotions are aroused and speaking of such groupings as needs. Social constructionists point out that the word emotions is only a word (as is the word need) and that all words reflect meanings that are local and meaningful only in the cultures that use and create them. The concept of need, I believe, requires the convenience of defining some cognitive-affective states common to all peoples regardless of language differences if we are to have a science of psychology. I now speak of a variety of needs as defined by specific cognitive-affective states as if they existed independently of the person's experiencing them, even though I know this to be impossible.

What are some of the human experiences that might behave as needs rather than wants? The organization of needs as described by Abraham Maslow (1968) and Erich Fromm (1947, 1950, 1980) are integrated into the following discussion. The biological drives are perhaps the easiest to agree on. The imbalance of homeostatic mechanisms leads to subjective states of hunger, thirst, fatigue, pressures to eliminate wastes, suffocation among others with a corresponding state of satiation that defines success in reducing, terminating, or avoiding these states of consciousness. As we evaluate our surroundings we learn that some events can affect our bodies in such ways as to cause physical (and later) emotional pain. Perceived threats to our safety are defined by fear and anger, where fear initiates some type of flight response and anger is expressed as one form of fight or another. Success at fight or flight will be experienced as a sense of safety or comfort. As we interact with others we may learn that the source of many of our satisfactions takes place when we are involved with other people. A wide range of emotions then might be defined as needs for love and belongingness with some defining success in our adaptive efforts and failure in others. Loneliness and hate, I would suggest, might define failure in these needs while feeling accepted and loved defines success.

How do we even begin to do justice to our sexual desires and the enormous number of adaptive problems that each person must learn to solve in their biological, psychological, and social arenas of living? Sexual desire is biologically created but does not share the characteristics of other drives because death would not occur to the individual who does not satisfy those desires. Much of the maintenance of desire becomes socially constructed and is shaped by a vast array of social forces. Western Christianity has not only demanded that its members not only learn to control sexual expression but abolish the desires themselves. Lust is defined as a sin punishable by eternal suffering in the afterlife, and where children are raised to literally accept such beliefs the adaptive demands to manage desire are prodigious indeed. All of our social relations involve sexual controls, complicated negotiations, and other interactions. Sexual desire can be used as a vehicle to express love or to express power. Sexual needs and the problems they invoke occupy much of the activity of those sharing intersubjective space, both on a descriptive and moral basis, and there are few problems solved with as much deception as sexual ones.

With the development of increased skills and an emerging sense of self there develops a variety of needs seen only in human beings. Biologists and others interested in evolutionary psychology are often guilty of reducing the concept of successful adaptation to our survival and reproductive needs and not recognizing that human beings seek satisfaction in those needs that are shared with other species but also seek to transcend their animal condition. For example, there are sets of needs in which individuals judge and assess their own skills and capacities to carry out individual initiatives. These needs can be referred to as esteem needs, where success might be experienced as pride, and failure as doubt and insecurity. I agree with many existential and humanistic theorists that a set of emotions exist that might also be defined as a need for self-actualization (Maslow 1968). Individuals may well develop intense desires to express whatever it is that only they can express according to the highest standards of which they are capable. Perhaps these needs might be defined as needs to be creative or become fully functioning (Carl Rogers 1961). Success at satisfying these needs, I believe, is represented by the emotion of joy while failure is best described by Jean Paul Sartre (1957) as nausea, an emotion that occurs when we do not keep good faith with ourselves.

There are needs directly related to the cognitive activities that define our scientific activities. Describing, explaining, and predicting are as basic to our survival as any activities, and when conditions exist that interfere with these activities strong emotions signal failure. Anxiety has long been a central concern of psychoanalysts who refer to the totality of our adaptive skills as the ego. Threats to the ego are signaled by the presence of anxiety. My own interpretation of this phenomena suggests that whenever individuals find themselves in situations experienced as ambiguous, explanations are contradictory, predictions are unclear, they are in conflict with their own motives, and it is unclear as to what actions will produce successful adaptations, anxiety results and motivates a set of searching activities designed to clarify and resolve the experienced ambiguity. I will return to the role of anxiety and the need to discover or create new answers to problems that are experienced in a kind of murky darkness when I discuss the concept of psychological defenses.

Other emotions which might motivate a need to seek new sources of information are confusion and doubt. The successful resolution of anxiety is defined by the emotion of certainty. One of humanity's most punishing emotions is anxiety. Anxiety creates a powerful need while certainty is one of our most rewarding affective states. The social implications of those who rouse anxiety and those who help people achieve a feeling of certainty are great. Those who can control the events that reduce anxiety and increase certainty have always enjoyed social prestige and power, especially when they promise to provide explanations concerning life and death. Teaching others to be scientists involves helping others tolerate ambiguity, uncertainty, and doubt and success depends on the instructor's success in doing so.

Emotions that are the opposite of anxiety are interest and curiosity. Many psychologists would not list these affective states as emotions but I feel it is useful to do so. Interest and curiosity are vital to intellectual activity, or any motivation to learn in that they emerge when we feel safe to play and explore in any given environment. One of my greatest challenges in working with people has been to help them find those aspects of the world which arouse their interest and curiosity, and if at all possible prepare to spend their lives in those places. When students are caught up in the god-thing stories of others and feel compelled to study topics that arouse little or no interest in them they are involved in a very difficult situation where learning is concerned.

Two additional emotions qua needs that relate directly to the adaptive process are stress and frustration on one hand, and boredom on the other. We experience frustration when we perceive that our efforts at achieving adaptive goals are blocked by physical barriers, time, efforts of others, or by our own inability to accommodate ourselves to the demands of an adaptive situation. Stress reactions occur when we experience that the demands of a situation are beyond our capabilities and we lack the resources to continue the adaptive struggle. Boredom arises when there are no accommodations to be made and no problems require solutions. We have all probably had the experience of feeling exhausted after struggling with a task that seemed overwhelming and then swearing that we would not move from our beds or easy chairs until we had fully rested only to discover that after a short period of time we went looking for something to solve in order to escape boredom.

I want to discuss the emotion of stuckness at this juncture because I have become convinced that it represents one of our most important and overlooked cognitive-affective needs. Feeling stuck can occur as we move from one place to another in time and space, from one relationship to another, or as Kegan (1982) points out when we move from one psychological organization of self to another. Often a move in one sphere demands moves in all others. We become stuck when we fear the consequences of leaving where we are and/or are fearful or anxious of where we are going. Stuckness, like anxiety, is a powerful motivating force for instigating a search for new information, help from others, or actions that lead to change. I have found that it is often just as important for people to understand the nature and sources of their stuckness as it is for them to understand anxiety.

Every cognitive appraisal may be either a description or a judgment of objects and events. Human beings constantly judge themselves and each other creating a host of moral needs. The need to be seen as worthy of life and love and the need to justify one's authority when making judgments represents pervasive ongoing needs and problems as people deal with each other in intersubjective space. An ongoing theme of this book has involved the human struggle to avoid guilt and shame and replace them with moral rectitude and a sense of worthiness. Attempts to be gods and things are often the outcome of the struggle to avoid the shame and guilt that comes from being judged by the self or others for committing errors in personal or social adaptation. Finally, we can mention the needs for spirituality and transcendence that seem a function of not only guilt and feelings of inadequacy, but which emerge as a function of our reflective consciousness. Ernst Becker (1973) has written eloquently concerning our need to cope with death and a variety of philosophers have dealt with our needs to be part of something larger than ourselves (Tillich 1952).

SELVES

I have been discussing needs and problems as divorced from the people who experience them. When we engage in an adaptive act it is motivated and organized around, and by, our selves. When others initiate an action (and we assume that they too have selves) then we refer to them as persons or individuals. We refer to beings we believe to be without selves as organisms, although among psychologists with their propensity to thing-a-fy us, we too, are organisms. I have already discussed the fact that selves are experienced and spoken of as if they are substantial and immutable, but on closer inspection we discover that they are comprised of cognitive-affective activities and, therefore, cannot be described by physicists, chemists, or biologists no matter how hard they try to do so. I keep wondering when the current craze to find ourselves in our brains will finally give way to the awareness that selves have brains (and bodies) but cannot be localized in brains. The interested reader is referred to Thomas Szasz's (1996) rebuttal of the fallacy of neurological reductionisms.

I have already suggested that we tend to see ourselves as the source of actions that we initiate and as both the observers and recipients of actions initiated by others toward ourselves. We are, therefore, both actors and objects to be acted upon. It is also clear that if ourselves are to be based on our cognitive activities then the bases of ourselves and how we experience ourselves must change dramatically as physical and psychological development takes place. Let me first attempt a more formal definition of the self and then briefly discuss how ourselves organize experience as cognitive-affective development takes place and as the self as object begins to take on descriptive and moral identity.

Isidor Chein (1972: 196–197) begins his definition with a statement by the Gestalt Psychologist Kurt Koffka

> what is there between the last thing just in front and the behind? Is space absolutely empty there? . . . Certainly not; between the "in front" and the behind, is that part of the behavioral world which I call myself. It has a very definite place in the world, and well defined, if variable boundaries. . . . "In front," "to the left and right," "behind," and "above and below" are charac-teristics of space which it possesses with regard to an object which serves as the origin of the system of spatial coordinates. This object, then, is funda-mentally different from all others, inasmuch as it determines fundamental space aspects.

Chein adds, "We might well add the time dimension since the self is always found between the 'already' and the 'not yet.' . . . Following this argument, we may say that *the self is that which is at the origin of perceived space-time* (origin, of course being understood in the mathematical and not in the historical or genetic sense); or, if you will, *the self is the hereness in the thereness*" (emphasis is Chein's).

Chein and others point out that there needs to be a differentiation between the I that thinks or performs the various adaptive operations and the I that is. The I that is, is the product of the I that performs the operations that create the I that is. The former is embedded in the processes that organize consciousness in such a way as to create the reflective I although the embedded I can become the reflected I if other processes now are used to organize these formerly embedded and nonreflected processes. Chein writes (1972: 198–199),

> An observed I is present in an experience as object; but, to be present as an object of awareness, presupposes a subject that is aware. The moment that the latter subject is observed, it is displaced to the position of object which requires a new subject. When I observe myself, there is involved an imme-diately present I and an I that is temporally displaced from the origin of space-time coordinate system; and even though that displacement maybe so minute as to escape normal attention, it is still there, with the consequence that the seeker after the immediate present I is engaged in the tantalizing activity of constantly almost grasping the object of his quest, only to find it eluding his grasp. Small wonder, then, that the problem of identifying the self has proved so difficult to philosophers and psychologists alike.

We must remember that the experience of being an entity at the origins of space-time is a psychological construction of processes that have evolved in such a way as to organize experiences as if selves really exist, and not of an actual entity capable of physical description. I suggest that the processes that organize experience in this way are the holons discussed in earlier chapters. Some of these organizing structures are capable of becoming the object of consciousness but many others remain prereflective or tacit to reflective consciousness. An exami-nation of Piagetian stages reveals how these processes exist as the means to various ends and then become themselves the ends of other processes which act as the means. Kegan (1982) points out that the early behaviors of infants do not exist in means-ends relationships and, therefore, there is no self. It is not until the actions of the infant become organized so that there are objects with whom the infant can relate that any notion of the self can be said to exist. The earlier self, however is embedded in the actions and affects, which define the nature of the objects, and it can be said that the self of the infant is his actions and affects.

The self at this stage is the result of the first of many evolutionary truces that continually define the self's experience in relation to the object world. In the preoperational stage, children's actions are organized by their perceptions of them. They no longer are their actions but now have their actions. The children are now embedded in their perceptions and therefore become their perceptions. During this truce the children's world is based on the descriptions provided above. With the development of reversibilities children now have perceptions but are now their reversibilities, a truce which continues until the reversibilities are organized by the processes which define the stage of formal operations. It is at this stage that children can reflect on their thoughts and feelings—they have thoughts and feelings rather than become them. Individuals are embedded in more than their thoughts and feelings. They are embedded in every aspect of their adaptation at whatever stage we are discussing. Therefore, we can be our social roles or have our roles, be our relationships or have our relationships, be our history and live within it, or have it and be able to make choices concerning the events that form our past. I will discuss Kohlberg's theory of moral development, which he based on Piagetian formulations, in a later chapter but for now I suggest that we can be our moral judgments or have them as well. I urge the reader to become familiar with Kegan's work which helps explain this theory.

I shift the discussion from the self as actor to the self as object. The self as object accrues an identity, that is it becomes identified first by others and later by ourselves. The self has a body, described and judged in a variety of ways. When we observe a part of our body it becomes removed from the self and becomes another object for our contemplation. One of the criticisms of the constructionists is that so much of our science describes people as disembodied intellects rather than fully embodied beings. We become aware of just how embodied we are when we become ill, our bodies are attacked in such a way as to threaten the continued existence of the self, or judgments are made concerning our appearance which simultaneously describes the body and the self.

Our identities involve many more elements than just our bodies. We are capable of measuring ourselves on the basis of our possessions, the home we call our own, the location of our home, the country we live in among others. Our identities are based on our age, sex, race, and the socially constructed judgments of each of these. In our culture identities based on material wealth or class are important but downplayed; our identities based on race and gender are the concern of most social scientists whatever their particular prejudices as to the origin of these problems in identity. The moral identities we develop as we struggle to adapt within the intersubjective spaces in which we are subsumed are of critical importance. We are either good or bad or maybe just not good enough. These conclusions determine the nature of the moral needs discussed above. How do we prove to ourselves and others that we are good enough to be loved, allowed to maintain our lives and standing in our families and communities, sane enough to be heard and have our opinions valued, or, for the purposes of this book, smart enough for genuine efforts to be made to continue our educations?

There is a clear relationship between our selves as experiencing agents and the manner and content with which our identities are constructed. Our descriptive and moral identities will create boundaries that delimit the actions permissible to us as agents. What we do, the activities we engage in, the roles we feel capable and worthy of inhabiting, as well as the actual cognitive-affective experiences we permit ourselves will be determined in part by the moral identities that we construct, and which are constructed with us by others in our lives, with the power to influence our identities. The goals we pursue in life, especially the goals which are comprised of changes we seek to make in ourselves, will be determined by the nature of our social and moral identities. An individual who lives by an identity that is dominated by negative moral judgments can spend a lifetime futilely seeking to change his or her identity to one defined by positive judgments as well as concentrate his or her activities on pleasing those authorities who are the source of moral judgments.

Many of the needs, problems, and dynamics that explain human behavior involve conclusions reached by individuals concerning themselves and the world in which they live. Is the world a good, safe, or nurturing place or a bad, dangerous, and demanding one? These conclusions determine whether or not an individual experiences hope or lives with despair. They will determine what Julian Rotter (1966) refers to as the locus of control of an individual's self. Locus of control involves both people's belief in the probability of their reaching their goals as well as the source of their success. Do their constructed truths suggest that their success in reaching their goals depends on their efforts (internal locus of control), or do they depend upon the gods, fate, their parents, teachers, or the political authorities in their community (external locus of control)? These conclusions can determine just how much effort individuals put into achieving goals or how much effort is put into influencing outside forces. The psychologist D. C. McClellend (1953) posed a similar set of ideas but on a societal level. McClellend suggested that individuals differed in their levels of achievement motivation, which was defined by the ability/willingness of individuals to see themselves as both capable and willing to work hard for their goals. Societies filled with individuals high in achievement motive tended to become wealthier than those with individuals low in achievement motive.

SELVES AND THE STORIES THEY TELL

As mentioned earlier, one of the critical new topics that occupies the professional lives of psychologists is known as narrative psychology. We seem to be natural storytellers, although culture has much to say about who tells stories and who does not and just which stories are to be told and how. One of the issues raised in the first chapter is the assumption that all people want to tell stories. This desire does not mean that all people get to tell stories. I believe that telling stories and having them heard is critical for the development of the self and the cognitive-affective processes which create and define the self. It is in the telling of stories that we come to have our lives, histories, roles, relationships and identities, rather than to be them. It is in the telling of narratives to ourselves that we bind the past, present, and future, express our moral identities as heroes or villains, and work out our explanations of the world as either theories or sacred stories.

It is from the stories told to us by parents, teachers, clergy, and others in our communities that we derive many of the elements of the narratives we, ourselves, tell. It is in giving voice to our stories, and retelling them to others in contexts different from those who would have us tell their story as if it were our own, that we find our own voices. We then find that we might develop and tell our own stories or perhaps learn to tell a new story whose ending is different than that which existed before the retelling. It is the retelling of our lives in a new intersubjective space to new evaluations, or perhaps, for the first time with descriptions of people and events rather than judgments, that god and thing stories give way to stories of human beings sharing their selves. This theme occupies the rest of this book.

WORK AND PLAY

All behaviors are motivated by some adaptive goal but not all behaviors are experienced as being motivated by an adaptive need. There are behaviors that we experience as having to be performed and others in which we want to be engaged. When we perform an act that we feel we must perform either because we will experience adaptive success or avoid adaptive failure we are engaged in work. In work, the goals of behavior are extrinsic to the acts themselves. We work to maintain our lives, protect our children, increase our esteem in the eyes of others, among other reasons. When we play, we engage in behaviors whose goals are intrinsic to the acts themselves. An act may be both one of work and play. If we eat to survive we are working, but if we eat because of the pleasure of the meal we are playing. If we engage in sex to have a baby we are working, but if we engage in a sexual act for pleasure then we are playing. If we tell stories to impress or convince others we are working, if we tell them for the joy of the telling we are playing. There are days that I teach only for my salary, and on those days I am engaged in very hard work. There are other, more pleasurable days, when my teaching is the activity I would choose above all others and on those days I am playing.

The differences between play and work have been noted in psychology in many different contexts and described with many different metaphors. Intrinsic versus extrinsic motivation was one way of noting the difference while psychoanalysts utilized the concepts of Heinz Hartmann (1958) to differentiate between ego and id needs. In the former, the individual is motivated by the sheer pleasure of utilizing an ego skill, while in the latter the skill is motivated to achieve satisfaction in a biological drive, sexual, or aggressive impulses. Hartmann's concept begins to make clear not only the difference between work and play but also their possible relationship. As we chart the descent of species we discover that the more complex the creature the more likely we are to find play as a regular activity. The higher mammals all seem to play, if it is at all possible for them to do so. Play is a distinguishing feature of infancy and whatever immature phases pass for what we call childhood. Whenever we find an aspect of behavior that seems to be directly influenced by evolution, and therefore is an achieved adaptation, we are bound to recognize that play is important to the development of that aspect of behavior and to the survival of the animals and species in which it is found.

Play exists, it can be suggested, in order for individuals to be rewarded in some important and immediate way to practice and develop those skills that will be needed when work becomes necessary. Piaget notes that infants begin to demonstrate their first acquired adaptations or first organized purposeful behaviors, when they discover that some actions are more affectively pleasing for one reason or another. Since the motivation to perform the actions that comprise the circular reactions are inherent to the actions themselves, they fit the definition of play. We discover that it is the function of play to see to it that the skills and cognitive organizations needed at later stages of development take place. The sensory motor play of infants is replaced by the imaginative play of the preoperational child, which in turn gives way to the social, rule-oriented play of later childhood. We see in all these forms of play the learning of skills and the solving of problems without the child being aware that these lessons are taking place. I believe that formal operations emerge when we read, write, and debate with others for the pleasure of the experience and hence, play with ideas as we once played with objects and later played with people. It is play, therefore, that provides some of our earliest and most important means of organizing and motivating psychological development.

Can infants be made to work and if so what might be the results of long periods of work in infancy? When infants are hungry they cry. Crying is initially reflexive (just like the patterns of motivated motor activity that are to become organized during the circular reactions) and exists, we might assume, as an acquired adaptation to alert caretakers as to the needs of their offspring. However, we must assume that infants soon recognize that their cries are followed by the appearance of what will later be constructed as a person, an adult, and probably a parent. They learn also that activity then takes place that makes further crying unnecessary. With the achievement of this insight, we might say that crying is the child's first form of work! We might also recognize that parenting or caretaking can be defined in terms of adaptation as involving those accommodations that the infants or children cannot perform for themselves. I will argue later that parents, teachers, and therapists have two important functions during the child's developing years, the first is to teach children how to accommodate those situations and events that children cannot learn for themselves except at great cost; and second, to perform those accommodations that are impossible for the child to learn at any given moment in time. In short, it is the function of the children's caretakers to see to it that they have adequate time to play and do not have to work too hard or too often. I consider parental success in raising children who play to be one of the great artistic achievements of any person's life.

Why is play so important? Are the psychological developments that take place when people work essentially different than when people play? Play seems to allow for subtleties of learning that cannot take place when we work and our survival or other significant consequences involving losses are involved. Individuals play when there are no perceived threats to their organism and, therefore, they can be motivated by the emotions of interest and curiosity which are as significant to the processes of describing, explaining, and predicting as the emotions of anxiety and confusion discussed above. (In fact, when seen from the perspective of work-play, anxiety defines cognitive work while interest defines cognitive play.) Jay Frankel (1998) discusses play not only in terms of the cognitive development of children but also in terms of its simultaneous role in the development of the image children have of their selves and their social relationships. The context of Frankel's discussion of play involves child psychoanalysis and makes clear the benefits of play in the context of any social relationships. Frankel suggests that play allows children to integrate various cognitive-affective modes of experience (called self-states) into their self identification rather than disavowing them and defensively consigning them to nonconsciousness and the not self. In short, play allows children to have various modes of experience rather than either being those states or pretending that they do not exist.

Science and art flourish when individuals are supported in some areas of their lives from the kinds of survival work that would otherwise occupy all of their waking hours. It is the lucky individual who has caretakers or sponsors and a stable home and community life that permit the benefits of play. There are few things and processes in this world that do not catch the interest of someone who, if left to his or her own devices, will not become expert in understanding that phenomena. Play seems to permit individuals the luxury of exploring many ways of accommodating to the situations of their choices and therefore developing a multiplicity of descriptions, explanations, predictions, and means of control. Perhaps most importantly, play permits the individual to make the necessary errors that define the accommodation process that are not too costly to make. In this sense, play represents Popperian intelligence and it may be true that the more play time an individual has the greater the degree of Popperian abilities will develop.

It is clear, therefore, that success in teaching must somehow involve helping students learn to play as well as work while they are involved in school. However, the use of grades and standardized tests (whose results can have huge consequences for the rest of a student's life) make school a place of work rather than play. One of the biggest problems that I face as a teacher is my student's need to work for grades rather than play with ideas that foster the kind of cognitive-affective understanding that defines what I judge to be real and enduring creative scholarship. When students are realistically aware that errors are mistakes and that mistakes lead to judgments that can follow an individual for a lifetime, then dramatic changes take place in the adaptive process in those situations. I will return to this problem at length in the subsequent sections but I can skip to the end of my story by saying that I have not been able to reverse the damaging dynamics caused by the use of grades and test scores to any appreciable degree.

7

INDIVIDUAL DIFFERENCES IN SELVES

INTRODUCTION

In Chapter 6 I described the continued evolution of human consciousness between infancy and adulthood from the framework provided by the Piagetian concepts of adaptation. The cognitive-affective processes which comprise consciousness change and reorganize as a result of the individual's attempts at assimilating the goals that represent successful adaptation and the accommodations necessary when the existing cognitive-affective skills of the individual are unable to assimilate those goals. When psychologists speak of the satisfaction of human needs they are using language that is parallel to the concept of assimilation; when they speak of solving problems in living they are also including the notion of accommodation. Finally, both needs and problems are represented by the cognitive-affective states of an individual's awareness and statements such as "I am hungry and can find nothing to eat." or "I am frightened of this and must find some way to deal with either my fears or the things that I fear." represent the adaptive situation and the problems that must be solved if adaptation is to be successful.

I outlined those cognitive-affective states that are generally experienced by people as needs. I defined needs as states of desire that preempt other wants or desires and tend to dominate behaviors until the needs that are biological drives are satisfied and the emotions that represent psychological needs are resolved. After outlining Piaget's description of the four stages of cognitive development, I provided a definition of the self as the central organizing construction in human consciousness and introduced a number of other topics I believe to be important for students of psychology to understand if they are to comprehend their own psychologies and personal developments. The chapter concluded with topics such as the intersubjective field and the difference between work and play.

It is now time to turn to an application of these same ideas and the roles they play in terms of their differences between individuals. Individual differences are critical for our understanding of why and how people become scientists and artists, or gods and things. While I believe that people share a common set of human needs and have a consciousness and a self that is shaped by their involvement in an adaptive struggle, in the final analysis no two people see or feel the same way or have selves that tell exactly the same story. Art and science emerge when individuals feel free to tell their unique story in ways that are comprehensible to others and told according to the highest moral and ethical standards of which they are capable. However, gods and things may also emerge as a result of certain conflicts and modes of conflict resolution which take place in the intersubjective field between these unique selves. What then are the sources of human differences and uniqueness that can possibly explain the highly disparate organizations of the self that eventually emerge, coalesce, and form the selves that determine a life of a poet or a life that is judged tragic?

THE SOURCES OF EXPERIENTIAL VARIABILITY

There is probably no topic about which we are so ignorant, but so passionate, as our insistence that we know the necessary answers to questions concerning individual differences. There is also probably no area where more god stories compete for dominance both within and outside of the profession than those concerning the source of individual differences, especially when these differences are judged to be morally repugnant and/or inadequate to the tasks of successful adaptation. In academia the theories concerning individual differences are so encrusted with ideological commitments that differences of opinions at professional meetings or even casual conversations are often met with stony silence, sardonic mocking, or overt hostility. I learned long ago that there were dangers in discussing religion and politics but I have added to that list the psychology of individual differences.

Why such passion about this issue and what might the contentious issues turn out to be? The basic arguments concerning individual differences revolve around the nature-nurture controversy and the mind-body dualism. They involve various interpretations of the roles played by biology and society in the shaping of human behavior. Passions are especially aroused because of the historical consequences to both groups and individuals as a result of social and political processes shaped by various beliefs of what might be called human nature. Carl Degler's (1991) history of the rise and fall (and recent rise again) of Darwinism and other biological theories of human behavior is indispensable at this juncture and is freely drawn upon in what follows.

The passions ignited on both sides of the nature-nurture controversy stem from the fact that almost every version of the story from both sides of the divide is told as a god story and casts its characters as either gods or things. In the nature stories, the behavior of people is either a function of their genes, nervous system, or some other biologically-created category such as belonging to their specific species. In the nurture version, human differences are a function of some societal or cultural configuration such as the child-rearing practices of their parents, religion, unfair practices instituted because of some biological difference such as race, gender, ethnic origins or, since Karl Marx, social class. In all of these stories the individuals as conscious agencies and beings struggling to make sense of their world disappear and are replaced by puppets or helpless artifacts that are endlessly buffeted by forces they can not comprehend or actively resist. These stories cast human beings in such ways as to justify treating them in ways congruent with their dehumanized status or as passive victims that will be fully reconstituted if only their environments can be appropriately restored. Casting human beings as lowly organisms, justifies their manipulation both by those who seek to hurt or exploit them or by self-proclaimed selfless crusaders who seek to save them. The gods in these stories do not consult those that they seek to control as they act to create one utopian vision after another that in every case turns dystopic for all participants. A brief examination of some aspects of human folly, fully, and morally justified by those who carried them out follows.

Slavery was justified as warranted by God and by the assertion that blacks were inherently inferior biologically. In fact, during the debates on our own American Constitution slavery was justified, as was the exclusion of those brought from Africa from the political process on the grounds that these individuals were only four fifths human. With the rise of Darwinian theory, it would now be argued that it was the evolutionary process not God who created the differences that made some men superior to others. The rise in industrial capitalism in the last century led to, in the interpretations of some, the degradation and manipulation of people as they labored in the production of wealth and in its unfair distribution between workers and management. More recently, Hitler's extermination of millions of people was justified on the basis of biological theories of master and inferior races. His extermination of six million Jews employed thousands of medical personnel who were to rid the Fatherland of the germs who were Jews. More recently we read in our daily papers of the hatred and suffering created by ethnic cleansing in the Baltic and a host of horrors unleashed in many other parts of the world justified by biological theories of human differences.

Other sad episodes in our history involve the manner in which sexual differences have been exploited by assuming that either men or women, more often women, were the inferior sex. Freudian theory is replete with biological concepts that continued the religious dogmas concerning women's innate and immutable inferiority. Women are cast in both the dominant religions of Western society and in Freudian psychology, which has dominated much of the debates among those in the clinical side of the field of psychology and psychiatry, as intellectually weaker than men, suffering from penis envy if they mistakenly and hopelessly compete with men, and mentally ill if they succeed or fail. Freud's final words on the subject of women were anatomy is destiny and it is this idea which fuels the rage of those who reject any biological explanations of human differences. In addition to theories on gender, the current theory of mental illness urges us to believe that all behaviors labeled pathological by mental health professionals are the direct result of brain

damage or chemical imbalances. Additionally, the justification to withhold education from those deemed biologically inferior still can be found in a variety of
doctrines concerning gender and race. I have already discussed some of the
assumptions used when testing children's intelligence quotients or IQ's that cause
much harm in educational practices. When professionals assume that these nonex-
istent IQ's are the result of biological factors the damage produced is that much
greater.

The biologisms used to justify the exploitations of people continues today but
has lead to its antithesis in what might be called extreme or radical environmental-
ism. The advocates of purely environmental explanations of human differences
have long had their champions. The English empiricists such as John Stuart Mill
argued that human beings were born as tabula rasa, or blank slates, upon which
human experiences are written. If differences exist then it is the unfair advantages
provided by one's circumstances that were responsible for any inferiority suffered
by individuals. These ideas generally find fertile ground among teachers and
therapists who try to influence human behavior. Environmentalists are set to despair
and reject any concept that suggests that biology is destiny.

As women and various minority groups in our society became more educated
and sought careers in teaching and other helping professions, the biological theories
that had been used to justify their oppression and make futile the efforts at social
change grew more anathema to larger groups within the professions. Biology
retreated to the study of genes, DNA, and other bio-molecular processes and left
the explanation of human behavior and its differences to the social scientists. Social
constructionism began to dominate the theories in the fields of social psychology,
sociology, and cultural anthropology. Degler points out that by the midpoint of our
own century sociological and environmental theories dominated the colleges and
universities of the United States (and, I would add, the psychiatric clinics).

Academic psychology was virtually dominated by radical behaviorism, which
hypothesized that both development and all individual differences were due to
learning which came in the two varieties known as operant and respondent conditioning. These theories created a heady optimism that education and psychotherapy
would end poverty and social injustice and usher in a new and shining millennium.
Utopian theories, which have always abounded, became nearly universal and
entrenched in the halls of academia everywhere.

The moral goals of the environmentalists initially appear more benign than those
that would actively exterminate or exclude individuals or groups on the basis of
biological differences, but because individuals are also conceived of as helpless
puppets, damage is done here as well. The picture painted is that of helpless victims
under the boot of inhuman monsters whose only source of rescue can be by their
saintly benefactors. Not only are the victims dehumanized in this framework but
individuals who disagree with any of the utopian social programs created by the
environmentalists are considered racists, sexists, or other dehumanizing terms.
Beth Azar (1997) describes evidence that suggests that research into sexual and
racial differences not only may be refused publication but its authors may damage
their careers in highly significant ways for merely conducting the research.

In the god stories of the environmentalists, the sympathies lacking for the victims of the biology stories are replaced by pity, which in its own way is disabling to those who now feel self-pity and endlessly bemoan their fates as victims. For the extreme environmentalists competition is to be abolished rather than worshiped as it is by the advocates of the biology stories. (Biologists love the idea of competition since those who fail at the competition did so because they were inherently unfit to compete. Therefore, biologists never have to worry about examining the rules of the game for signs that they are unfair.) For the environmentalists, not only should the playing field be level for all if they choose to compete but the outcomes for success must be assured for all as well. The utopian visions of the environmentalists lead to differential standards for individuals and groups thought to be victims of the gods in biological stories. Kurt Vonnegut (1988) has lampooned the environmentalists in a story set in the future when governmental policy and the handicapper general sees to it that the smart, the beautiful, and the talented are not allowed to be more successful than the rest of the population. Among the environmentalists those who dare suggest that there are better and worse among students, arts and sciences, or schools are immediately labeled elitist, a most serious moral condemnation. I will return to this theme in later chapters when I discuss educational standards seen from the god stories of the biologists and environmentalists in education.

This does not mean that those who advocate for biological theories of behavior have gone quietly into the night. Beginning in the 1970s Darwinian thinking appeared once again in the guise of the sociobiological theories of Edward Wilson (1975) and others who argued that the study of the behavior of less complex species such as ants could be incorporated in attempts to explain human social organization. Once again the consciousness of human beings is reduced to that of an ant or some other species and the qualities that make us human are ignored. I have earlier presented the basic ideas of evolutionary psychology, which is in my opinion a much more sophisticated outgrowth of sociobiology. Unlike sociobiology, the new evolutionary theory places human consciousness as its focus of attention. If one believes the media's daily deluge of reports, medical science has found a gene to explain all sorts of human differences, which creates a very different impression than that found on academic campuses. In short, the nature-nurture wars rage on in the helping professions and in the public arena.

The evidence, as I assess it, is that we must recognize that all human differences are the product of both nature and nurture and that there are no differences between human beings that do not bear the stamp of both. Biology and culture contribute both to the expression of differences and both biology and culture act to constrain the expression of those differences. I believe that any culture that tries to ignore human needs and modes of problem solving that have evolved over time, or which evolve within the lifetime of a given individual, will either face rebellion as they try and force people to behave in ways that run counter to their needs or destroy them if they do not take into account the limitations in problem solving that exist for any individual. The schemes of the biologists fail when the Hitler's among them assume that the inferiority of those they seek to mutilate are irremediable and the utopian visions of the environmentalists fail when they institute some environmental change and expect massive overnight differences to appear in the populations affected by the changes. The biological utopians crush many individuals under the unbending standards that they set while the environmentalists prevent development as they destroy standards in the name of democracy and fairness.

We do not know which change in the environment or which policies will release changes that will be judged growth or judged monstrous and destructive for all involved. We do not know which changes in policy inhibit differences that might have otherwise come to exist for the betterment or destruction of both the individuals and cultures involved. We do not know which differences in human beings are expressions or constraints of either biology or the environment. Before we can create intelligent educational policy we will have to know much more than we currently do.

We are also essentially ignorant of how genes help shape differences in various modes of human experience. To suggest that genes do so is perfectly reasonable but to ignore the fact that biological organs such as the brain are as much a product of the environment as the genes which direct their construction is patently absurd. From the moment an embryo is a multicellular organism it is shaped by differences in the intrauterine environment. If that environment is changed, as occurs when drugs such as thalidomide or alcohol are introduced into it, the development of the emerging human being is radically changed. At birth a baby is born with a brain that is different from all other brains not only because of variations in genetic structure but because of the diet of the mother and a complex of factors that differed both in their contents and in the sequences that were brought to bear on the developing fetus.

Even after birth we must avoid the error that suggests that either the form or physiological operation of the brain determines the nature of an individual's functioning any more or less than the nature of the same individual's functioning affects the form or physiology of their brains. Kittens raised in total darkness beyond a given length of time do not develop the necessary brain structure that leads to meaningful sight. It has been recently reported that soldiers suffering from post-traumatic stress disorder reveal changes in their brain structure. Psychiatrists are quick to suggest that the disorder is a function of the brain changes which are themselves diagnosed as brain dysfunctions or damage. But it is equally logical to assume that the adaptive demands of battle define the cognitive-affective structure of the soldier and that the changes in neurophysiology are both normal and necessary to meet the demands of combat. It is logical to assume that every subjective psychological state requires a specific neurophysiological state to allow it to exist. If this is true then it is a person's sense of depression or sense of joy which lowers and raises the level of neurotransmitter in his or her synapses and not, as psychiatrists claim, the other way around. If what I argue is so, then drugs (euphemistically called medicine) used to artificially change the normal and necessary brain functions that permit states of sadness that result from people's appraisal and cognitive construction of reality must be doing terrible damage to the bodies and lives of millions.

Perhaps, any theory of how we are shaped by our biology and environments must, as I have outlined earlier, include the view of active human beings capable of responding to and co-constructing their world even as they are shaped by the powerful and often unjust forces impinging upon them. We must focus upon the manner in which biological and environmental forces shape human consciousness as the proximate source of behavior. If we ignore consciousness as the source of behavior and instead explain behavior as a function of impersonal biological and environmental forces we have described a puppet or machine, not a human being. And in assessing the differences between people we must be scrupulous in recognizing the difference between a description and a moral judgment as well as recognizing our own tendencies to dehumanize others in justifying our actions to help others. We must be as aware of our cruelties when we see people as things to be helped and pitied as when we see them as things to be excluded, discarded, or destroyed. I recognize that these arguments will probably do little to resolve the anger aroused in the true believers on both sides of the nature-nurture controversy.

BIOLOGICAL INFLUENCES IN HUMAN DIFFERENCES

Every parent who has had more than one child has had to contend with the fact, whether they reflected on it or not, that their children were born with differences in the expression of their needs and the manner in which they solve problems. In short, each child seemed to experience and organize their world and their selves differently from one another. I believe there is compelling evidence to suggest that children are born with fairly wide variations in the thresholds or sensitivities of their sensory and motor modalities. While the basics of experience itself are the same for children born with healthy species-specific biological equipment, the sensitivities, colorations, and balances among the various senses and holonic systems vary from child to child. From the very beginning, therefore, no two children experience the world in exactly the same way even though there are great overlaps of similarities in modes of experience.

I believe that research will eventually demonstrate that there are three different types of thresholds that assure no two individuals experience the world in the same way. The first variable relates to the lower limit in which cognitive-affective appraisals begin to operate, such as the point at which individuals begin to experience some type of affective pleasure or pain. The second variable regards the speed with which information is processed and the intensity of pain or pleasure rises. The third variable involves the threshold differences with which pain is disconnected from reflective consciousness and individuals experience numbness or apathy. I will return to this idea below because I have long believed that the difference between those diagnosed as mentally ill and those who live lives of quiet despair involved the manner in which emotional pain was experienced. In the latter, numbing took place at lower threshold levels than in the former.

Some of the earliest studies on temperament (Thomas and Chess 1968), which is the common term used for these differences in sensitivity and organization of experience, isolated distinct differences in activity level and responses to parental handling independently of the style of that handling. Researchers grouped babies as difficult, slow to warm up, easy, and uncategorizable (since this group appeared to be a mixture of the characteristics of the other three groupings). More recently Jerome Kagan (1994), has suggested that children born with a vulnerability to loud noises or other intense stimuli are usually the same children who show higher than average levels of social shyness or timidity when they are of school age.

The problem with much of this research is that it creates categories that should be descriptive of differences in experience, but instead are judgments of the essence or the self of the child. In short, all descriptions of traits act as god stories not as descriptive, dynamic science. Easy, difficult, timid, and shy are judgments and not descriptions. For whom is the child easy or difficult? Do the children feel distress as they experience and organize the world or is it the parents, teachers, and researchers dealing with the children? Is timidity a problem for the child so labeled because her differences in experiencing her world have been labeled timid and shy and led her to be treated differently than if such a label had not been applied?

The psychoanalyst Anthony Storr (1988) writes in his book Solitude that today's standards demand that children be sociable and have many friends and acquaintances compared to earlier times when people lived in more rural areas and had to adjust to fewer people in their lives. He goes on to point out that individuals who enjoyed solitude may well have benefitted by having fewer distractions and in turn having more time to develop their skills and interests. If Beethoven were more gregarious and less shy and difficult might we have never heard the ninth symphony because he would have had less time to write it? Might a child today who prefers to be alone be psychologically damaged by attempts to change his shyness because his differences in response to others has been defined in negative rather than neutral terminology? Would we even call a child shy if the culture in which he lived rewarded a more introspective and outwardly quiet demeanor?

A difference does not become a problem unless it is labeled as such by someone who objects to the difference or the adapting individual experiences a failure in adaptation and thereby makes the same judgment. The recognition of innate differences does not imply that these differences cannot be modified because the same research (Kagan 1994) that suggests that temperament exists and is stable also reveals that these differences can not only be modified but that the ability to predict the later behavior of individuals described with the difference is not great at all. All that can be implied by the study of individual differences is that the emerging person would have revealed a different self and told a different story were he born with another mode of experiencing and organizing his world. A problem exists when the individual described as different is forced to operate in contexts that are not friendly to the existence of his or her differences. I believe that we are all born experiencing our common world differently from one another but when these differences are allowed to find expression in environments that maximize their success rather than their potential for failure then the individuals involved do not find reasons to judge their differences as problems. From the point of view of the adapting individual it is the context in which differences operate that always determine if something is judged as wrong although as we have seen many times it is the individual and not the context that is labeled as having the wrongness.

But where our differences lead to increased error, longer and more difficult adaptive struggles, and even failure in adaptation we cannot as scientists pretend that the differences do not exist. But as educators we can recognize that if this or that particular environment favors a particular difference, and if we cannot modify these differences in individuals, we can still help people see the differences for what they are and not define their whole beings as defective, thereby suggesting that there are no environments that might favor those differences. If persons do not object to being less successful in a given environment we might also find ways for them to remain in that environment if it is of benefit to them.

In recent years the awareness that infants seek their own way of organizing their consciousness has lead to the need for caretakers to adapt to those individual styles with mutuality and sensitivity rather than follow rigidly prescribed rules of infant and child care. An increasing number of theorists have recognized, at least implicitly, that inborn differences in modes of experience require a dance of mutuality between adult and child. These last sentences prescribe behaviors that make sense only if these infants are seen as not only an active co-constructors of their world and their relationships but individuals who from conception will see the world in ways differently from all other human beings with whom they will interact. We are almost ready to begin a discussion concerning how differences in the events that take place in the intersubjective spaces between people contributes to differences in participating individuals.

There is one final issue that begs for a brief statement. I can address it now that I have created a framework for it. The question is whether or not differences exist in groups of people rather than individuals, specifically groupings based on race and sex. I will not review the growing literature that suggests that little girls and little boys will demonstrate differences no matter how hard we try and make them disappear or no matter what efforts are made to treat them the same. My conclusions on these differences are the same as Marie Fausto-Sterling (1985) whose work is quoted by environmentalists as proof that differences based on the biology of sex do not exist. Fausto-Sterling suggests that differences based on biology do exist but are smaller than they would be were not culture so active in enhancing them or as they are reflected in the biased reporting of those committed to believing in their existence. Fausto-Sterling shows that the research designs used to demonstrate that differences do exist are most often so flawed that we cannot rely on their results. But demonstrating a flaw in the design of a piece of research in no way invalidates the hypothesis the research was attempting to test.

The issue of race is far more problematic, especially given the history of injustice and enslavement of African-Americans in our culture. It is not unreasonable to assume that genetic variations in the biological equipment that shapes the modes of an individual's adaptive experience does exist in groups of individuals struggling to survive in vastly different environments over long periods of time with no opportunities to mix genes with individuals from other groupings in other adaptive environments. These are the very conditions of speciation, and one of the great anthropological questions has yet to be answered is why human beings are still only one species. What is clear, however, is that we are one and that is the salient factor when establishing educational or social policy of any kind.

It is both scientifically and morally wrong to assume that such differences justify treating individuals from any of these groupings, based on sex or race, as inferior or denying any individuals the right to try and succeed wherever, and whenever, they wish. Educational policy should never involve only the desires of the policy makers but must also include the wishes of those affected by the policy. As long as the standards used to measure success are equally applied to all who attempt a task, I see no reason why individuals of any group cannot be respected if they wish to compete with individuals from any other group. Moreover, it is wholly incorrect to treat differences between people as absolute rather than distributed in both groups according to normal curves with enormous degrees of overlap. It must also be realized that the average degree of intragroup genetic variability is greater than the average degree of intergroup genetic variability. What we must be most scrupulous about as scientists is to use language that describes these differences that is not inherently judgmental.

In the case of race, differences are said to exist in intelligence, a concept already discussed. Intelligence is an inherently judgmental term which exists as a word and nothing else. Finally, and perhaps most importantly, is the assumption that one can even discern who belongs to what race. In the hundreds of years since slavery began, and in the years since its abolition, there has been so much gene mixing for so many reasons that the very idea of separate races becomes suspect. Current research then gets based on skin color, not race. In our society I defy anyone to examine the range of skin colors and come up with firm criteria for race. The search for racial differences in our culture seems to be based on god-thing stories that are far from the goals of science. As a teacher, I see it as my job to teach individuals to respect their differences as individuals and not as members of groups and measure all of them according to the same criteria of success. As a scientist, however, I defend anyone's right to conduct research on any topic of interest regardless of objections to the research and as long as the science inherent in the research is good science.

FIXATION AND DEFENSES IN ADAPTATION

One of the most important topics to be transferred from the clinical to the educational side of the field of psychology involves the idea of psychological defenses and the fixation of various modes of an individual's being in the world. Defenses contribute much to the emergence of individual differences in modes of experience and they bring us back to the fact that all emerging differences after birth are constructed by individuals regardless of how biology and genetics create differences in basic experience. Defenses demonstrate the self regulating nature of consciousness. To discuss these ideas as related to the adaptive struggles of individuals they must be purged of the moral judgments used by clinicians that cast these activities as pathological or as related to mental illnesses and disorders.

A common definition of a psychological defense was, and for many still is, the denial and distortion of reality. The definition provides insight to what is meant by defense: individuals confronting a situation that will not yield up adaptive success somehow deceive themselves into believing otherwise. The reason that defenses are considered pathological are twofold. First, the consequences of using defenses are often judged to be more painful and destructive to those who utilize them than the original adaptive failure, and second, the reality constructed by individuals as they use defenses often differs radically from the experiences of those making the judgments that pathology is in evidence. In fact, it has been my experience that it is more the refusal to share a common reality with others, particularly the professionals acting as arbiters of reality, than the suffering created as a result of the using defenses that most often motivates the moral judgments that a person is demonstrating symptoms of mentally illness. I define defenses as the denial and distortion of the reality of others, although it would be equally true to define defenses as the creating of a reality different than the one that would be experienced were the defenses not to have been utilized.

The word defense in this context has a specialized meaning from the more common use of the word. To defend is to ward off attack. Much of human existence is spent defending the self and others from the experienced dangers of the natural and human world. We spend more time warding off noxious situations than pursuing pleasant or helpful ones. Behaviorists point out that human beings are motivated more frequently by negative reinforcers (that is the successful reduction, termination or avoidance of painful stimulation) than by positive reinforcers which involve attempts to add various forms of stimulation to one's experience. I believe that work is inherently defensive because it wards off unwanted experience. Most of us are forced to expend more effort at working than playing, the latter being the potentially least defensive form of human behavior. But not all forms of defense imply the specialized use of the word discussed in this context. In the more usual sense of the word we experience others as successfully satisfying needs and solving problems, in the narrower, more technical use of the concept we see others as deceiving themselves as to the success of their adaptations. In the more ordinary use of defense we see individuals increase the range of their skills and grow as new forms of mental organization seem to emerge. The more technical aspects of defense mean we judge others as fixated, stereotyped, driven, and unable to reorganize their modes of experience.

My definition clearly leaves open my recognition that individuals may assimilate unwanted aspects of the world into their own belief system without modifying or adapting their belief systems to the meanings implied by the unwanted situation. But my definition also recognizes that my truth of the world's meanings are also constructed and I have no privileged position from which to judge reality as reality. That being said, I do believe that defensive behavior requires its own discussion, both as a source of individual differences in human modes of experience and because of the different aspects of defensive behavior such as non-defensive coping or behavior that permits mastery of a situation. I am clearly making a judgment in this instance, one that has its basis in moral philosophy rather than science or medicine. I believe that people use defenses as adaptations when they experience them as both necessary and unavoidable and when their adaptive skills permit them no alternatives, however, defenses lead to adaptive solutions that more often than not involve the construction of gods and things rather than artistic, loving human beings. How do defenses operate and why are their consequences so often destructive both to those who use them and to those associated with them?

If we reinvoke our earlier discussion on adaptation (see Chapter 6) we can see that defenses may involve changes in the manner in which the threatening situation is evaluated or appraised, the manner in which the emotions which define the individual's needs or problems are experienced, or the secondary appraisals and skills that are utilized to deal with the situation or events in question. Let me begin first with the types of appraisals often used in defenses. Individuals using defenses often appraise offending situations with preoperational rather than the expected formal operational forms of thought and perception. (The typical clinician's judgment of defenses is that they are irrational. I believe that it is the expectation of operationalized thinking in the adult individual that draws this moral judgment. There is no irrational thinking although there is thinking that is unwanted and misunderstood by a variety of onlookers who then judge what they neither like nor understand.) I believe that preoperational modes of appraisal underlie defenses for two reasons: the first reason involves defenses that began in childhood and have been maintained into adulthood; the second reason is explained by the fact that with preoperational thinking the rules of logic that define formal operations are not in evidence and therefore the individual can utilize the magical properties inherent in preoperational thought.

Preoperational thought allows an individual to assimilate the meaning of events into beliefs while minimizing attention to detail while utilizing concepts that are broadly based and overgeneralized. In such thinking, fantasy is easily confused with perceptual activity allowing the individual to assimilate perceptual experiences into wish fulfilling daydreams. Moreover, preoperational thinking does not permit seriation or other mathematically-based evaluations and it freezes the experience of time in the present, thus avoiding unpleasant conclusions based on predictions of the future. The failure to use scientific logic permits individuals to justify actions, turn failure into success, shame and guilt into pride and doubt into total certainty.

Preoperational thought allows for perceptions of the world far more egocentric than if individuals relied on formal operations. Individuals maintain and insist on their points of view to the exclusion of all others. Preoperational thought allows for the mechanisms of repression or motivated forgetting as well as selective inattention to aspects of a situation that arouses painful emotions. Preoperations permit an individual to experience another person who is demonstrating anger to be experienced as a different person than when the same person is behaving pleasantly, thereby utilizing the defense that psychoanalysts call splitting. Therefore, in effect, the individual can more easily eliminate unpleasant aspects of the world by creating an experience in which painful accommodations no longer seem necessary. Finally, preoperations allow individuals to concretize and hence make real for themselves abstract metaphors. Metaphorical gods provide as little comfort as metaphorical bread satisfies hunger.

Defenses also allow individuals to organize their interpersonal relationships differently than would be possible without the magical preoperational properties utilized in the defensive constructions. Parents and leaders can be seen as all-powerful and capable of protecting us under any circumstances as well as fulfilling any of our physical needs, our scientific requirements for understanding events, and our needs for moral worth and justice. Defenses simultaneously allow parents and other authority figures to construct beliefs that they are indeed as omniscient, omnipotent as their dependents wish them to be, and justify whatever actions they deem necessary to maintain their authority. The nature of social adaptations based on such defenses will be discussed in the next chapter.

Other defenses change the manner in which emotions that follow appraisal are experienced, even if preoperational mechanisms are not utilized. Human beings seem able to dissociate and disconnect from their emotions rendering the appraised situation less painful than it would be otherwise. These defenses also leave the individuals using them as intellectually in touch with the situation but emotionally detached therefore seeking ways to make decisions to act based on other cues than their own wants and desires. Emotions may also be given new labels and interpreted differently, such as in the case of anxiety which may be interpreted as sexual desire and sexual activities are then utilized to calm and soothe the anxiety. Equally common are feelings of loneliness, anxiety, fear, and a variety of affects being experienced as hunger. How many pizza pies must be eaten in order to feel loved? Unwanted emotions may be deadened while positive emotions enhanced with the use of drugs or by engaging in mind-numbing or otherwise diverting activities. Human beings may engage in a wide variety of activities over long periods of their lives without being aware of which powerful emotions they are escaping. This is a simplified discussion of the myriad ways in which humanity regularly and successfully reconstructs reality.

What situations seem set the stage for the utilization of defenses? I believe defenses may be employed in any situation where individuals believe that they lack the skills necessary to achieve adaptive success. Success and failure in adaptation are in the eye of the beholder. Teachers are always involved with youngsters who disagree with the teacher's assessment of what they are capable of in any given situation and will, from the teacher's point of view, utilize defenses against failure prematurely and unnecessarily. The same is true of the experiences of parents and psychotherapists who regularly deal with individuals whose operating stories of life cast themselves as things unable to perform tasks that they might easily master if they saw themselves with more human qualities. However, over the years I have concluded that there are certain interpretations of situations that almost always bring forth the utilization of powerful defensive action on the part of a very large number of human beings. I have called these experienced situations the "psychotic landscape" (Simon 1986, 1994). The following situations most often provoke extensive defensive constructions of reality.

The Knowledge of Our Own Deaths

Ernst Becker's (1973) *The Denial of Death* is mandatory reading on this topic. We construct all manner of defensive arrangements concerning death for two reasons. First involves dealing with the terror that our own loss of self and consciousness might entail. The second involves the extreme anxiety engendered by the unimaginableness of what death might be like.

The Extreme Loss of Moral Worth

Ernst Becker (1975) has also suggested that human beings have difficulties accepting those actions and motives in themselves and others that are judged to be genuinely evil not merely immoral. There are several questions raised concerning the problem of, as Becker puts it, escaping from evil. First, how do we define evil and is there a place for such a concept in modern scientific psychology? Second, are there any behaviors or motives that might be universally accepted as evil? Third, what issues are raised when we differentiate between having to defend ourselves against judgments of our overt behaviors rather than defend against our cognitive-affective needs that motivate behaviors? This last question has significance that goes beyond defending against evil and relates to the problems created when individuals judge as morally wrong what they and others do and also judge as equally wrong what they think and feel.

There is, of course no privileged position from which to objectively define any actions as immoral, let alone evil. Therefore, evil is in the eye of the beholder and any set of actions or motives might be judged to be evil. I believe, however, that if we remove evil from its original usage in religious contexts it refers to acts of immorality that are seen as so reprehensible as to remove the individuals who perform these acts from being seen as human by those making the judgments. We are once again in the garden of the god-thing narrative. Once individuals are defined as evil they become a thing and the thing that they become is a monster. We defend against evil because to do otherwise would be to confront the fact that we can either be the victims of monsters or define ourselves and our identities as monsters.

It is clear that as a scientist the terms *evil* and *monster* are moral judgments and not descriptions and violate the demands that my explanations of behavior be both naturalistic and non-dualistic. Differentiating between human beings and monsters violates my scientific principles. However, even as I struggle to remain scientific in my outlook and recognize that monsters are only metaphorical in nature I cannot prevent myself from literalizing my metaphor and experiencing the existence of human monsters. It is the same problem discussed earlier in relation to self: I know that I do not have a self that is describable as a noun but I cannot help but experiencing myself as if I were a noun. Therefore, there are no actual monsters but there are metaphorical monsters.

What behaviors qualify as monstrous? I agree with Becker that we become monsters and commit evil when we dehumanize our fellow human beings, inflict pain and even death on them, and either become incapable of empathizing with their pain or even enjoying their pain, humiliation, suffering, and dying. In short, we become monsters to others when we play God and turn them into things. I believe that when we hear stories about evil we tend to deny their validity. Some of our most significant reconstructions of reality involve creating a world in which we, or our loved ones, do not fall prey to monsters.

Just as we try and avoid, by whatever means possible, experiencing ourselves as the victims of monsters, we also utilize any and all means to avoid being defined as monsters or evil. We find ourselves in a paradox: when others see us as monsters we are defensively playing God and have little insight into the nature of how we are perceived. In fact, we see ourselves as morally correct in our behavior and our victims deserving of their fate. We might be engaged in these moral acts because we have defined the others, now cast as "its," as the monsters. Therefore, when we see ourselves as monsters it is the result of agreeing with judgments made about us that we are not quite human. We are also agreeing that we are irredeemably flawed morally, not deserving of love, forgiveness or mercy. When we see ourselves as monsters we are playing God with ourselves. The defense employed against seeing ourselves as monsters is to recreate ourselves as morally pure gods immune to the evils inflicted on us by others or those we have inflicted on them.

We now come to the ultimate paradox concerning defenses: when we escape from our human condition for any reason, but particularly to defend ourselves from the evil in others or in ourselves, we create the very conditions from which the worst human transgressions spring and the experiences that lead to the next round of defensive adaptations. By not accepting our vulnerabilities (and the fact that we can be hurt by, as well as hurt, others) we bring about the very conditions we seek to escape. Most evil is the product of the god-like manner in which we deal with the behaviors and motives that we judge to be morally wrong. The cause of the worst human transgressions are committed in the name of morality, religion, national defense, goodness, and purity.

The final issue discussed is the consequences of defining as evil actual behaviors and the cognitive-affective needs that motivate them. We can think of ourselves as monsters for what we do, think, and feel. It is difficult enough to control the expression of our desires but infinitely more difficult to eliminate our needs and other wishes. In order to eliminate desire and needs we must, in effect, eliminate consciousness itself and with it the processes that literally define us as human. In our culture, many emotions have been equated as immoral and unacceptable both in overt expression and inner experience. This is most true where human sexuality is concerned, especially sexual feelings directed toward close kin and, therefore, incestuous.

The theories of Sigmund Freud (1957, 1966) make the most sense when viewed from the perspective of trying to explain the adaptive behavior of individuals trying to solve the moral problems created when their evolved sexual feelings define them, to themselves, to their significant others, to society in general, and to those who claim to represent God, as evil. While I disagree with many of the specifics of Freudian psychoanalysis, I believe we must pay attention to the manner in which individuals are asked to deal with incestuous and other sexual desires. All societies prohibit incest suggesting that it is both a universal desire and one perceived as dangerous to our species if acted on. But like the equally evolved and universal desires to dehumanize and enjoy the destruction of those who are our enemies, the need to rid ourselves of the desires themselves rather than learn to control their expression has lead to a constant need to utilize defenses associated with the psychotic landscape.

The Knowledge That We Might Be Unloved by Our Own Parents, Especially Our Mothers

Years of working with children has led me to conclude that many children (and adults) would rather die than admit that the parents who hurt and abandoned them did so because they did not love or care for them, and even hated them. For years I worked with groups of mothers who had to contend with children who blamed them for the fact that their fathers did not see them when it was very clear to all concerned that the fathers could have maintained their relationships with their children had they chosen to do so. It was easier for the children to blame their mothers or their own moral failings for father's disappearance than the fact that father may not have loved them.

The Belief That the Universe Is Not User-Friendly

There is no meaning or purpose to our lives except that which we create for ourselves, and that we live and die by accident rather than by events planned or under the control of any type of intelligence.

The Awareness That Morality and Justice Are Human Creations and Are Not Discovered

Bad things can happen to good people and good things can happen to bad people. We do not always live happily ever after. It is the experience of these possibilities as real and true that motivates defensive reconstructions of reality in very large numbers of individuals and further seems to motivate whole groups to agree to the reality of these reconstructions with harsh punishments meted out to those who disagree with the reconstructed realities. It is my belief that the god stories that exist in such variety and profusion in every culture (and which are defended to the death by their believers, usually the death of the non-believers) are defenses against the possibility that the psychotic landscape might be true. I believe, too, that these god stories not only justify human morality, which in turn justifies human necessity, but also justify and disguise the desires, wants, and even the whims of those who utilize the god stories to aid in the transmission of their own genes and memes. I agree with Erich Fromm (1947) that humanity tries to escape from the burdens and responsibilities of being a vulnerable human being by seeking those who would offer them the protection of the gods. Their tragedy begins the moment they find those who speak for the gods, for with the illusion of protection comes the loss of their freedoms and the beginning of their lives as slaves, puppets, and things.

How can we discern the difference between a defense and a non-defense? We cannot say that we recognize a defensive construction by its lack of truthfulness or its violations of reality as we have no privileged position from which to do so. (In the case of alterations of basic perceptual experience such as the hearing of voices or seeing of objects that nobody else experiences we usually find ourselves on firmer ground when questioning the reality testing of an individual.) When individuals create a god story that only they believe it might be experienced as absurd by those who do not share their construction of reality; they might be called psychotic, mad, or schizophrenic. If individuals instead share the defensive beliefs of others then they will probably be called religious, patriotic and well-adjusted by those with whom they share a common reality. I believe that none of us is equipped to say just how many of the religious, scientific, and other socially accepted truths revered by humanity are defensive constructions and if held by individuals rather than by multitudes would be judged madness, not wisdom. We do know that of the 2,000 or so organized religions on this planet each refers to itself as the truth and the rest as heresy, which is the religious equivalent of the term psychosis or delusion. I now describe the criteria by which defenses may often be distinguished from non-defensive beliefs. I also describe the price we pay for living those areas of our lives based on defenses.

Defensive thought and other adaptations tend to be non-negotiable, non-debatable, absolutist, and able to invoke rage and even violence when they are directly and continuously challenged. Defensive beliefs and other modes of defensive adaptation represent work and therefore cannot be played with. When individuals believe deeply in ideas that are meaningful to their lives but are held non-defensively they hold such ideas playfully and joyfully. They defend them with humor and tolerance even though the ideas have much gravity and consequence for those who live by them. Non-defensive adaptations can be debated and even argued without the discussions turning ugly and personal. Such adaptations are far more likely to be held as theoretical and open to change if new information becomes available. As Kuhn (1970) might put it, the non-defensive paradigms will be modified by the presence of anomalies rather than the anomalies explained away in order to protect the paradigm. Good science is non-defensive while defenses are in effect the enemy of science.

Karen Horney (1950: 39) described the modes of being in the world created by the extensive use of defenses, although she never integrated Piagetian thought into her own framework. Horney described the childlike concepts of perfection that were used by individuals to justify their modes of escaping from what she called basic anxiety, a mixture of fear, loneliness, and helplessness that the individual can neither tolerate nor find the means to resolve except by adopting neurotic trends. Horney described the defensive justifications of dominating others, living under the domination of others, or living isolated and alienated from others as seeking perfect mastery, perfect goodness, or perfect independence. She called the search for such perfection the "search for glory" and labeled the life styles that emerged as a result as "the devils pact." What Horney and other clinicians had accurately described were individuals who continued to feel like frightened children well into adulthood while acting like all-knowing, all-powerful, perfectly moral gods. We will now consider the role of defenses in what clinicians call fixation.

Adaptation is an essentially conservative process. Individuals do not seek to accommodate and change their skills arbitrarily. Most individuals do not risk change or create conditions in which costly errors and mistakes become possible unless confronted with an emotion or drive that represents a need or problem or they are convinced there is a better way to satisfy a need or solve a problem. When individuals perceive that they are relatively safe and needs and problems are not manifest they experiment in those activities called play. But the situations that represent play are relatively rare for most people and the activities that comprise play are usually required for later adaptations. From this point of view, even play is a conservative activity. When individuals cannot conceive of new ways of solving a set of problems, they are content with existing solutions to a variety of problems, others solve problems for them or forbid them to solve them for themselves, or defenses are used as their best solutions, then development may be judged fixated. I believe that if one examines the lives of any of us we discover that in any given situation we may be utilizing sensori-motor, preoperational or concrete, or formal operations to appraise the various events and situations that comprise our lives.

A student reading the developmental literature might be lead to believe that it is inevitable that each person move from one stage of intellectual development to the next, and that the achievement of a newer stage means the replacement of the previous stage. An impression is given that while the ages that different people achieve later stages may differ, eventually the transition to the later stage is achieved by everyone. There is also the implicit idea that earlier stages disappear once later stages arrive. Finally, there is a commonly held belief that later stages represent progress and are superior to the earlier stages in some essential manner. (A similar belief exists in relation to Darwinian evolution which implicitly or explicitly holds that the newer, more complex species at the top of the food chain, particularly humankind, represent both evolutionary progress and the inevitable direction that evolution had to take.) I reject all such notions of individual and species evolution. The child is not a defective, unimproved version of the adult and development is not inevitable. Development of cognitive functions is potentially available for all healthy members of our species but will not take place unless each individual experiences an environmental or social demand for it to take place, is motivated, and if necessary is helped by tutors, to make the accommodations that represent the learning of new skills that define new intellectual functions. Development takes place only in relation to those situations, classes of situations, or events in which the conditions necessary and sufficient for development exist.

When individuals are content with their adaptations to a situation, lack the necessary instruction to proceed with the development of their skills, hold on to those defensive operations that protect them from experiencing memories that represent terrifying and threatening past events or the guilt and shame for what they believe they have done to others, then development of the later stages will not take place. In the next chapter I discuss at length those relationships that involve god-thing stories for their existence. The defensive nature of the god-thing narratives often demand preoperational thinking and the punishment of the things by the gods if certain learning and development is to take place. It is important to remember that during the era in which America practiced slavery the only crime a master could commit in relation to his slaves was to teach them to read. Therefore, development is not automatically driven from within but does or does not take place depending on both the demands of the situation and individual and socially collective interpretations of those situations. As each of us moves through our day we are constantly shifting the developmental mode of our experience of various people, places, and things.

We drive home from work feeling in control of our lives and proud of the research that we have done in our laboratory only to stand cowering and terrified when stopped by a policeman who informs us that our car needs inspection or we whine for our suppers when we meet our wives at the door. We may or may not reflect on these discrepancies in our own behavior. We return home to confront our parents with what we feel is their unfairness toward us. We are firmly committed to utilizing the new skills of accommodation and negotiation that we have learned in psychology class only to find ourselves shrieking and crying as we have done hundreds of times before the moment we begin discussing our complaints with our parents. We wonder why it is so difficult to remain adult when our parents speak to us as if we were still six years old. We wonder why at the moment of our shame and undoing we feel exactly like we were six years old in this (and similar) situation. How is it possible for any of us to appraise and respond to situations and events in such disparate manners. Why do we feel ourselves to be of so many different ages as we move through the time and space of our lives?

In general, I have found that most individuals have a better developed sense of the inanimate world than the animate, a better understanding of animals than people. People are threatening if others learn to understand their deceptions. It is people who are able to hold one idea while stating its opposite with genuine conviction. People create what Horney called idealized self images and then demand, upon pain of death or abandonment, that others share that vision as if they too believed it to be absolutely true. One of the major sources of fixation involves individuals remaining totally embedded in relationships with powerful figures who demand and reward them for absolute allegiance with the authority's memes.

People are hard to explain, predict, and control therefore it is people, especially ourselves, for whom we have such difficulties developing a science based on formal operations. We want to learn about all aspects of our world but ourselves. Psychology is the last of the great sciences to develop and developmental psychology is the last of the psychologies to appear as a formal discipline. The criticisms that I have been leveling at psychology throughout this book are criticisms of the defenses we have employed as individuals, and as professionals in the field, that have left us fixated as a field. The self-critical development of evolutionary psychology and constructionism lead me to believe that we are ready to become a full-fledged science based on formal operations and humanistic principles.

The next chapter deals with the social construction of individual differences by reiterating the profound ignorance with which we seek answers as to why one individual experiences a situation, plays with it, and makes new discoveries one after another while another individual, in what we judge to be the same situation, feels such dread that he constructs an appraisal of the situation that will not change for the next fifty years. Perhaps more interestingly, why two individuals seem to be utilizing similar defenses and one begins to play, invent, and discover while the other continues to defend and remain dependent on the same sets of skills and interpretations. In all my years as a teacher and therapist I can never predict who will grow and who will not, nor explain why growth suddenly takes place in an individual. What is in the narratives of some people that will cause them to reexamine their lives while others tell the same story over and over with its same sad ending? Why do some people tell stories in which they are heroes and agents, others relate tales of being victims and villains, while still others tell no stories at all? The biology that structures their modes of experience must play a role, but so too must the nature of the social interactions which comprise the more interesting aspects of their environments. We now turn to the social construction of experience.

8

THE POLITICS OF EXPERIENCE AND THE
SOCIAL CONSTRUCTION OF SELVES

INTRODUCTION

We now turn to theoretical descriptions of how individual similarities and differences are shaped through social interactions. As has been noted numerous times there are no human behaviors or modes of experience that are not the product of a genetically structured, biological organism seeking to deal with a physical, and perhaps more importantly, social environment. We are dealing with human consciousness, an emergent process that is created and recreated each moment of its existence through the incredibly complex interactions of processes provided by biology, social forces which are the product of other conscious human beings, and the reflective self-regulating properties of consciousness. This chapter attempts to achieve descriptions concerning the manner in which different types of social interaction lead to a variety of means and modes by which individuals come to understand themselves and their lives. My goal is to achieve these ends while avoiding the common error of many social environmentalists—to lose sight of the fact that while individuals are inevitably constructed by their family, friends, community, and other social institutions comprising the society and culture of which they are a part they never stops being active agents with prior biological constructions and their own emergent, self-regulating internal activities. All individuals are constantly at work constructing those who would construct them.

RELATIONSHIPS, ATTACHMENT, SEPARATION, AND
CONFLICT

This discussion is anchored in a number of interrelated concepts seen through the lens of heterophenomonolgy. I define social constructionism as the collective processes by which human experience and differences between those modes of experience are shaped by various aspects of the adaptive struggle in contexts provided by different types of human relationships. I agree with the cultural psychologists Ernst Boesch and his colleagues (1997) that no human action can be understood outside of the context in which it takes place and that it is our culture that provides our collective social context. To study any aspect of human psychological functioning is to study culture! Human beings become aware of the world in a context of other human beings being aware of them as they become aware of the world. The developments that shape growing children's adaptive efforts are the adaptive efforts of others, especially as they relate to these children.

The narratives which define our selves, make clear our descriptive and moral identities, organize and prioritize the goals that we believe will satisfy our needs and solve our problems, begin as subjects within the narratives of others well before we reach storytelling age. At birth we represent the adaptive needs and problems of those whose narratives are now focused on us. In one way or another it matters to those who precede us as storytellers what story we learn to tell, as well as those stories we do not tell. Developing children can be conceptualized as holons within the context of ever more complex groupings of holons, all with similarities and differences in their conscious experiences of each other and the larger aspects of the world that enfolds them.

The genes we inherited from our parents shape both the cognitive processes with which we first begin to perceive and understand the world in which we live as well as the drives and emotions that define the needs we will have to satisfy and the problems we will have to solve, so too, do those human beings, whose concerns we are, also possess the goal of shaping those same cognitive and affective processes. Many of the needs we will experience and the skills we will develop are in part the result of evolutionary selections demanded by the role social organization has played in successful human adaptation. We are, therefore, born ready to join the human species as members of families, societies, and cultures but cannot do so unless we find ways to satisfy our needs and solve the problems preventing us from achieving our place in human society. We cannot achieve a place within the human family without the cooperative efforts of others because we are born with the need to join but not the means. We possess the rudiments of skills and desires that make us human but not the specific variations that have evolved in the particular time and place of our birth and represented by the society and culture which, in turn, represents the collective outcome of the adaptive struggle that we are to join. The specific shaping of our consciousness will be the result of how we satisfy the totality of our human needs and solve the totality of our human problems with and without the help of others. Our consciousness will also be shaped by the means and modes employed by others and approved of by the culture of which they are a part, in their attempts to teach us how to be human.

I begin this discussion of the social construction of consciousness with those evolutionary cognitive-affective adaptations that might underlie the interactions of an adult of our species and a newly-born infant. Becoming part of human society begins at birth and must include descriptions of the developmental processes by which adult consciousness is reached. I am assuming, as did John Bowlby (1969,

1973, 1979, 1980, 1988), that the extreme helplessness of the human neonate, and the long childhood that follows, have the adaptive purpose of demanding the social construction of each human being. We are born dependent on others and remain so for a long time because learning to be human in the manner prescribed by the particular culture we are to join is a long, arduous, and complex process.

I also assume along with Bowlby and others who approach the study of infancy from an ethological perspective, that the interactions between infants and their caretakers, made necessary by that long period of dependency, exist because of the survival advantages they provide for the individual members of our species and which are realized by the child's capacity to become a member of a cultural group. It is through the collective efforts of cooperating human beings that the individual members of our species become successful at passing on their genes and their memes.

I also agree with scholars such as Thomas Sowell (1995, 1996) that the extreme dependency on our caretakers makes the transmission of culture, and the differences these contribute to our view of the world, as basic to us as the ingestion of mother's milk and parental languages. Our induction into our culture begins the moment we are born and the very means used by our caretakers to nurture and shape our development simultaneously describes our social interactions and our socialization. We can describe the interactions between parent and child in psychological terms or in social terms but whichever terminology we choose we are also implicitly utilizing the other. The effect of cultures is not only as powerful and persistent as the effect of genes but almost impossible to separate from one another. In the light of previous discussions, I reiterate my belief that we are 100 percent the result of both our genetic inheritance and our cultural heritage.

The narrative by which students of psychology begin (and often end) their understanding of the social construction of the infant involves what is defined as attachment and separation-individuation. This is one of the hottest of hot button topics in psychology because so much may be at stake for our society if the manner in which we raise our children, and especially deal with our infants, is as important as those who share this particular narrative have claimed. Therefore, a caveat is required before discussing this topic. For a long time the only professionals who were concerned with the way in which social interactions determined human functioning were psychologists and psychiatrists working with so-called mentally ill patients.

Clinical models of personality development divide all types of mental and social organization into the healthy and the pathological. In the dominant clinical theories, the etiology of health and pathology involves the manner in which mothers and infants form emotional bonds and then negotiate the separations necessary for the child to become either the type of adult that is respected and successful in our society or the type favored by the subsociety of clinicians. When mothers and/or infants refuse or are unable to interact according to the prescriptions of clinical theory it will be assumed that these relationships are pathological and will lead inevitably to some form of mental illness or disorder. Moreover, when clinicians judge people to be mentally ill they often assume that the etiology of the illness involves relationships within the sick persons' primary families, especially with their mothers.

Adolf Grünbaum (1984), and Jerome Kagan (1996) among others have demonstrated both logically and empirically that there is neither evidence to support nor refute the suppositions that early childhood experiences *by themselves* can determine the behavior of an adult many years later or that adult forms of unhappiness and behavioral deviancy can ever be proven to derive from specific childhood experiences. Other critics point out that the placing of blame on parents, especially mothers, if developmental pathology exists, absolves society in general for the totality of injustices that might also create unwanted adaptations. Focusing exclusively on mother-child interactions ignores the other relationships in which mothers are engaged that can alter the manner in which they care for their infants, and the other relationships involved in the infants and growing children's lives. My own complaint adds the fact that the labeling of so much human behavior as pathological does not permit us to understand the consciousness of those who have adapted to social situations of which clinicians and other politically liberal academic types disapprove nor the nature of those situations which bring about variations in mother-child intersubjectivity, which in turn might lead to adaptive processes that differ from one another.

I believe that what transpires between infants and caretakers has consequences for later development in the sense that these earliest of adaptations begin to shape the interpersonal skills, expectations of the self and others, and the nature of the infant's identity that, in turn, shapes the manner these developing persons seek to construct relationships from their side of intersubjective space. The earliest of relationships may be responsible not only for the manner in which individuals assume that later relationships must and should be shaped but also may determine with whom it makes adaptive sense to engage in any given relationship. By pursuing those individuals who continue the pattern of previous relationships, avoiding others who threaten the established adaptive patterns, and demanding of all who engage in them that they adapt to their modes of need satisfaction and problem solving, individuals may well reproduce early patterns of behavior judged by others to be pathological. All individuals seek to assimilate new situations into existing adaptive organizations. This remains as true for situations comprised of the consciousness of others as any others. What remains open for interpretation, however, is whether or not these early interpersonal situations carry a greater weight in creating and maintaining adaptive patterns than relationships occurring later in people's lives. With this in mind, I turn to the nature of these early interpersonal patterns and the differences they may help to create in adaptive consciousness.

The following is based not only the work of John Bowlby as well as Mary Ainsworth (1985, 1989), L. A. Sroufe (1987), Margaret Mahler (1968), Heinz Kohut (1971, 1977), D. W Winnicott (1965), Daniel Stern (1977), Jessica Benjamin (1989), Malcolm Slavin and Daniel Kriegsman (1992) and too many others to mention in so short a space. I begin with a general definition of attachment which is an emotional bond between individuals in which one or both of the individuals also depend on the other to satisfy a host of other social needs. Emotional bonding represents one type of intersubjective experience and define one important type of relationship. According to Ainsworth, there are four criteria that define an emotional bond and the cognitive-affective experience that acts as this type of social need. When babies are born they are likely, but not necessarily, to become conscious of others in an intersubjective field defined by being the object of at least one intense emotional bond. Any given infant will discover that (1) he or she is irreplaceable to those who are bonded to him or her; (2) unplanned separations will cause those who hold him precious emotional distress; (3) being reunited with him or her will lead to comfort and even joy on the part of those who experienced distress; and (4) permanent separation as in the case of death will lead to the experience of grief and the process of mourning in which the loss will be made real and the emotions that make him or her irreplaceable lessened. To become bonded with (or to love) another in this manner and to define as one of the goals of life the continuance and expansion of other bonded relationships is to assure one's lifelong need for others and to define a mode of conscious experience in which other human beings remain important.

The purpose and importance of emotional bonding seems obvious when viewed from the perspective of the parents or caretakers of the young; it dramatically increases the chances that the young will not only be cared for and protected but also provided opportunities to develop the desire to form emotional bonds with others with whom long term cooperation will be necessary. The love and loyalty of an adult for a child during the long period of childhood dependency also increases the chances that the young will learn those skills that will allow dependencies to be lessened. In addition, the bonds between adults and children also assure that children will be amenable to learning these new adaptive skills in the manner in which the adults and the society they represent wish them to be learned. In every social group children are required to adopt the social behaviors that pass for adulthood in that social group. In effect, attachment promotes bonding and bonding leads to the reduction of attachment. One major difference between people can be assumed to be the directions that development might take given the presence or absence of opportunities to develop emotional bonds with others. Another difference would be created by the nature and difficulty of problems children would be asked to solve both with and without consistent and affectionate attention from those more skilled than the child. One of the differences I have long been interested in involves a child's experience of adults who experience their ministration of him or her as play compared to the experience that one's needs are to be satisfied as a form of moral obligation or just plain hard work.

Much of the charting of adaptational growth and the judgments made of this process involve the manner in which children and caretakers renegotiate their relationships and reduce the attachment while evolving new forms of their bonds. The physical and cognitive-affective developmental changes that permit infants and then older children to rely less on adults and more on their own abilities is termed separation and the process that permits the developing youngsters to define their own identities and senses of self is referred to as individuation. I believe some form of attachment and bonding between individuals has been made inevitable by evolution, that some form of separation-individuation will be experienced as necessary by all individuals as both needs to be satisfied and a potential set of problems to be solved. We must all find ways to cooperate and influence how others are to be of benefit to us. We also learn to solve a growing variety of problems by ourselves as well as learn to effectively compete with others when situations demand it. If our genes and memes are to survive we must be prepared to care for the next generation as well.

If we examine the process of separation we find that it is defined by the development of new forms of adaptive behaviors made possible by biological development known as maturation and the simultaneous influence of those care-takers in whose interest it is for these new skills to emerge. Learning to walk, talk, and manipulate tools with hands made free by being newly upright, all increase the types of play and explorations that might arouse the interests of children. These skills, in turn, stimulate the development of still newer skills as well as variations in older skills. The increase in skills and new forms of cognitive-affective con-sciousness will require new responses from caretakers and inevitably begin to alter their relationships with their offspring. A myriad number of factors will shape the direction that separation might take. These might include how much time children will have for play compared to work, and if the children must work (that is, engage in activities in order to survive) how many and what types of problems will they experience while working. It is in the nature of children's relationships with their caretakers and the degree to which comforting protection is guaranteed as a result of the existence of strong emotional bonds that may well determine the balance of work and play in children's lives.

If we observe children with parents with whom they are securely attached enter what Ainsworth called the strange situation we see a dance begin in which the children initially cling to their parents for reassurance, protection, and comfort. They then begin to push away from their parents to explore and play with the objects and contents of the now less than strange situation. Play continues until the children assimilate all that interests them in their immediate surroundings or until they discover something that again frightens them. At that moment, the children turn to their parents for comfort by engaging in eye contact, and perhaps physical contact as well. Children attempt to read their parents emotional assessment of the fright-ening objects or events. If they read danger or disapproval in their caretakers they might return and cling, or simply make eye contact in order to seek comfort and guidance until they make their own decision to continue or break off explorations. If nothing frightens the children they continue the exploration until other needs make themselves manifest or other demands are made on them by their caretakers. Observing children in this way we see that play is an adventure and the adventure continues until fear or another need turns the adventure into work. At that moment, the children seek comfort and aid from those with whom attachments exist.

We can cast the entire life cycle into a framework in which developing individu-als increase the adaptive range of their abilities, move further and further from their attachment figures in both physical and psychological space, exercise increased independence in terms of skills and the individuality of self expression. As this progression continues the psychological boundaries that define the horizon line between adventure and fear expands. This expansion occurs in all areas of life including the interpersonal and the intrapsychic. Human relationships, and the relationship individuals have with their own selves, must be constantly renegotiated. Each individual becomes more adept at becoming a storyteller and as the cycle continues back and forward, toward and away from traditional sources of comfort and direction the narratives that explain, organize, and justify life also change. Once the line representing fear is crossed individuals once again seeks those places, things (individuals become bonded with objects other than human), and most of all people with whom comfort, security, and new direction can be achieved. With each change in adaptive skills and the reorganized consciousness that represents those changes, there arises new needs, problems, experiences of success and failure, narratives, skills including new defenses, relationships, and so on in a never ending intertwined set of events and situations.

As these cycles continue there are changes in the intrapsychic organization of interpersonal experience that are worth noting. With the development of memory, those objects with which children have become bonded and attached become available internally even when they are not to be experienced externally. Children can now interact with these people, places, and things even when they are away from them. They may be comforted by them, or criticized and threatened. An important determinant of differences in separation involves the capacity of individuals to self-soothe or self-criticize when confronting difficult and threatening situations. The experience of internalized objects also changes as a function of the type of thought organization utilized by the individual. Preoperational children have difficulty separating fantasy and dream figures from ones perceptually experienced and, therefore, interact with their internalized objects of attachment differently than when operations come into existence. With the emergence of operations, the interactions between the self and others within fantasy become less a function of attachment and more of two equals. Images of the self and others are replaced by words and an internal dialogue that often lasts a lifetime. These internal dialogues represent Popperian adaptations within the social realm. Another difference in the social construction of experience involves how and when our interpersonal relationships are experienced in fantasy, especially in relation to soothing and comforting, criticizing and threatening.

The concept of dialogue leads us to another aspect of the social construction of individuals and their differences, the discursive nature of human relationships. The narratives by which people live may be seen to exist as scripts when narratives are shared in intersubjective space. By gesture, body language, words, and emotional tone attachment and separations are negotiated by a variety of forms of communication. Communication is essential for human beings to teach and otherwise influence each other, and the manner of these communications powerfully determines the nature of human consciousness. Because the direction of human adaptations is in the interest of those with whom we interact, all communications and scripts are, in part, rhetorical as well as moral in nature. Those seeking to communicate attempt to convince others as to what they should and should not do as well as how things should be done. There are two functions involved in the discursive

nature of human communications: instruction and conflict resolution. We now turn
to the differences in adaptive consciousness created by these two activities.

The child must learn the skills and the rules that govern the expression of those
skills involved in coming together with and separating from people, as well as the
skills for cooperation and competition. Everything discussed thus far is a potential
cause of interpersonal conflict. Conflict is inevitable whenever and wherever the
human species become socially organized. The rest of this chapter discusses the
differences that exist in conflict resolution as it relates to the construction of
adaptive differences.

THE POLITICS OF CONFLICT RESOLUTION

The sources of human conflict are many as are the needs for mechanisms of
conflict avoidance, reduction, and resolution. Conflicts exist at all levels of life on
this planet and derives from the competition for resources necessary for the
maintenance and reproduction of life. The typical resolution of conflict involves
some form of combat in which one party to the conflict is defeated and either
withdraws or is killed. The moment a species relies on cooperation among its
members for survival or other benefits, there must be some form of social organization that demands far more complex forms of conflict resolution. Killing the
competitor or driving it from the environment is still a way of resolving differences
but this form of resolution means the destruction of the social organization on which
all the members depend. Under these circumstances there must be a means of
dealing with competition that balances the needs of individuals as individuals with
their needs of the group; it is after all need satisfaction and problem solving of
individuals that leads to satisfactions and solutions by individuals and groups. At
the human level, conflict resolution takes a much more complex turn because of
the human need for others, which includes bonds such as love and the inherent need
human beings have for ideas such as fairness, justice, and morality.

Human beings compete and conflict not only for the resources to transmit their
genes successfully but also their memes. Even within similar gene groupings where
strong love, affection, and loyalties exist there will be conflicts. Siblings compete
with each other for the physical and psychological nurturance of their parents even
as they protect one another from nonkin. Fathers and mothers may compete on
many levels, not the least involving the different sexual strategies developed
through natural selection. Parents will struggle with their children over the demands
made by the children on resources the adults need for their own survival and
developments of the self. There will be inevitable conflicts as children choose
modes of separation and individuation that conflict with parental or societal
expectations or which parents consider dangerous for the survival or growth of the
offspring. In these cases, the conflicts may be intense but the needs to resolve them
with both individual and group life continuing are just as intense.

Conflict resolution is one of the main determinants of the structure of any group
organization and, therefore, it has a determining effect on how the other adaptive
processes of interpersonal life succeed, fail, and are shaped. Conflicts are resolved

or avoided by the creation of policy which results in moral rules or codified laws. Group life is, in part, determined by who creates and maintains policy and how political ends are achieved. The individuals who set and maintain policy represent the authority of that particular group. One of the most prevalent types of conflict involves determining who is or who is not to have political authority and how that authority is to be shared. Another key conflict will involve the use to which authority is put when policy is set. Will that policy aid in the satisfaction of the needs of those who require the presence of authority in their lives or will the rules established by authority benefit mainly the authority? Every organized group has an internal politics, therefore Philip Tetlock (1992) is correct when he opines that one way or another we are all politicians. Every social interaction, no matter for what adaptive reasons it exists, is a political act. There are three forms of political organization practiced on this planet or wished for: Anarchy, Authoritarian/totalitarian and Democratic/Humanistic. I believe that every society, community, school, church, and family practices, or hopes to practice, one or more of these types of politics to maintain social organization and avoid, reduce, and resolve conflicts among its members.

ANARCHY, AUTHORITARIAN/TOTALITARIAN, AND DEMOCRATIC/HUMANISTIC ORGANIZATIONS

I begin by describing the authoritarian/totalitarian mode of social organization because it is, I believe, the one that is predominate in most social groups on this planet and most described by any study of the history of social organization. Anarchy is wished for by many as a reaction to the horrors visited on those not having power as they participate in social structures defined by authoritarian and especially totalitarian systems. I believe anarchy is impossible to institute as long as some must be dependent on others, as is certainly the case with children, although anarchy does exist by default when other forms of social organization fail. The democratic/humanistic mode also exists more as a wish than actuality although some forms of democracy/humanism may exist from time to time. Much of the conflicts that currently exist at all levels of society involve those that would maintain the authoritarian and those that would replace it with democratic institutions. In many current societies, especially our own, we see a mixture of all three types and the conflicts that attend them at all levels of social organization from within individuals, families, schools, and communities to the most macroscopic of social organizations.

I believe that the authoritarian systems predominate because they evolved during the long prehistoric epoch when humanity lived in small hunter-gatherer groups that were in constant danger of extinction. Everyone in these groups depended on everyone else, bonding many relationships and basing a large number on attachment. Decisions had to be made swiftly by those with the knowledge to make them and the skills to win the necessary and frequent combats with the human and animal foes with whom the group competed for survival. Individuals who assumed authority were usually self-selected by their adaptive skills at violence, decision making, and their abilities to project characteristics that earned the favor of those they must lead. They maintained their leadership only as long as those led believed it necessary or until they were successfully challenged by those believing they were better qualified to lead.

Leaders soon discovered that the powers and freedoms confirmed on them by their positions of authority carried enormous burdens of responsibility toward others, many of whom were not kin. The leaders of such groups were constantly confronted with choices of carrying out their responsibilities toward others or caring for their own needs or those of their immediate kin. Viewing the problems of authority from a gene's eye perspective suggests that the solution to these internal conflicts, as well as challenges to authority, might very well be modes of leadership that maximized the freedom to aid the self and kin while simultaneously decreasing responsibilities for others. From the leaders point of view, anyone who challenged their authority were considered enemies and the more effectively they prevented enemies from challenging their right to lead the more they would be able to maintain their authority and gain advantages for their genes and memes by being in positions of authority and power in the group.

In order to protect their authority, the leaders had to have the motive, means, and justification to use force. Force meant killing or forcing from the group individuals whose cooperation was required for the groups continuance and for the continuance of authority; it makes no sense to be a leader without followers. These problems could be solved only if the authority could appeal to the followers in such a way as to convince them that they benefited from decisions that in fact benefited mainly the leaders. It meant convincing the followers that they needed the leaders more than the leaders needed them and that they had the skills required to justify continuing their tenure as authority even when they did not. The success of such dilemmas required two elements: first the leaders' capacity to utilize deceptions of the self and others; and second, to find and/or create conditions in the followers that would insure that they would co-create the beliefs that were based on the defensive deceptions being structured by the authority. The needs of children for their parents and of citizens for leadership could always be utilized by those in authority to create the psychological conditions necessary to assure their continuance as authority if disobeyed and challenged. Children threatened with starvation, abandonment, or the brute powers of their parents or other adult figures are prime subjects to be convinced to obey authority without question and experience as true whatever the adults would have them believe.

Before continuing with a description of the means and modes by which authoritarian/totalitarian systems operate, as well as the dynamics which are derived from these activities, let me differentiate between an authoritarian and totalitarian form of leadership. In an authoritarian system the leader is generally content with outward, behavioral displays of loyalty and unquestioned compliance with policies. In a totalitarian system the leadership seeks to be convinced that loyalty exists in the very thoughts and emotions which comprise consciousness itself. George Orwell (1949) described the nature of the totalitarian system as it seeks to control the very language used to communicate, redefine emotions such as love and sexual desire, and even creates conditions wherein if an individual is shown four fingers and told that he is perceiving five he will believe what he is told. In working with individuals over many years I am convinced that those labeled with the worst of psychiatric diagnoses are the products of totalitarian families, religions, and schools and that every authoritarian system is to some degree totalitarian.

Authoritarian systems operate with narratives that are god-thing stories. The language adopted involves the use of moral judgments that pose as descriptions. Moral judgments are applied to the identities of those interacting and, therefore, act to define various individual's essences rather than specific behavior taking place in specified contexts. Those in authority are flattered and told that they are good, geniuses, heroic, beautiful, and even appointed by the gods to their exalted status. Those who are led form a hierarchy based on who is closest to the highest authority and, therefore, shares similar superiority. The lower that one is placed on the hierarchy the fewer positive qualities one finds associated with their essences. One becomes unclean, sinful, ugly, and despised by the gods. In our culture it seems that the iron rule of psychology is that the poor are always to be found lacking in "intelligence" but make up for that lack by a plentitude of "mental illnesses." In short, the higher we rise in the vertical hierarchies of the authoritarian system the less able we are to apply words suggesting weaknesses or faults, the lower we descend on the hierarchy the less able we are to find anything but words that connote weakness, faults and defects. Those who are in power and practice authoritarian politics are described as pure and perfect while those below exist in various states of defectiveness. Defects can be changed to perfection but require the aid and the control of those who are pure and perfect.

Those at the top of the hierarchy make decisions while those below are good as long as they are obedient to their betters and superiors and do not forget their place or who they are. Places may be formalized, as in the case of caste systems or economic hierarchies forming classes, or exist as subtexts that are maintained without being discussed or reflected upon. When individuals behave disobediently they are punished but first they are made to agree with authority that the punishment is called discipline and is being done for their own good. Authority creates conditions in which the followers experience needs that only the authority can satisfy and creates problems that only the authority can solve. By inducing fear in those who are dependent, or terror when it serves its purposes, authority defines the conditions that limit the terror. "Recognize my authority and I will protect you," suggests the authority, demanding that all ignore who created the terror in the first place. "Accept me as perfect," demands authority, "and I will save you from your inherently defective essence, soul, self, and so on."

Authoritarian systems employ the use of scapegoats on whom the terror created by the authority can be blamed. External enemies can be dehumanized permitting the authority to wage war, a process that solidifies the followers belief in their abilities and necessity as leaders. Any visible minority can be dehumanized, despised, and used to provide the illusion that they are the source of all terrors. In our society, those of African descent have been the main despised minority, although at other times Jews, the mentally ill, and other social groups have filled in to serve the needs of authoritarian structures. Any biologism can be used to create moral hierarchies by using judgments instead of words to describe biological differences. Sexual differences have long been the basis for struggles over power between men and women as authority sought to describe the god(s) as either male or female. Family therapists have long recognized that any child in a family might be designated as the bad, crazy, violent, or oversexed and play the role of the despised child blamed for causing all of the family difficulties.

This extortion game may be played with any set of needs, not just fear and terror. Children may learn that they are loved only so long as they comply with either adult demands for outward obedience or with adult perceptions and definitions of reality itself. "Daddy is not drunk, he is sick." intones mother as she subtly makes clear to the children that they either conform to her definitions or lose what little love they now receive from her. Carl Rogers (1961) described such interactions as being raised under conditions of worth. Mother's needs to define her children's reality in this way may well be predicated on her fear and terror of being physically abused by a much stronger male as well as being abandoned financially by him and left with small children. The extortion game may involve needs for moral approval created by the authority's definition that one is morally defective or even a monster of one type or another. "What is the matter with you?" roars an angry parent, leaving the child to chose his own moral defect from among others he or she might have been labeled with in the past: lazy, weird, crazy, brat, bum, good-for-nothing, or some of my favorites from my days of working with families: lazy bag of shit, and the result of a failed abortion. Churches can define errant parishioners as sinners, heretics, and damned for all eternity, while governments claim that the disobedient are treasonous and not worthy of being citizens.

Psychological descriptions of inner emotional states disappear and are replaced by moral terminology. Children learn to fear their own emotions, even as they lose the language to describe them, when emotions themselves come under authority's attack and control. "Daddy, I am scared." "Don't be such a baby, what is wrong with you? There is absolutely nothing to be afraid of." "Eat, you are hungry!" "Go to sleep, you are tired!" Gregory Bateson (1979) and other communication theorists described the adaptive problems confronting children when authority demands obedience to their moral definition of the child's cognitive-affective processes. In this context, the knowledge of the authority is cast as always and absolutely true while the knowledge of those lower in the hierarchy are increasingly suspect in their essential validity. The professor, the teacher, the parents, the clergy, the politician are not to be disputed by their students, offspring, parishioners or citizens. If they do their minds will be declared defective in some way by the authority. Many religions teach children that their moral worth depends on their pleasing gods and human authorities that can read and judge their minds. These same religions insist that there are no differences as to moral infractions based on thoughts and feelings or overt behavior., I believe these religions are creating psychological problems whose solutions are massively difficult and create the need for the worst type of god-thing narratives as defenses.

There are certain consequences that I believe grow from the extortion and blackmail that mark the authoritarian system. The defenses that comprise the adaptive interpersonal means and modes of interaction often require the use of preoperational thinking to be achieved. The result is a fixation in the relationship between those involved, not only in the individual modes of adaptive behavior. The authority remains the authority with all the freedoms and responsibilities while the followers rely on the authority and fail to develop those skills that would permit them to have their own freedoms and responsibilities. The relationship between adult and child, leader and follower, does not get mutually renegotiated. Interpersonal perceptions are marked by a continuance of god-thing, I-it, rather than person to person, I-thou.

The skills that might define an individuated identity are not only shaped in the process of development to reflect the needs of authority but those skills that would permit individuals to perceive themselves as separate from authority do not come into existence. These individuals live out the stories and narratives told to them rather than those they might tell to others. They remain embedded in a mode of consciousness in which "I am my identity, moral and descriptive." is not replaced by "I have an identity." "I am my emotions." does not get transformed into "I have emotions." "My emotions [such as anger] make me hit you." does not get transformed into "I am angry but how I express my anger is a separate issue from my feeling anger. I cannot help but feel angry but I have an infinite number of choices as to how I reveal my feelings to you."

In an authoritarian/totalitarian system there is little opportunity to play! Pleasing authority becomes the main form of work which may become all consuming. Often individuals find themselves working endlessly at keeping their own thoughts and feelings from straying into sinful, crazy, or treasonous realms. When individuals internalize a set of rules to govern their consciousness, the necessary conditions to create and become artistic seem to vanish. Creativity exists only to the degree and in the directions approved of by the authority and then only if the authority defines the limits and intersubjective spaces where intellectual play can take place. While the necessary standards to create might exist in these systems, the freedom to explore, express, and develop the individuality required for artistic achievement often does not.

We now turn next to the interpersonal spaces created by anarchy. Anarchy exists as the result of those who desire relief from the pain of the authoritarian/totalitarian form of interpersonal relationships and through the inadvertent consequences of the failure of other types of social organization. Anarchy is wished for by some but is rarely realized for any length of time in practical terms. Those who plan the downfall of authority or escape from it are exercising what Erich Fromm (1947: 121) called "the freedoms from." But being free of fear or oppression, for example, does not define "the freedoms to." Erik Erikson (1968) recognized that identities defined by what they are not and what they are against can only be maintained as long as there is something to be against. In such circumstances, individuals do not become aware of their needs to define who they are and for what they stand.

As a result, planned anarchism, usually expressed in utopian visions, emerge as chaotic or more totalitarian than the organizations they replace. The fixations created by totalitarian systems do not permit individuals to figure out alternative ways of solving conflicts if extortion and blackmail are not used. It is one thing to resolve a problem differently than the manner in which it has been done in the past, it is quite another matter to figure out or learn how to do it. The ever present pressure of evolution creates desires in those who would be leaderless and maintain equality with all others to seek ways to express the individual memes that define their personal positive visions by which the group should live. "Freedoms to" eventually are defined and while these freedoms are defined differently than before it is not long before they are demanded of all who express themselves in ways other than their new leaders expect. Once again those lower in the social hierarchy are expected to do what is good for them and the group as a whole.

History teaches us that it is impossible for anarchy to exist for any extended period of time and when the worst tyrants are removed they are often replaced by even worse dictators unless an alternative form of social organization replaces it. Hitler and his Nazi Party replaced the Kaisers, Stalin and the Communist Politburo replaced the Czars, and Mao Tse-tung stood in the place of the Mandarins. Older siblings terrorize their younger brothers and sisters when the feared parents are not around.

There are many who see our culture's form of social organization being attacked by anarchists who would impose, by default, a tyranny based on the rejection of all authority and the pursuit of hedonistic pleasures and self indulgences. An economy that forces both parents to work while providing no alternative forms of rearing children is, in effect, raising those children in an anarchy. It is this form of anarchy, seen within many of our families, that concerns many professionals even though it is these same professionals who are, in part, responsible for the disorganization of these families. I agree with feminists who argue that the anarchy of children's lives created when they lack caretakers should not be called maternal separation or deprivation thereby implying that the anarchy is the fault of mothers and women. However, these youngsters are still experiencing anarchic surroundings.

The problems to be solved by individuals adapting to an anarchic social structure are quite different than in an authoritarian/totalitarian social unit. The lack of consistent caretakers makes bonding a far more difficult task and changes the relationship to be more businesslike and less familiar than in other types of structures. There can be no consistent attachments without emotional bonds and without attachments we cannot really speak of separation. Just as the individual does not learn to relate to others within an interpersonal field of experience, that same individual fails to learn to express adaptive differences within the norms required of being a member of a social group. As a result, there can be no internalization of moral standards against which individual expressions of behavior or cognitive-affective experience can be measured. For most of us in the helping professions, raised as we were in authoritarian or perhaps democratic systems, contact with children who could not predict the behavior of adults, whose modes of adaptation were often highly idiosyncratic, whose willingness or ability to even establish a relationship with consistent rules no matter how authority behaved toward them and whose social and cognitive skills are so disparate and inconsistently developed, has been a dislocating and disorienting experience.

It is hard for me to imagine what life would feel like if caretakers and authority had not been present in my life. I can easily relate to the sudden disappearance or inconsistency of authority, but these are events that have followed my own development within organized systems and the internalization of my own skills and identity as an authority. As a professional therapist I became used to enraged teenagers committing acts of violence as they opposed the very authority they were emulating and then attempted to morally justify their actions. What I was not used to, and which upsets me even as I write about it, were children inflicting damage on others or themselves and simply saying, "I felt like doing it." I believe that such behaviors result from adaptations to real anarchic situations. I extend the discussion of the outcomes of anarchy in addition to those of authoritarian organizations in the next chapter.

Let me conclude this section with a brief discussion of the social construction of experience as it relates to democratic/humanistic forms of social organization. My discussion is of an ideal in much the same way that anarchy exists as an ideal. I live in a society that holds democracy to be its ideal and many reading this will become enraged as I state that I see moments of democracy in practice, but more often than not what I experience is either anarchy or an authoritarian system. To quote Shakespeare, "it [in this case real democracy and humanism] is more honored in the breach than in the observance." Unlike anarchy, however, democracy seems to be a viable long-term solution for our needs for social organization in that it provides for necessary leadership, rules to govern cooperative behavior, and mechanisms for conflict resolution when individual forms of self-expression and competition for resources threaten to destroy the fabric of the group itself. I believe that the main difference between democratic and authoritarian systems involves the rejection of god-thing stories in the democratic system and the use of science (in its broadest, nontechnical and artistic sense as well as its more formally defined activities) to define its membership and their structuralized relationships. At their base, democratic forms of organization are created by individuals who are socially constructed according to the principles of psychology rather than through the moral worth of their essences. What defines the consciousness of individuals as they develop in a democratic/humanistic system is a theory of mind made up of motives and reasons for behavior based on descriptions of cognitive-affective processes rather than hierarchical moral judgments of their essential worth.

The bases of interpersonal organizations, like so many other forms of individual and collective adaptations, have been uneven and varied from place to place and person to person. Why our culture became increasingly organized around the memes that all human beings are motivated by thoughts and feelings rather than supernatural forces or moral essences is a mystery, as are all the reasons why individuals and societies move in this or that direction. It is clear that the enlightenment, the scientific revolution, the industrial revolution, and urbanization were steps along the way but what role each played as cause and/or effect is unclear. But it seems clear to me that in Western society we are still moving in the direction of more widespread belief that science and psychology are the sources of human understanding and the morally correct way to deal with ourselves and each other. There is much conflict over this direction and on any given day I would not take bets on how long this trend will continue. I am, however, morally committed to the correctness of this direction. I believe that educational and all other childrearing efforts should be geared to its continued development even though neither I nor anyone else can say with certainty that in the long run the democratic/humanistic form of governance will be best for the success of our genes or our memes. I take this stand out of conviction and faith!

In a democracy, individuals submit themselves voluntarily to the authority that they have selected, elected, and with whom they have a contractual relationship. They do so in a belief that what they give up will be given back in the form of benefits provided by group cooperation. They believe that their genes and their memes will ultimately benefit by submitting to the society's contractual relationships. All relationships are contractual even if some of the rules remain unwritten. The specific relationships establishing authority at all levels of a democratic society become codified and expressed as laws. These laws supersede the authority of any individuals in the societal system so that even the highest of authorities voluntarily submit themselves to the laws. Authority is selected on the basis of the describable intellectual and moral skills that are needed to achieve the clearly defined goals that authority is to achieve. Authority is not defined by superior essences and all citizens are permitted to aspire to leadership roles if they are willing and capable of demonstrating the skills necessary to carry out the responsibilities of their offices.

Authority maintains its position for as long as preexisting contracts determine or until the authority is unable to fulfill the terms of its contract. When any citizens of a democratic society violate their authority with any other they are dealt with by their fellow citizens as equals and human beings. If individuals are deprived of their freedoms because of violations of law or other moral transgressions it is done according to the rules of evidence and voted on by their fellow citizens who then act in clearly defined roles as judges. There are no attempts to punish others based on the innately superior wisdom of the judges and the inherent immorality and inferiority of the accused. People deal with one another with languages based on descriptions and opinions separated from facts, not as gods defining ultimate and absolute truths about some type of thing or another.

All individuals in a democratic system are not accorded equal status as voting citizens. Those who have been found guilty of a crime and whose behaviors (not their essences) have been judged to be criminal are excluded from participation until they have fulfilled their debt to society or otherwise judged worthy of rejoining their fellow citizens. Children are another category of individuals that are not accorded the freedoms of full citizenship nor demanded the full responsibilities that exist as a function of having the full range of adult freedoms. Unlike in an anarchy, children in a democracy are asked to submit to the authority of adult figures and are held to morals concerning right and wrong and standards that define excellence and high quality. Unlike authoritarian systems, children are seen as human beings lacking learnable skills rather than being inferior, defective versions of adults who have yet to be perfected. Children in a democracy, based on science and psychology, are seen as motivated by the same cognitive-affective processes as adults and having needs to satisfy and problems to solve. Therefore, when children fail to live up to the morals of their society or perform according to standards of quality and excellence it is the psychology of the child, not their moral worth, that needs to be redirected. The redirecting of an individual's psychology requires different efforts than the use of force and moral intimidation required to create obedience and submission to adult authority.

The language of interacting adults and children in a democratic-humanistic social structure reflects the same scientific-psychological underpinnings of these relationships as in adult-adult interactions. Children are told by adults that, "I am pleased or disappointed in your behavior because." This is followed by a description of the consequences of the child's behavior on which pleasure or displeasure is based. Children are given clear choices by adults who establish different consequences for behaviors considered immoral or substandard, only after efforts have been made to help the children see the consequences of their actions and make sure that the children are capable of performing the actions required of them by adults. The adults are also careful to make clear to themselves just who is helped or hurt by the actions of the children. Is it the children who are hurt by their immoral behavior, other individuals, or is the offense to the authority of the adult making the moral judgments of the children's actions?

Adaptive errors on the children's part do not make them stupid or lazy but in need of help in making necessary accommodations to situations and events experienced as difficult. Errors and transgressions also relate to describable behaviors and their consequences, not to the cognitive-affective processes which motivate them. "I think you are feeling thus and so," or "Are you feeling thus and so?" replaces "What is the matter with you that you cry, laugh, or engage in some other expression of behavior." There are never sentences that begin with, "You think" or "You feel." I wish space would permit me to expand on these linguistic differences but I believe I have given the reader a flavor of what might be involved in the social construction of consciousness within the contexts of differing political systems.

There is, however, one additional topic to be introduced as it relates to social interactions and the politics of experience. When children are loved, and later respected, for having thoughts and feelings that motivate them, when differentiations are made by adults as to the moral transgressions created by thinking as opposed to behaving, and when children are not made to fear the adults who care for, teach, and discipline them, these children experience what the Psychoanalyst D. W. Winnicott (1965: 29–37) calls a "holding environment." A holding environment allows the child to define himself as motivated by psychological phenomena rather than moral labels. It permits a tolerance of their own thoughts and emotions and the awareness that necessary moral and intellectual changes require new forms of learning rather than changes in their essences that somehow remain impossible to define, let alone achieve. Most significant is the children's ability to play with adults and in the presence of adults rather than spending endless amounts of time working hard to please adults and other authorities.

A holding environment also creates conditions that permit individuals to experience themselves as both part of and separate from others. It allows for definitions of the self that are defined by how the individual is the same as others and yet simultaneously unique. It is these individuals that learn to tell narratives that reflect both uniqueness and a common humanity. Finally, I believe that play within the interpersonal space of a holding environment permits the fullest development of Popperian intelligence. While these remarks involve an implicit criticism of authoritarian systems they also have meaning for those children of anarchy who lack those who can provide a sense of safety and comfort as well as descriptive forms of noncoercive direction and discipline.

MORAL DEVELOPMENT

I close this chapter with a short introduction into the work of Laurence Kohlberg (1984) concerning moral development as well as some speculations on his work as it derives from the preceding paragraphs. Kohlberg based his work on moral development on the stage theory of Piaget. He looked at the morals of children from the manner in which children of differing cognitive development are able to comprehend any set of specific morals, not from the specific content of the morals themselves . In short, he recognized that morals are constructed by people and their construction should change based on the cognitive stage in which a youngster constructed any or all of his or her moral beliefs. Based on his research, Kohlberg concluded that one can organize the developing constructions of children's morality into three large stages each based on two specific developmental substages. He was able to demonstrate that there were preconventional, conventional, and postconventional modes of moral understanding.

Preconventional morality is based on egocentric hedonism. The child begins to define as good anything that feels pleasurable and defines as bad anything that is painful. With continued development, the child soon learns that his or her actions produce both the pain and the pleasure but these good and bad consequences come from the actions of others as well as the effect his or her actions have on the objects of his or her actions. If the child missteps and falls he or she might learn that this action is bad because the misstep lead to pain but also because mommy or daddy were angry because the child was clumsy.

The second stage of moral judgments involves the manner and interaction with caretakers who now teach the children that rules exist governing moral actions and that they, and even higher authorities, are the source of these rules. If the child learns and follows the rules then his or her actions are defined as good, and if he or she does not then she or her actions are bad in one way or another. During the conventional stage, the consequences that most control children's behavior are the actions or the prediction of actions taken by authority that define good and bad. It is the pain and pleasure inflicted by authority, both physically and psychologically by the application of moral judgments that are the consequences of their actions that become most meaningful to children. Unlike the preconventional stage, where it is the children's experiences that comprise the source of moral judgments in the conventional stage the source of moral judgment moves from the children's point of view to that of authority.

If postconventional morality develops individuals become their own moral authority. However, the basis of good and bad have been transformed as people now recognize that others also have consciousness. With newly emerging empathy, the capacity to decenter from their own points of view to that of others, these individuals now recognize that inflicting pain on others, as well as on oneself, is also bad. The now grown children come to recognize that not only are they their own moral authorities but, those with whom they must interact are too. Since all parties in any social interactions are both equal in power and possess the ability to feel pleasure and pain, all interactions are seen as contracts with justice and fairness the best means of carrying out the contracts.

Kohlberg's work, like Piaget's, did not properly describe development in a social and cultural context. The stages of moral development are tied to the stages of cognitive development and the development of the latter are described as a function of the time it takes for the child to learn the underlying rules of any particular stage. The dynamics of power, the role of deception and defenses, and the adaptive demands made on any interacting group as it faced its struggles for survival, were not adequately factored into the development of these stages. As one studies these and other stage theorists, one is often left with the impression that there is an inevitability about development that is pushed more from internal evolutionary rules rather than pulled by the adaptive contexts themselves.

I am suggesting that both the push and the pull are necessary to understand all development, including moral development. I speculate that the preoperational thinking that underlies conventional morality is an evolutionary adaptation that has an important function to play during the long dependency of childhood. Children of this age see adults as omniscient and omnipotent gods. I believe that this adaptation makes it more likely that children will learn from their caretakers as they depend on them for survival and spend long hours observing how the caretakers go about the business of adaptation. Preoperational thinking helps insure that children have faith in their adult caretakers, that they feel safe to play, and that the games that interest them will be the right games to learn. Therefore, it is natural and necessary for children to cast their parents and other teachers in the role of gods.

Kohlberg pointed out that most adults remain in the stage of conventional morality even though each has the potential to move to the more desired (by Kohlberg, myself, and many of the professional who are psychologists and committed, at least in principle, to democratic humanistic politics) postconventional stage. Why does this final stage emerge in so few individuals? The explanation involves the failure of formal operational modes of thinking that are required for empathy and more decentered types of perceptions. I believe that this failure is dependent on the fact that the caretakers of the preoperational children are themselves still preoperational because of the use of defenses and their own fixations at this stage. Each generation fails to develop postconventional morality because each generation requires god-thing stories for its continued functioning and continues to play the role of gods with their own offspring. The dynamics of god-thing interactions does not permit a psychological set of explanations to replace the moral labels used by those at differing levels of the social hierarchies based on these stories. What should be a transitory stage in which children learn to replace their view of their godlike parents with perceptions of human beings never takes place for most people.

IV

STORIES AND LESSONS FROM EDUCATION

9

CHANGING STORIES AND NEW LESSONS, PART I

INTRODUCTION

These final chapters are the most joyful for me to write but also the most difficult and reflective of intense anxiety, confusion, and uncertainty. To scientifically/artistically describe a physical or psychological landscape, the scientist/artist must do so from a stable position that permits a clear, unobstructed view of the intended subject matter. If the observer is moving in relation to the landscape to be described then the descriptive efforts become far more difficult just like if the landscape is moving relative to the observer. Relativity theory demands that we see these two conditions as the same; it is impossible for an observer to know if he is moving relative to the observed or vice versa unless only some aspects of the landscape are changing and not others.

If the artist also realizes that the landscape that he or she is observing is constructed by the act of observation then he or she also becomes aware that in changing his or her physical and psychological position relative to the observed means he is reconstructing the landscape as well as observing it. That is exactly what I experience happening to me as I write these words. The actual writing of these words is both a cause and effect of changes in how I view my role as a psychology professor in a large community college in New York City. I find that my activities in the classroom and the content of my curriculum are constantly being revised creating opportunities to change both my teaching and writing over and over again. I have suggested to myself (and rejected for many reasons) that I should wait to write this book, especially these final chapters, until I retire and can construct a more stable platform from which to organize my ideas related to teaching.

Along with the revolution in my thinking that occurred when I realized that the term mental illness was a moral judgment rather than a medical or descriptive concept, and that all too many patients were finding psychiatric harm when they sought psychiatric help, I have also come to see the present mode of educational procedures to be more harmful than they are helpful for the cognitive-affective adaptational development of those who pass through its sequences. My unhappiness as a clinical psychologist led to a vast redeployment of my efforts in relation to my work as a therapist. The net result is that I have lost almost all contact with my former colleagues, and despite an occasional individual who will work with me without being diagnosed and reimbursed by third-party insurance payments, I am virtually out of the clinical field. Since I have no other professional endeavors to enter if I leave the educational field, (and have no chance to teach outside of a college setting), my growing unhappiness with my former means and modes of teaching as well as the structure and function of the system in which I am enfolded increases my anxiety. I have never been happier with who I am and what I am learning and doing as a teacher and never more discontented with what I see going on around me. I have never been more hopeful of change and, simultaneously, more pessimistic and cynical concerning the realization of the changes. Let me describe what I believe is necessary for the kind of humanistic and scientific educational process I would like to see, the efforts I have made to realize my vision, and the discrepancies between what I believe should be and what is.

I believe I owe my readers an explanation why I wrote many of this book's chapters in the first person. The training of scientists, and this is true of scientific psychology, demands that the descriptions of events be dispassionate, impersonal, and objective and, hence, be placed in the third person. Scientists as observers must keep themselves at a distance from the observed. The use of the third person narrative assumes that the observer is separate from the observed and has a stable platform from which to make observations. The advent of science studies as discussed in Chapter 2 has raised questions concerning the use of language as it appears in scientific journals. These criticisms suggest that the use of the third person implies and constructs the subjects of science from the vantage point of the aloof, Cartesian, otherworldly observer, which as we have seen is no longer a tenable position for many of us. The impersonal third person voice often implies a god-thing story with the observer speaking some universal truth that the observed has no voice in co-creating. I hope I have made clear that such a position is especially untenable in psychology where the observed is also an observer of the observer. The use of the first person, which implies a human perspective, is therefore appropriate as long as the material to be described is not replaced with the material comprising the life of the observer. The use of the first person narrative also implies that the scientist is not speaking as a god figure that floats serenely above his subject matter but suggests that the observer, in a real sense, has constructed the observed and that the subject and object are the same. The use of the third person also implies a subjective feeling that one is describing something from a stable, fixed position vis-à-vis the object of study. I write in the first person not only out of principle but because the day-to-day intellectual struggles that create for me a shifting educational landscape demand that I do so.

For the rest of this chapter, and the following chapter, I wish to discuss a variety of subjects that reflect on some of the new directions my teaching has taken me as I have applied the insights developed when the walls between my life as clinician and educator collapsed. I attempt to make clear a model of education based on the psychological theory or curriculum explicated in the last five chapters. I write in the belief that the more aware any of us are of the processes that define our work the more in control we are of these processes and the more they can be modified to attain both our descriptive and moral goals. As a clinician I learned to take for granted that my scientific role included reflecting on my techniques and my relationships and that success in these appraisals allowed me to have my role as therapist rather than to be my role. My teaching dramatically changed the moment I demanded of myself the same level of analysis that is taken for granted in the therapy field but which did not exist in any meaningful manner in my life as an educator. I am hoping these words will be of help in creating the kind of dialogue that I feel is necessary if schools are to become, in my judgment, better, more joyful places.

The changes in my teaching reflect simultaneous changes in how I experienced myself at all levels of my life. The moment I found my own voice as a theorist, I also found it as a therapist and professor. I became aware of how frightened I had always been arousing the anger and disapproval of authorities in the various institutions in which I worked and how intimidated I felt comparing myself to former professors and other professionals working in prestigious universities and hospitals. I now realize how my working-class roots (we all pretended to be middle class, but this shared American myth acts as a defense mechanism for those too fearful to expand beyond their upbringing and those wishing to justify the unfair Darwinian practices that often define business in our society) and upbringing in an essentially authoritarian system had left me fixated, defensive, and reactive to life's pressures rather than active and proactive in utilizing my skills and resources to shape my own life. I realize now just how many years I spent lamenting what I did not have rather than enjoying what I did possess. I also realize that it could not have been any other way because of how my beliefs and the ideas that expressed my truths were shaped and organized.

I do not wish to describe my childhood or the events that shaped me but two thing are crystal clear: I was a victim of many unfortunate circumstances and deprivations, however I have been incredibly lucky in the biological, social, and psychological assets that were in my life. I have discovered that I have a right to my pain but compared to the majority of people on this planet, my pain has been minimal and often inconsequential. I do not fully understand how and why the transformations in my thinking and feeling have taken place but I do know that my study of psychology has two goals. First, to understand these changes; and second to learn how to control them and stimulate them in my patients, my students, and all those who enter my life seeking change and growth without their being able to say why or how. Let me turn to some of the transformations in my teaching, making it clear that I see education's primary goal the reorganization and transformation of human adaptive consciousness so that my students can feel as proactive, creative, and joyful as I now feel.

THE ZONE OF PROXIMAL DEVELOPMENT AND INTERSUBJECTIVE SPACE

I now introduce and modify the ideas of the Soviet educational psychologist Lev Vygotsky. Vygotsky demands that we recognize the essential social nature of the learning experience when he writes (1978: 88) "Human learning presupposes a specific social nature and a process *by which children grow into the intellectual life of those around them*" (my emphasis). I have been compelled to recognize that the relationship between teacher and student, just as the relationship between parent and child, therapist and patient takes place in an intersubjective space of their mutual construction. We work together in intersubjective space whether or not we are aware of the space, its construction, or the politics practiced within it. I am suggesting that the intersubjective space of the educational relationship of teacher and student be democratic, humanistic, and conform as closely as possible to the interaction of a loving parent-child relationship and the professional relationship of patient and psychotherapist as I previously defined it (Simon 1994). It is in these types of relationships that we learn to see ourselves as worthy and able to be the equals of all human beings and become the kind of scientists and artists that make life worth living.

The politics of any relationship, the manner in which we compete and cooperate, come together and separate, work out the conflicts that must emerge as individuals, negotiate the means and modes by which they satisfy each other's needs, help each other solve problems related to living with each other, define every aspect of every relationship including those aspects related to the teaching function. My life has been comprised of three types of relationships that involved being taught and, in turn, teaching others: parent-child, therapist-patient, and student-teacher. I have been on both sides of all three of these types of social interactions. I find Vygotsky's concept of the "zone of proximal development" (1978: 86) to be most useful in defining the nature of intersubjective space as it relates to the educational or tutorial aspects in the three types of relationships in which there is an imbalance in power and adaptational abilities and the assumed stronger and more able must teach the assumed weaker and less able. I will define the concept of this zone and then discuss how the dynamic issues that define all relationships affect what does or does not, should or should not go on within it.

Vygotsky noted that the performance level of children varies if they are asked to take a test by themselves or if they take the same test with other children, or more importantly, with an adult in a tutorial capacity. If the adults question the children's work in such a way as to broaden the children's approach to the problems, without in any way giving the children the answers or solving the problem for them, the children usually score much higher on the exam. Vygotsky defines the difference between the children's achievement alone and their achievements in the presence of others as the zone of proximal development. He writes (1978: 86), "the zone of proximal development is the distance between the actual developmental level as determined by independent problem solving and the level of potential development as determined through problem solving under adult guidance or in collaboration with more capable peers." It seems clear that Vygotsky has created an interpersonal and intersubjective model of learning that can give us guidance as to the structure of our teaching activities while simultaneously gauging the effects on our teaching of the myriad dynamics that effect human relationships.

We can examine the zone of proximal development from a number of contextualized vantage points. We can hypothesize as to the children's experience of working alone on what they know to be a test that measures not only their abilities to solve problems in a given time and place, but is also believed to be measuring both their capacities to solve problems anywhere and their self-worth in their eyes and those that claim to love them. Children learn early on that these measurements of intellectual prowess are valued for much more than the cognitive abilities they are supposed to evaluate and that these judgments are used for other purposes than setting the goals and directions that future educational activities might take on their behalf. They soon learn that the willingness of their teachers to teach at all might rest on their performance.

We can conjecture as to the experiences of these same children sitting across from Vygotsky or an associate and being aware of the adult's excitement and interest in the outcome of their efforts to solve these problems. We might wonder what happens to the experience of problem solving and its outcome when children work with concerned others who are not judging them, compared to sitting alone and worrying about passing or failing a variety of intellectual and social criteria. I cannot prove that the zone of proximal development as described by Vygotsky reflects dynamics such as these but the view of the learning process seen from this vantage point has proven both a logical and useful one to explore.

From years spent as a psychotherapist I believe that it is necessary to understand the dynamics of intersubjective space. Vygotsky's model gave me a starting point with which to understand what might be going on between myself and my students in order to improve what I experienced in that interpersonal set of spaces as well as improve the outcomes. (I believe that psychotherapists would do well to employ the concept of the zone in their work with patients, but that is another story and one that would depend on therapists seeing their work as educational rather than related to medicine.) The immediate advantages of examining the nature of the teacher-student relationship from what is essentially a psychodynamic perspective is that the teacher can pull back from the relationship in such a way as to have various aspects of these interactions rather than be these aspects. It makes an enormous difference, for example, to understand the politics that one is engaged in and thereby have one's political processes available for discussion and justification than to be embedded in these same processes and have to defend oneself if one's politics are criticized. After all, these political processes define the very nature of one's self as it interacts with others, in this case with students and colleagues. Let me now discuss the intersubjective space of the zone of proximal development from a dynamic point of view and relate the changes that have taken place as a consequence of my using this type of analysis with my students.

THE ZONE OF PROXIMAL DEVELOPMENT AND THE EDUCATIONAL PROCESS

When teachers and students meet for the first time, they enter the subjective space of one another with a mode of consciousness that reflects the adaptive processes as they have evolved and developed. Each individual has a history of which they can speak, as well as a history of which they are unaware but which has, nonetheless, shaped their conscious experiences. Each individual's history reflects the interactive products of biology, sociology, and psychology and, in effect, carries with it their pasts as individuals, members of a culture, and of the evolutionary process itself. As teachers and students first perceive each other they do so in the light of past memories and future expectations. Each sees the other from the perspective of an ongoing narrative and different interpersonal scripts. Each individual represents a potential for various types of need satisfaction as well as a potential for various problems to be solved alone or in mutual effort, in cooperation or in conflict. Each is prepared to use various political means to achieve their individual adaptive ends and deal with the inevitable conflicts that will arise between them. Once again I lack a vocabulary of simultaneity with which to capture the exquisite complexity of this moment in time. I do know, however, that more happens in that instant than any of us are aware of and the more we are aware of that the more we are able to determine the unfolding of what occurs between us both in descriptive and moral terms.

The teacher-student relationship, just as with the parent-child and therapist-patient relationship, exists as a means to an end and not as an end in and of itself. While the parent-child relationship might last a lifetime, it still exists for the purpose of helping children become adult members of the human species and a particular culture. The parent-child relationship, like the other two relationships, has as its goal, or as we will discuss below should have as its goal, a decrease in the need of the child for the adult. The child in each case develops the capacity to be their own parent, teacher, and self-therapist, and if they choose, be able to carry out these same functions for the next generation. Teachers and therapists are expected to part company with their charges as soon as possible, children are expected to see their parents as human beings in their own rights as soon as possible. The child-parent relationship usually, but not necessarily, continues longer than the other two, but hopefully on a much different basis. I have defined what I believe to be the legitimate goal of all three relationships: the transformation from interactions based on inequalities of abilities to adapt to the world, to interactions based on equalities of abilities even if they are defined by differences in adaptive skills. The proposed analysis of the teacher-student relationship is to further the goals of the teacher in helping the student eliminate the teacher as soon as possible; assumes that the student and teacher never know too much that can be used to improve the cognitive-affective and moral aspects of their work together.

As I discuss the nature of the educational enterprise let me not arouse in the reader any expectations that I am successful in achieving most of my goals with my colleagues or my students. The institutions that I have attended, and have worked in professionally, are largely authoritarian and conservative and reflect the basic values and organization of the culture that they serve. In order for me to realize success with my methods they would have to be widely applied. My attempts at converting the viewpoints of my clinical colleagues was no more successful than was Szasz's or the others who came before me arguing that mental illness is a myth. My attempts to point out to my educational associates that we in education give lip service to democratic/humanistic ideals are merely modern attempts to change the educational system and follow the work of John Dewey and other educational reformers. Society is not easily persuaded to give up comforting god-stories and the traditions which spring from and reinforce these sacred stories. Moreover, my students reading at grade-school levels may begin to work to improve their academic skills once they accept that they are not too stupid or lazy to do so. However, it will take years of renewed efforts by themselves and their teachers for them to develop skills or to bloom as scholars.

BEGINNING THE EDUCATIONAL ENTERPRISE

I have in mind a relationship of two or more individuals of equal moral worth, one of whom is superior to the other both in an area of knowledge and the skills necessary for successful adaptation with regard to a given set of situations and events. I believe it is critical for the teacher-student relationship to be defined for both in terms of a description of these differences. Concerned participants must also be aware of the difference between a description and a moral judgment. It must be clear to both the teacher and the students that the goals of education are moral in nature, that is, it is good for the students to learn that which the teacher wishes them to learn. However, it must be equally clear that achieving, or failing to achieve, the educational goals that have been defined does not make any individual's essence any more or less valuable. We are all to be treated as if we have sacred souls whether or not we pass algebra or calculus, study Shakespeare, or understand Skinner's concept of negative reinforcement. Teachers are not inherently more or less morally worthwhile for their skills and their apparent knowledge than their students. Just as I have had extreme difficulty in getting my patients to reject the moralism inherent in their dehumanizing diagnoses, I have had much difficulty in getting my students to understand that their cognitive skills and academic knowledge need development, instead of their belief that their intelligence and moral character need replacing.

At the beginning the term, I engage my students in the creation of a contract that will govern our interactions. I do not impose a set of rules or punishments that would swiftly follow transgressions. The contract is one negotiated by both sides and agreed to by all involved. Contract negotiations are another set of skills that can be developed but will not be unless they are given an opportunity to do so. I do not give up my authority as teacher but I try to be authoritative and not authoritarian. My students are my moral equals and must be heard, but I still choose the course materials and set the course's methodologies. However, I must justify what I have chosen and the philosophy behind my methodology, and listen to objections the students might have.

I have discovered that while most comments are made from consciousness that reflects anger, a sense of powerlessness, and no real experience in thinking from a position of authority, many students will, if given the opportunity to be part of the contract process, come up with ideas that are enormously helpful to my teaching. Recently, a student suggested that the ongoing written projects which are so important to my methods of teaching should be more valued toward the final grade than the four short answer tests that are equal to each other and the final paper that was the summation of the terms writings. I agreed and changed the balance between various types of tests in all my classes based on this insight. It is anxiety provoking for me to share this aspect of authority with my students, especially since they are untutored in these processes. However, if my goal is to change their consciousness then the direction their adaptive efforts take must include the same behaviors that I value as a teacher, scientist, and psychologist.

The discussions related to the contract involve my efforts to get students to become aware of just what level of commitment they possess to study the topics comprising the course. The biggest problems that I experience in setting a contract involves anger and resistance to being in my class or in school. I have discovered that a majority of my students would rather be elsewhere but are in school because of their parents, and others important to their lives wishes. Many have learned the same lesson that I learned by the second grade, that my parents would sooner accept me committing murder than failing math. Like the children of many immigrants, I attended school not only for me to be educated but for my relatives to be redeemed by their lack of formal education. My students enter the school building with one or more relatives perched on each shoulder. These individuals need an education in realizing how different their goals in taking the course are from mine. "I am in school because my parents would kill me (or die) if I leave and join the marines." "Go to work." "I am taking psychology in order to fulfill my course requirements." or "to get my degree in education." "I have no interest in this course." We must understand our desires as we work out a contract or else conflicts will arise whose sources will be mysteries to us, but no genuine contracts can be drawn.

In the discussions concerning motivation I hope to negotiate a contract with my students that will establish my relationship with them as based on principles of non-coercion and mutual cooperation to the degree that these are possible in a school setting. I defined psycho"therapy" as that form of individualized educational procedure that exists only to the degree that all parties to the procedure are there of their own free wills. I have long recognized that to the degree that force is involved in a relationship pleasing the stronger and avoiding his or her wrath replaces or becomes primary to all other topics with which that the relationship might deal. My students cannot play with the ideas of psychology and experiment with their emerging academic skills any more than my patients if they must first work hard to gain the approval of the teacher or therapist. My patients usually left therapy the moment they discovered that I was not going to be the focus of their work and that pleasing or hurting me would gain them little if these were their only reasons for attending treatment. My students rarely leave my class when they make similar discoveries because they might still seek course credits even if they are not interested in learning psychology. However, if we are aware of our differing goals as we interact, and we all remain true to our purposes, there are few misunderstandings and very little anger. I will delay discussing the inherent coercion in my role as teacher and the fact that I cannot give up the power of making public judgments of my students until I discuss the issue of grades below.

As suggested in Chapter 1, some of my most successful moments as a teacher or a therapist come when students or patients begin to discover their own motives for remaining in or leaving school, or therapy. The moment I see that large numbers of students are disinterested, hostile to my purposes and goals which have been clearly stated, and are using a variety of means (such as passive resistance) to defeat my efforts to teach, I refocus my discussion on the class dynamics without making judgments or attacking individuals. In one such recent discussion a young man told me how disinterested he was in psychology or any other subjects that he is studying. "It goes in one ear and out the other—I hate this Piaget stuff." Another joins in and states, "He speaks for me too. I can't read any of the words in the book and I'm worried it might be too late for me." Still another student, a female adds, "It doesn't matter, if I fail with you, I'll just find out who the easier teachers are and pass the course with one of them." By the sessions end the first student was exploring his desires to become a chef and wondering whether or not his parents might still love him if he pursued his own dreams (they did and he has applied to chef school). The second student was convinced to seek out tutoring for help with his reading. I had privately given the third student the names of teachers who would surely see her as society's victim and just as surely not make her work too hard to pass.

The success of these discussions creates a very different mood in the classroom than would exist if they had not taken place. It is not that everyone is now happy and involved in the learning process, but those who are unhappy with the course now understand that they are unhappy and perhaps even why they are unhappy. If they continue with the course they have more of an understanding that it is their choice to do so. The students are no longer their resistance; they have and can reflect on their resistance. Learning feels differently if motivated by an intrinsic desire to play with the subject material and the skills necessary to assimilate the material than learning out of fear, shame, guilt, or a sense of duty. But it makes a significant difference to the teacher-student interaction if those who are not in the class of their own joyful accord understand whose anger, shame, and guilt is motivating them and just whose needs they are dutifully satisfying if not their own.

TEACHING AND LEARNING IN THE ZONE OF PROXIMAL DEVELOPMENT

All educational activities take place in a zone of proximal development whether or not we are aware of it and whether or not we take care to manipulate the zone for maximum effectiveness of teacher and learner. I am assuming that all involved in a given educational interaction are aware that they are pursuing a common goal, are aware of their own personal motives for doing so, and understand the means by which these goals will be sought. In short, I am assuming that the issues related to motivation, discussed in the last section have been worked through, although later I expand my discussion to what happens in the zone if these issues are not resolved. If this is the case, then what we see happening in the zone is one individual—the teacher—trying to guide both the pace and direction of the adaptational struggles of another individual, the student. The reader might be objecting to such a description since in a classroom there is usually one teacher and many students, and I am describing the zone between teacher and student as if it is individualized and one on one. In fact, the teacher and student are always involved in a shared intersubjective space regardless of how many individuals are also present and engaged in intersubjective spaces with the teacher. We can all sit at the table and eat our food together but each one eats only their own food, tastes it in the particular manner that we as individuals taste flavors and then digests only those calories we took into our own bodies. Teachers may claim to teach a class of students but that class is comprised of individuals, each of whom co-constructs an intersubjective space with the teacher, and with each other, as only they are able to construct it. Even if we ignore the nature of the zone when we try and interact with thirty, forty, or more individuals it does not mean that the rules of learning which govern the intersubjective nature of the zone have been changed or obviated by our ignorance.

Let me discuss this topic from the perspective of a concerned, loving parent or a psycho"therapist" that is working with an individual patient. How does learning proceed under these circumstances? The process is engaged when the student enters the intersubjective space of the teacher with his or her existing adaptive skills, which includes the organization of those skills as well as the cognitive-affective content toward which those skills are directed. The teacher makes clear to the learner, often directly, but more often indirectly, that they seek to change both the skills of the student as well as aspects of the content that define the reasons for the skills existence. The teacher seeks to change what the student knows and how they know it and realizes that changes in one necessitates changes in the other. To increase the content of someone's knowledge inevitably demands new ways of understanding the material and trying to change the skills a person has cannot take place without discussing and changing the perspective on what the skills are concerned with as content. The teacher must start where the student's knowledge base ends and engage the students cognitive-affective organization as it exists when engagement in the zone begins. To teach content to an individual lacking a conceptual framework in which to place the content and demand comprehension based on skills that do not exist is to submerge the student in a sea of meaningless sights and sounds. It is as if the teacher were to speak to an empty room and pretend that such an activity represents productive education and not some form of madness or cruelty.

Teachers begin where their student's adaptive mechanisms locate them but simultaneously make clear to the students that goals exist that will define success when the lesson is over. The teacher must, therefore, be able to set goals representing the upper level of the zone of proximal development that might reasonably be achieved by the student given the time involved and the modes of instruction being utilized. In Piagetian terms, the teacher sets the degree to which disequilibrium will exist as the student discovers a need to accommodate in order to assimilate. There are many considerations that now begin to govern the process by which the student seeks to attain the upper limit of the zone, as defined by increases in both the content of the student's knowledge and the transformation of the adaptive processes that define their consciousness.

The first of these considerations involves the flexibility of the teacher to modify the upper limits of the zone in the light of the student's progress. In short, it is the teacher who sets the size of the gap that defines the intersubjective zone between themselves and the students or the students need to make necessary accommodations to learn a given set of materials. It is the values of the teachers that not only defines how large the zone should be at any given moment but the speed or timing that is appropriate for the gap in the zone to be closed. Teachers who love their students, as in the case of some parents, will be endlessly patient about the time that is necessary for any given student to achieve the goals that define the successful closing of the intersubjective gap that defines that particular zone. Teachers less committed to their students, who become frustrated with the student's progress, who see their students as defective things not worthy of further attention, or who because of the time constraints placed on them by schools and academic calendars, will more likely seek ways to terminate the struggle that almost always defines the teaching effort. They might then fail the student and declare them unable or unwilling to learn or move ahead in the creation of new zone upper limits regardless of what the student can assimilate.

Another consideration related to the teachers manipulation of the zone involves how well the teachers are willing or able to read the efforts it takes students to achieve new knowledge or the reorganization and transformation of specific skills. The students struggling in the presence of their teachers are trying to assimilate the teachers goals utilizing existing skills and upon experiencing difficulty attempt to accommodate their skills to the demands being set for them. It is one of the real arts of being a teacher of children in any capacity to know when to intercede and help the children in their accommodations and problem solving and when to allow them to continue to struggle. It is often the teachers emotional fixations, defenses, and dynamics that determine the manner and degree of effort that they make on their student's behalf. At other times it is the teacher's unavoidable sheer ignorance concerning their student's consciousness that determines the overindulgence and overprotection committed on the one hand and the deprivations and neglects on the other. I am employing terms from psychoanalysis because children who have too much done for them often become bored in school or other educational contexts while children given too little help experience intense stress and frustration. In both types of situations the resulting development of the children's knowledge and skills are less than what they would have otherwise been had different choices been made by the teacher.

When teachers deal with children's learning (which involves affecting the adaptive processes that transform human consciousness) in the manner being proposed—descriptively, scientifically, with patience, respect, affection and even love for the learner, the material being learned and the process of learning itself—

then they cannot but help turn the intersubjective zone that they both share and are co-creating into a holding environment in which both feel free to play as well as work hard to achieve new adaptive goals. The interaction between people changes dramatically when they feel free to laugh, express the selves that they experience as real, and perhaps most importantly, make the inevitable errors that adaptation entails. I reject the current idea among some that we each have a real self beneath the layers of our pathology awaiting discovery. I do believe, however, that we each have a self or even multiple selves that feel real and honest to each of us. But all these selves are bio-social-psychological constructions. They are not discovered, they are invented. It is always an implicit goal of human educational processes to develop Popperian forms of adaptation, which are defined by a willingness to make errors in play prior to engaging in the actual situations in which adaptation takes place.

Moreover, if our goal is to include a curriculum in which developing individuals are helped to become scientific psychologists, then the individuals concerned must be willing to reflect on both their knowledge and the cognitive-affective processes on which their knowledge is based. Conducting critical self-analysis and recogniz- ing the errors in one's own thought processes requires an internal and interpersonal holding environment in which errors are seen in descriptive terms free of moral judgments that tell individuals they are defective instead of telling them that they must play around with their own processes with an eye toward modifying them. I consider it vital to the educational process that people learn to see their adaptive errors in descriptive rather than moral terms, in narratives concerning human beings rather than gods and things.

If we chart the course of growth in the type of zone where dynamics are being explicated, we observe that as soon as the student achieves the goals of the particular zone in which the teacher and student have been working, the teacher reestablishes a new ceiling on the zone. What was the student's initial goal has now become a new entry point directed to new goals representing increases in knowledge and new transformations of adaptive skills. A perfect example of this can be seen in a mother's attempt to guide the language development of her children. When infants signal that they are ready for speech, mothers speak to them in simple sentences, spoken very slowly in high-pitched, sing-song style. Linguists refer to this language system as motherese. As soon as the infants comprehend their mother's communi- cation, the mothers lower the pitch of the language and increases the speed of their speech as well as the size of the vocabulary. This process of renewing the upper and lower limits of the zone continues until the child has reached the level of skill the teachers, or in this case the mothers, feel that the students need to achieve at this time or until the children have reached the upper level of skills and knowledge any particular teacher is willing or able to provide. However, the pacing of the renewal of the zone is based on an exquisite dance of mutuality that takes into account both the skill level of the student and the knowledge base into which new information must find its way.

The dance of mutuality that I feel is so essential to effective instruction depends on teachers who simultaneously balance two easily contradictory and conflicted attitudes. The teachers that I have admired the most are both loving and supportive to the efforts of their students to learn but simultaneously demanding of their success and guided by the highest standards of excellence. Parents are often the teachers most patient with their students but they are also aware that it is important to find ways for their children to develop skills that will permit successful social, academic, financial, as well as moral adaptations. I am concerned with helping my students become artists and scientists of their own lives, which means that I must create conditions that maximize their abilities to reflect on their own thoughts and emotions as they seek ways to express themselves. However, I believe that art is more than self-expression and I decry the commonly-held belief that children who freely express themselves are true artists. Art requires standards of excellence and must be based on comparisons to those qualities that manifest both substance and quality no matter how difficult it is to define these terms. Often the art that appears to be the freest and most natural is based on painstakingly careful and detailed work done in the spirit of play.

One final set of considerations concerning the dynamics surrounding the zone is the idea of a meaningful knowledge base. Space considerations have forced me to end a topic that in itself is probably inexhaustible. As the developing individuals move from one set of skills organization to another, and master and organize new information into useful knowledge they also reconstruct narratives that define their selves and provide theories by which they negotiate and live their lives. The scripts that define their roles in interpersonal relationships change as well. Students learn, and turn into knowledge, information that relates to the ongoing narratives that define their selves and the world and organize both into a meaningful whole. Each of us learns and remembers best that which we find adaptive reasons for doing so. We assimilate and struggle to accommodate information that relates to ourselves. Given the definition of self provided earlier, the hereness in the thereness, we might say that learning involves making the thereness into the hereness and we incorporate from the thereness only what makes sense and is useful in the hereness. Nothing enters the hereness from the thereness unless it is invited in. One of the teacher's most important functions in the intersubjective zone where learning takes place involves the co-construction of a narrative that makes the information in any curriculum available to the student.

When students approach a topic that does not relate to the narratives that define themselves and their place in their world then assimilating the material is the same as trying to memorize nonsense material or perhaps a telephone directory. It is, therefore, not enough for teachers to create a zone whose upper and lower limits are coordinated in terms of the level of the student's adaptive skills and to pace the movement of development in the zone with patience and sensitivity, but they must find ways to connect the meaning of the material to be taught with the meaning system of the students as reflected in the organization of their selves and the narrative which expresses those selves. I have found this aspect of my teaching to be the most difficult since the forty or more students with whom I share intersubjective space in the classroom not only come from vastly different cultures than I do but approach me and each other with all manner of god-thing stories. The challenge of creating a narrative or interpersonal script that we can all share and into which we can all interrelate the stories of our respective lives with the philosophical and psychological narratives which comprise a psychology (or any academic course) is most daunting. I find that these difficulties are as, or even more, profound than trying to teach students with preoperational thinking concepts based on formal operations. I must rely on my clinical training to keep from giving up the whole educational enterprise and protecting myself from failure and threats to myself by playing God and turning my students into things. I will describe my adaptive struggles with both my student's level of adaptive skills and the types of narratives that I experience them bringing into our shared intersubjective space after I describe the psychotherapeutic concept of transference which hopefully allows me to prevent defenses from forcing me to lose sight of the adaptive goals I am trying to achieve.

TRANSFERENCE, COUNTER-TRANSFERENCE, AND CO-TRANSFERENCE IN THE ZONE OF PROXIMAL DEVELOPMENT

One of the most important concepts developed by psychotherapists, especially those who define themselves as psychoanalysts, is that of transference. Transference has been defined in almost as many ways as the therapists who have used the concept. But if there are any commonalities in the manner in which transference is used it is that therapists must be aware of how the patient's pathology interacts with the therapist's own emotional problems to sabotage the patient's benefitting from treatment and eventually recovering from the mental illnesses that brought them into treatment. While my own definition requires that I translate these ideas into descriptions free from the pseudomedical terminology that masks a host of moral judgments, I feel that the concept of transference is vitally important because it demands that therapists, and in this case teachers, examine the nature of their relationships with their charges for those activities that defeat their best efforts or create goals not in anyone's interest, especially the students. Therefore, I believe that teachers or anyone else that works with people be trained to think of their professional interactions in terms of transference.

When therapists learn about the concept of transference they are taught that it is the patient who initiates transferential difficulties when they behave toward the therapist with feelings transferred from figures involved with the etiology of their pathologies. Thus, the patients may expect similar abuse or neglect from their therapists that they had experienced with mothers or fathers, or make unrealistic demands of their therapists hoping that the therapists will fulfill needs left unmet by caretakers. The job of the therapist is to resist becoming an accomplice in the patient's infantile wishes, needs, expectations, and manipulations and thereby taking over the role of a feared or wished for caretaker. When therapists lose their professional objectivity, and instead of helping patients develop insights into how their fixated and defended behaviors are sabotaging their lives, then the therapist is guilty of acting counter-transferentially toward the patient. Important to the psychoanalytic training and practice is the therapist's own treatment as well as ongoing supervision with peers or a supervisor that are both designed to reduce counter-transferential problems with patients.

I have made several alterations in these concepts that make them congruent with the concepts being developed in my work. First, therapists and teachers carry as many pathological concepts into intersubjective space as students and patients. I prefer to think of transferential behaviors as mutually constructed and therefore use the term coined by psychoanalysts such as Donna Orange (1995), co-transference. I interpret concepts such a pathological as moral in nature. I recognize that transference in a relationship involves moral judgments of unwanted and misunderstood behaviors. I suggest that both students and teachers see behaviors in others and in themselves that are unwanted because they interfere with achieving the goals each seeks from the other. It is pointless to blame others for the destructive effects of their immoral or unethical activities in a relationship because that most often leads to defensive self-protection and the best defenses which are usually offensive in nature. Finger pointing and mutual recrimination are not as helpful as mutual self analysis as to each participant's role in damaging the forward motion of a working relationship. The usefulness of co-transference involves each participant in a relationship examining, pointing out, taking responsibility for, and taking steps to change their own unwanted behaviors.

Finally, I reject the psychoanalytic contention that co-transference results mainly from unwanted behaviors shaped in early childhood in relation to mothers and other primary family members. The process of postmodern deconstruction demands a wider analysis of the phenomenon of co-transference. It is not that an examination of the roots of any set of behaviors do not benefit from an analysis of childhood experiences but I believe that any attempts to understand the origins of a person's adaptive modes of understanding their world must include the ideologies and political methods dominating the culture in which parents and all other family members were steeped. The parent's social class, religion, attitudes toward gender, age, and race, the neighborhood in which they all lived, the era in which development took place including whether war or peace prevailed and the politics practiced as a result of all of these factors, and the many more variables that have not been mentioned helped shape the cognitive-affective mode of adult adaptive experience and the narratives expressing these modes. We see the world through lenses shaped by the socially-constructed history of our pasts and while that history usually begins through the ministrations of mothers and fathers any analysis must include the broader aspects of that history if we are to understand why we behave morally or immorally in the present.

What do I consider transference in my own behavior? I believe I must make efforts to change any attitude or behavior that in any way implies or openly states that I am above or below the human condition and that those with whom I work (or live) are anything but human beings. I must change any activities that simultaneously prevent individuals from exercising their freedoms and/or acting to prevent them from being responsible for the consequences that result from the choices they make. I must conduct a difficult self-examination of all the defenses that I regularly employ that create god-thing stories that I find to be sacred but should instead, see as myths.

I discovered to my chagrin that an examination of many of the intellectual fads that have affected my consciousness over the years contained many god-thing stories directed at many groups of individuals, especially those I was supposedly committed to helping. The god-like stance built into my role as a scientist, especially one with a Ph.D., was one I had to struggle years to overcome. I believed I knew more than my patients and my students (and almost anyone else I came in contact with) simply because I had been given the tools to uncover so-called truths hidden from less worthy beings. I am embarrassed by the manner in which I used my Rorschach ink blot test to divine the true unconscious beliefs and motives of those I tested. I am just as embarrassed by my gullibility in believing my clinical instructors who claimed that these ten ink blots were the true key to the unconscious as well as my participation in case conferences (now I call them character assassinations) in which I joined the arrogance of my colleagues in saying things such as, "The patient thinks he loves his wife but WE know that this is a reaction formation and that he really hates his mother." The whole diagnostic system comprising the Diagnostic and Statistical Manual (DSM) of the American Psychiatric Association is one gigantic professional counter-transference.

I am equally appalled at the IQ tests I have administered and the judgments made about the capacity of children to learn without first examining the conditions of their lives, the cultures and subcultures from which they came, or whether or not they had breakfast before their late morning testings. I am upset that I tested without inquiring further how their intelligence had been affected by sitting in a strange room with a strange man being asked questions for people whose interests may or may not have been the same as the children being sent for evaluation. In the next chapter, I wrestle with my conscience about the exams that I have administered to thousands of students without carefully gauging the effects of variables such as those mentioned above. For whom were these tests being administered? For the good of my students and their struggles to learn or for the authority that paid my salary and whose desires for me to educate my students as I unquestioningly did, ran counter to the humanistic and scientific goals of both me and my students?

Similarly, I wish I had remained more neutral in the ideological culture wars that envelop the university system of which I am still a proud member. It is interesting to note that my progression in these transformations of belief are mirrored for me in the writings of Neil Postman, particularly those related to education (1969, 1979, 1995). Postman and Charles Weingartner initially would have us be subversive to the society in which we lived and which had just discovered that racism and the war in Vietnam were symptoms of previously unexplored moral pathologies eating away at the fabric of society. I went through a period of extreme liberalism which meant joining with those who not only saw our society as having serious problems to address but possessing no moral worth whatsoever. All authority was bad authority. The students attending schools were seen as victims of society and in need of saving from a school that had no interests other than indoctrinating them into the very society that abused them. The schools were to be turned into engines of social change that were the leading edge of utopian plans to rid society of racism, sexism, and poverty. There were those who proposed that we would have to deschool society entirely. There were wonderful moments of delicious innocence in those heady days when it seemed possible to transform society and with it human nature. The attacks on authority, any and all authority, felt good indeed and to this day seem mostly justified.

But my liberal days waned almost as soon as they waxed. While I am forever grateful to have been rescued from my childhood beliefs that my country and its leaders could never be responsible for immoral and evil actions, that Franklin Delano Roosevelt was God incarnate, that if we went to war it must be for pure and noble reasons, and that I and everyone I knew weren't racist to the core, I could never quite accept the rhetoric surrounding the new academic liberalism. I could never accept that we were the worst country on earth, that suspending the educational processes and not giving homework was educationally sound, that setting any standards of academic excellence was elitist, racist, and made one a fascist. I couldn't fully believe that suspending final exams while hating white, male authority figures would bring about the golden age of equality. I have come to agree with Richard Rorty (1994) that an open mind does not mean an unpatriotic stance toward my country and the university that nurtured me.

I could never accept the core of Marxist theory wafting through the hallways of academia that suggested that God was not in charge of our lives but some anthropomorphized view of history that was bringing about our heaven on Earth. This view of history-as-God always seemed nonscientific and unacceptably dualistic. It also seemed that the various communist systems, the supposed advanced example of economic paradise, made any immoralities committed by my country pale in comparison to the horrors perpetrated on its citizens by Stalin and his political decedents, and Mao and his loyal minions.

I was relieved to read Shelby Steele's (1990) treatise and similar missives by Thomas Sowell (1995, 1996) and others suggesting that white guilt and reverse racism would not solve our racial problems. It was just as racist, or sexist, to suggest that any minority that had been (or was still being) victimized would profit from educational policies that did any more than give victimized members of a group an equal chance at success with other members of society. Equal opportunity did not mean equal chances of success. Equal entry into a system could not guarantee equality of exit from that system and changing the exit criteria for some and not for others was unjust to all concerned, including the former victims. Such policies would subvert, and have subverted, the very system that was supposed to engineer the desired social changes. I had to recognize the manner in which I victimized my students but that did not mean celebrating their victimizations and then victimizing all other groups as the means of creating equality. I believe that all students need to be loved and given individualized opportunities to learn but that in the final analysis if they are to be graded then the grading must be done on the same criteria for all, or if differences in exit criteria are utilized then they must be made public.

I soon learned after my days of liberalism that pity is not love and setting standards of excellence for my students, especially if I apply them to myself first, is not elitism or undemocratic but means that I expect from my students no less than I expect from my own children. I will not save or improve democracy by helping all sink to the same low level but rather contribute to the raising of all to the same high level. Moreover, I learned that if authority was deconstructed simply because it was authority, if bad gods were destroyed and not replaced with good gods, then I had deprived myself of authority as well. I realized that I was creating an anarchy with my liberalism not a democracy.

Twenty years of talking liberalism but behaving conservatively (I was still diagnosing and testing patients and students for the very authority that I was publicly attacking) left me defensive, exhausted, and confused. It must have done the same to Postman who announced that the role of the teacher was no longer to subvert but to conserve. But what were we to conserve and how were we to do it? We had analyzed our authority and found it (and all authority) often to be genuinely corrupt and transferential. I had then deconstructed the deconstructors and found the beliefs of the Left with its pity and utopian notions of what it would take to educate our students, these victims of cruel authority, to be simplistic and stated in the most authoritarian of manners. We were deconstructing traditional authority but speaking of these human beings in the most authoritarian, hate-filled manner according to god-thing stories of our own making. Moreover, according to my allies in the battle for truth and goodness I found myself hated by many feminists because I was male, hated by the civil rights establishment blacks because I was white, and hated by most of the Left because I was Jewish. Where could I turn and from what platform could I operate without identifying with co-transferential philosophies? Is there any way for one to be an authority without playing god in the lives of those one is supposed to lead? Is there any way to create positive commonly agreed on beliefs that give people reasons to live and struggle without god and things, fear and deception?

I could not turn to the political right, who were, at the time being led by Ronald Reagan, an actor turned politician. The Right hated the Left who in turn hated the Right. The Right hated me because I was a teacher and an intellectual. I discovered during this time that Richard Hofstader (1963) was correct when he recognized that most Americans admire intelligence when it is used to solve problems and make lots of money but distrust those who enjoy intelligence for its own sake. I was hated because I was a Jewish intellectual. I also could not accept a political philosophy that could not criticize itself as a philosophy and hated anything or anyone who espoused differences. America, went the god story of the Right, could do no wrong and if you didn't love it you should leave it. (The Left also hated everyone but at least they had the good taste to hate themselves as well.) My students, according to the smug self-satisfied millionaires on the Right, were not poor and uneducated because they were victims but because they were truly inferior in God's eyes. God, it seemed, was himself a millionaire and could not abide the poor. God wanted us all rich, and in the America of the 1980s one could not be too rich or too thin, which is another story not to be pursued here. We pursued the God of money like never before often leaving me genuinely bitter and self-pitying because as a teacher I could never get rich. I began to have trouble with my students because only rich people could be authorities. Rich actors, rich sports figures, rich rock and roll musicians (all of whom were dubbed artists superior to figures such as Beethoven, who had died poor) became the authority to a whole generation of my students.

We had subverted authority, Postman and me, we had participated in the final death of God as the philosophers had suggested we were doing a century ago but had not counted on the need for people to have faith in the authority who must inevitably lead them. As the 1990s dawned and we approached the new millennium, we were all our own authority. Some are still pursuing god-money and the celebrities whose life styles mark them as rich and famous, others are embracing gods more hostile to science and the life of the mind than any of us would have thought possible thirty years ago. I have students whose beliefs in spirits, visiting aliens from other planets, and the pronouncements of horoscopes reflect mental outlooks that would fit well in the thirteenth century. Still others believe that we will have discovered utopia once we are all wired to our computers-television-high fidelity-stereo-quadraphonic-home entertainment-systems and never have to leave home or see another teacher or human being again. My most troubling students are those who seem to exist in a psychological space that was created while being literally raised by electronic media, which according to Joshua Meyrowitz (1985) has left them disconnected from people, the history and culture of those of us raised in interpersonal communities connected to a larger social structures, and with no sense of place whatsoever.

Postman tells me it is too late to conserve anything and that we are at the end of education. I agree with Postman's nihilism and his attempts in the second half of his book to take his nihilism back by suggesting that love for each other, and for the planet we all share that we are now destroying in the name of the god-dollar and because once online we won't be needing it any more, might provide a curriculum and give us the authority to bring our educational system and ourselves back from the brink of extinction. Having analyzed all of my transference reactions and being left with neither authority nor god-justified educational goals to pursue, I can only hope that love is enough and that I will not deconstruct this last poor platform from which I now narrate my story. If we fail to find ways to reconnect ourselves to traditions of academic community and excellence without resorting to destructive god-thing narratives then I fear what "rough beasts might well be stirring" (Yeats 1920).

10

CHANGING STORIES AND NEW LESSONS, PART II

INTRODUCTION

It should be apparent to anyone who has spent time in our schools that nearly everything seems constructed to reflect the maximum degree of co-transference and the minimum of individualized and caring teacher-student relationships. Attempts to realize an educational structure built along the lines I am suggesting will be met head on by most of those participating with furious indignation, overt hostility, or passive neglect. There are millions of teachers who feel as I do but feel compelled to remain silent and cooperate with the rules of the system out of fear, loyalty, and a clear knowledge of where power resides in the system. The god-thing stories, which seem derived from selfish genes and memes, appear to predominate in the organization of most, if not all, human social structures and may never be replaced by human narratives reflective of science and art and modeled on humanistic principles. I suggest that we find being just human almost intolerable and our educational institutions, all too often, reflect our attempts to rise above or sink below our human condition rather than find ways to live within it.

Why do I write a book concerning education that must describe more failure than success? The answer to this question is derived from the theory of human adaptation developed thus far in this book. All of our social institutions and the justifications that maintain them are individually and socially constructed. What has been constructed by some can be reconstructed by others. If our schools do not reflect the will of the gods then there is nothing inevitable or eternal about them. If they are based on god-thing stories that were created with the use of self-protective deceptions then it may be possible to create social conditions that permit the individuals involved in these systems to rely less on fixating and preoperationally maintained belief systems. We may be able to help people feel free to explore their own thoughts and feelings, develop their own Popperian adaptive devices, and imagine alternatives to those aspects of their lives and their selves that they believe oppress them.

I defined psycho"therapy" as a process that recontextualizes the experiences of those who enter into the process. I define education in the same terms. I write this book in part because I believe I have found ways to increase, to some small degree, classroom conditions that allow some of my students to increase the sense of authorship in their own lives along scientific, artistic, and humanistic lines of development. This has given me faith to try and convince others to pursue their own therapeutic and pedagogical efforts in similar ways. I write this book because for the first time in my professional life I can talk about my role as an educator without anger toward the system, feelings of personal failure and self-loathing and most of all without judging the students who are supposed to be the justification of my professional life. I write as a scientist and (hopefully) not as a moral prig.

DESCRIBING EDUCATIONAL OBSTACLES

I have already described what I believe to be the source of obstacles in realizing an educational process modeled on parent-child, therapist-patient interactions. These are the same enemies of science, art, and moral humanism in any social structures. They derive from our human vulnerabilities and our inability or unwillingness to accept the forms of experience that exist when we have to accommodate and adapt to events that cause intense suffering, disease, meaninglessness, the death of our genes, memes, and overall consciousness, as well as the shame and guilt we feel when we hurt others in our attempts to adapt and advance the cause of our own interests. The social transactions that most resist the advance of democracy and humanism reflect the defenses created and deployed to deny and justify our pain and immoral actions. In this chapter I describe some of the specific academic procedures that, in my opinion, reflect these defenses and the god-thing stories in which defenses most often appear. I then discuss some actual and proposed changes in procedure that have for me ameliorated some of these problems. I finish this chapter by describing the goals I envision from a truly scientific, artistic, and humanistic educational system. Once again I wish I had a language of simultaneity that would permit me to discuss the problems I encounter at the level of university organization, students, faculty, administration and culture at large as they create and reinforce each other rather than having to describe them as if each subset of the university exists fully independent of all the others.

It is impossible to interact and be a participant in shared zones of intersubjectivity with more than several students, patients, or children at one time. When classes reach forty, fifty, or more students are on their own and the teacher speaks at a level and pace that might satisfy the needs of all or none of the students. I am told by colleagues in large, prestigious state and city-run universities that introductory classes in a variety of subjects may run into the hundreds or even thousands. This is not education. The multitude of students are better referred to as audiences and listening to the professors as they describe teaching these throngs describes an entertainer not an educator.

My own classes of forty or so are usually comprised of students of such varying levels of preparedness, interests, values, cultures, and even languages that I despair when I stand in front of a room and deliver the same lecture to all of them. It is not the same lecture for all. For some students there is a negative zone of proximal development, in that I am presenting material that is already known to them at a pace and in a linguistic style that they mastered years earlier. For other students the zone is not a gap whose upper limit can be gleaned and struggled toward but a chasm and an abyss whose dimensions the student can't even begin to fathom. These individuals have taken my course for some purpose and deserve my attention to either clarify or change their goals if we both agree that other goals might better serve their purposes or be helped in a manner that fits their needs and modes of problem solving. Under the current system, I perform educational triage as much as I teach.

While I used to justify my actions by blaming the victims, "They deserve to flunk out, they don't deserve to be here, why can't I be sent good students or go teach in a real school where good students go" I find that I can no longer content or torture myself with such rhetoric. The collapse of the god-thing stories that sustained such intellectual efforts leave me struggling to find ways of individualizing the education of all my students. I am now working much harder at the job and the emotional payoff seems well worth the effort.

If the size and variability of my classes makes teaching difficult then the manner in which my classes, and the educational process in its entirety, are structured in terms of time increases those difficulties exponentially. Our schools are modeled on the factory system and resemble an assembly line. For many important social processes, including medicine and psychotherapy, education is a product and those who benefit from it are consumers. We educate our students in units of time, with speed and efficiency being the most important indicators of productivity. The students move, lock step, in strict chronological order, one year at a time in grade school, one semester at a time in college. They move through this system under an implicit assumption that their individual psychological developments are the same, that they are all entering their respective zones of proximal development at the same place, and will all accommodate to the adaptive problems they find there in the same style, sequence, and pacing. I have often referred to our school system as the great sausage maker.

Student's success and failures are measured by tests and grades and issued on report cards to parents. A permanent and public record is kept of these grades along with other moral judgments made concerning conduct and classroom behavior. Every several years progress is measured by standardized tests; these rituals are growing in number, frequency, and urgency. When the students reach the age of graduation from the high schools of the system, a new round of frantic testing takes place to see who will attend the most prestigious colleges and who, therefore, will be entitled to a legitimate economic future. I wish time and space would allow me to describe the holy rites surrounding the Scholastic Aptitude Test (SAT) and the emotional stress and damage done to those who take it and do well, do not do well, those who fail to take it at all, and response and reactions of the families of the students involved.

Those who are capable of adapting to the tasks demanded, and benefitting from the style and pacing available from the teachers in the school settings as they are currently constituted, and those who do well on the growing number of academic tests are judged to be smart, intelligent, gifted, and good students. Some teachers of these students feel that they are lucky to be blessed, while others seek to demonstrate how their teaching accounts for the success of the students. Administrators and politicians always take responsibility for the success of the good, A students. Those students who move more slowly and cannot benefit from what is available will be judged slow, learning disabled, emotionally disturbed or just not too smart. In this case, the teachers, administrators, politicians, students, and their families all scramble to place blame on everyone but themselves. Each group has the power to scapegoat the others but in the end responsibility falls squarely on the shoulders of the weakest link in this chain, the poor students. The system failed because "The students did not want to learn, were lazy, lacked natural aptitude, and what's wrong with these kids today anyway?" But changing the system with its large classes that inhibit any real success at individualizing the teacher-student relationship, its lock step system of moving large herds of children from grade to grade while ignoring individual rates and styles of adaptive growth (especially the normal growth differences between preadolescent boys and girls) is never considered. What is rarely if ever, discussed is the third and most devastating impediment to a creative humanistic educational process—the unexamined use of grades and the standards they are supposed to represent.

GRADES, GOLD STARS, DIPLOMAS, AND STANDARDS

I am either trusted or ignored by the administration of my college and the university where I am employed as to the content of my courses and the methods by which I have chosen to teach. I am either enjoying the benefits of a true democratic process or I am enfolded in a true anarchy. There are times I wish that more of a dialogue could exist between myself, other faculty members, and the administration (change as I envision it in education cannot take place without a joint effort of all concerned and without the leadership provided by administration), however, when I listen to most administrators discuss their visions concerning education, or observe their policies and politics, I opt for anarchy. My academic freedoms end the day that grades come due.

If I do not hand in my grades in a timely fashion I will find myself under the scrutiny of the administration who will first inquire as to my physical health and then to any other reasons my grades have not appeared ready for entry in the university computers. It is clear to me that what is most important to the university, and the society that has fashioned these educational institutions, is that I grade my students. I must boil down our entire human interaction to a single letter. If I do not do this, regardless of whatever justifications I might have for my behavior, the administration and the wheels of education will come to a halt, there will be mass confusion and much anxiety, anger, and consternation, and I will be in real trouble!

There are fewer more important indicators as to the nature of the authoritarian hierarchy of the educational system in which I toil than the pervasive role played by testing, grading, and certifying, and the incredible amount of importance attached to these procedures and moral rituals. Because the use of grades and other similar reinforcers are inherently authoritarian they are simultaneously inimical to creativity and democratic principles of development. I suggest that the reader become familiar with the work of Alfie Kohn (1993) who extensively summarizes the evidence that demonstrates the counterproductive effects of utilizing external rewards to increase individual's motivation to complete a task or improve learning. I will limit my discussion to the effects of grades in terms of the politics of the teacher-student relationship.

Grades shift the attention of both student and teacher from the changing nature of the shared content and developmental processes comprising the intersubjective space between them to the effects they have on a goal that is controlled by the teacher and which is external to the learning process itself. Instead of concentrating on the efforts required to reduce adaptive errors students are focused on the reactions and judgments of the teacher. Instead of developing their own authority to make judgments of success and failure based on the specific outcomes experienced as a consequence of their own efforts students rely on the judgments of the teacher. The rules of the learning situation become defined in Kohlberg's terms of conventional morality rather than postconventional modes of thinking. It is the teachers who determine what is right and wrong, good and bad, not the students. (A student recently admonished me for my hostility toward grades. "How will I know how I am doing without grades," he queried? I answered, "How did you know you were learning to ride a bicycle?")

The efforts of students to please teachers makes the learning situation one of work rather than the kind of play that results when students are able to rely on their own judgments as they experiment with different means to achieve their adaptive ends. Unlike play, where an activity is enjoyed or valued for its own sake, with grades the activity is valued for the grade and often only for the grade. If the grade or other external reinforcer is withdrawn, the activity collapses because it is entirely motivated by that external reinforcer. As I have discussed at various intervals in this book, the adaptive process changes dramatically when individuals develop their own critical capacities as they play in a situation than when they learn under conditions of fear and the moral judgments of others.

Grades are powerful weapons that teachers possess to praise or punish students, especially since these grades become public knowledge and are so easily interpreted as judgments of the essential worth of the self of the learner and not merely an indicator of success failure at a particular time and place. I hate the power that I possess based on the common belief that my having failed students has literally ruined the rest of their lives. No matter how I try to develop an authority based on respect my students fear me. Unlike parenting and therapy where my criticisms are private and temporary, and relate to the specific behaviors that I am trying to guide, the grades I must submit at the end of a term hang like a generalized shroud over every aspect of the learning situation and my relationships with my students.

It is not that criticism and feedback from the teacher are not necessary for the student to learn. If such feedback were not necessary then there would be no need for the teacher. However, in the therapeutic environment corrective feedback comes in the form of specific questions that allow the teachers to refocus the efforts of the students by making them aware of the relationship of their efforts to the specific outcomes being judged. In short, it is behavior and its consequences being judged, not the learners themselves. Moreover, the teachers in such situations can demonstrate the correct behaviors creating one of the most powerful means of teaching, that of apprentice and mentor. I believe that all individuals who learn any complex set of adaptive skills learn them best in a shared learning experience. It is important to note that all of these forms of correction are based on shared descriptions rather than moral judgments, and on shared perceptions and activities not the activities of one and the godlike distant criticism of the other. In a mentor-apprentice relationship, such as the one being described, the mentor can set the highest of standards but because of the manner in which learning is paced, demonstrated, and set in descriptive rather than moral terms, the individuals involved experience constant success as the long as the interaction between the teachers and students continues. The learners experience failure only when they, the students, decide it is in their interest to discontinue their adaptive efforts.

When educators discuss standards without taking into account the context in which standards are being applied, two distinct ideologies begin to emerge, both of which have already been discussed. Teachers who were themselves successful in the academic system and are proud of having succeeded come to the defense of the institutions, and by implication, the culture that has created them. These individuals, often filled with anger that defends against much guilt, rail about the inadequacies of the students and that the students must fail if standards are to remain high. The finest gift these students can bestow upon their teachers is to drop their courses early and in great numbers. We all complain bitterly about insensitive administrations and politicians, as well as a public that gives more lip service to education than real support, but it is the students who in the end are judged lacking because these teachers, and the rest of us, lack any real political power to change the conditions that inhibit educational change from taking place.

The other ideology, espoused by those who are just as politically helpless, takes the side of the students and claims that the standards are unfair to those who are disadvantaged and victimized by the cultural institutions that were supposed to help all students reach their maximum potential. These teachers often actively subvert any attempts to set any standards as racist, sexist, or otherwise discriminatory. The rhetoric of these two groups is often deafening but no matter how loud the din, it is the students who suffer and are unable to develop their adaptive skills to genuine levels of excellence.

My students seem to be overly represented by the terms slow, disturbed, and unprepared. The number of troublesome students varies class by class. Many students come to my college because it is close to their homes, relatively cheap, are seeking a second chance after leaving home before they are ready to separate or deal with more academically competitive schools, or are adults returning to school seeking new career paths. These students are a joy to work with because they require no special efforts to teach. The students that I am writing about, and who have become my concern as a teacher, are those who are in my classes as a last resort in one way or another. They are the ones who have failed or done poorly on the endless rituals that are supposed to measure school success, but instead measure loveableness, self-worth, and teachability. They seem to be so fearful of further failure that they make few efforts to even try to learn .

Many of these students come from homes broken by death, divorce, drugs, and alcohol. They are the students who speak of poverty, both economic and spiritual, as well as discipline carried out by enraged parents who use insults and physical violence to resolve conflicts with their offspring. They often appear numb to physical or emotional pain. They seem to be the same students most disconnected from the culture of the school and most connected to the wasteland of commercial television and popular entertainment. (A friend and colleague teaching history recently told me of a class of more than forty in which the number representing the year 1492 had no historical significance. "How is it possible for people growing up in our society not to know Columbus's birthday, he asked? "Easy," I replied, "they might have been born in our society but they were not raised in our culture!")

Finally, these students appear to have come from school systems that judged them failures in the most authoritarian manner while simultaneously passing them along the assembly line ignoring their own quality control standards. The students were promoted or passed in spite of failing to achieve the standards that were set for them; in spite of being evaluated by a parade of professionals who found their IQ's to be low, their emotions disordered, their brains damaged, and their social surroundings impoverished. The schools and the politicians who advance their public relations played politics and created the illusions of academic success, instead of admitting to failure in their attempts to teach the content and skills that would represent traditional academic standards,. These same schools and their teachers function like an anarchy that ignores the values they espouse. My students feel like failures but have no real idea of the standards that many of their college teachers hold for success for their own children or which have been set for the good students. Totalitarian control mixed with anarchic indifference and pity seems to be a deadly combination for developing minds, to say nothing of the incredible hypocrisy of those running such a system and mountains of existential nausea felt by those teaching in the system.

CHANGING LESSONS

In recent years I have been involved in exploring whatever degrees of freedom might be available for me to establish a high quality educational experience for my students that embodies the principles that derive from parent-child, therapist-patient interactions. I have utilized pedagogical techniques to create a *holding environment* in my classroom. I feel confident that I do not explicitly, or even implicitly, suggest to my students that they are defective in any way, either cognitively, emotionally, or morally. I have learned how to describe and use descriptive psychological concepts when being critical of my student's behavior. As discussed earlier, the first topic that I discuss in any course is geared toward helping my students understand the difference between descriptions and judgments and to understand that they are studying a science that is geared toward describing, explaining, predicting, and controlling, but not judging. The discussions are integrated into classroom and take home exercises that give hands on experience in recognizing the difference between describing and judging. Some of my student's most excited responses come as they develop insights into how much their intrapsychic and interpersonal lives have been affected by the confusion of describing and judging and how much of their identities are defined by negative moral judgments.

I either begin with, or shortly into the course, introduce an analysis of the political structures created by authoritarian hierarchies and how they differ from democracies and anarchic systems. This topic also creates much anxiety and a sense of liberation as my students begin to analyze their own experiences at home, school, and in their social lives along these political dimensions. I discuss grades and the role of testing in their lives and make clear that while I wish I did not have to give them grades I cannot keep my job unless I do so. I ask them to be creative and suggest ways to get around this problem. What I find interesting is that in almost every class someone will suggest, at times seriously, that I give them all A's. I ask my classes how they would feel about this as an option and I have never had more than two or three in a room that would even consider getting a grade they didn't deserve. Some are horrified at the thought of not being able to get an A and simultaneously being able to enjoy their grade in the light of others getting failing grades. The competitive nature of grades fosters attitudes such as these. I believe that these discussions concerning grades create horror and anxiety for some but a genuine shift in priorities for others. It does seem to help create an atmosphere in which more students can focus on the material as it relates to their lives and as it poses a problem to be solved rather than another opportunity to just pass or fail.

I have already discussed the contract that I work out with my students when they are informed which books they will need and the content of the course. I hate textbooks almost as much as I hate grades. I will use textbooks when the number of students in my classes threaten my sense of sanity. A textbook almost always comes from the publisher with teacher materials, including short-answer tests that derive directly from the text. A textbook and the short-answer tests make a teacher's life much easier especially when the tests can be marked by machine. True, the texts are almost all dull and incoherent. Short answer tests only measure the student's ability and willingness to memorize facts mostly disconnected from the body of knowledge that is organized by the student's personal narrative and, therefore, forgotten minutes after the tests are over. I feel guilty for teaching this way, but I want to be a committed teacher not a teacher who gets committed.

Whenever I find it feasible I utilize primary source materials or books such as "The Moral Animal" (Wright 1994) which is written by a professional science writer. Such books are usually well-written and cover a great deal of material in a coherent fashion. When I select books written by professionals for professionals or the general educated reader I make sure that they are being sold in large trade stores and therefore are being sold to non-professional audiences as well. I try to order books that are in paperback to reduce costs and because books are not culturally valued by most of my students. This process tends to assure that the books are beyond the current reading levels of most of my students but are not insulting to those students who read at or near adult levels. In this way, the level of reading required presents a ceiling on the zone of proximal development that represents a worthwhile adaptive goal for the students to try and achieve. Increasingly, I use books or other materials that I (or colleagues) have written with students such as these in mind. By making the readings as narratively coherent and interesting as possible I have chance to motivate my students to read. Most students come from anarchic schools where the readings were assigned but the material was covered in advance by the teachers. Tests were then constructed to make sure the questions reflected material covered by the teachers. In effect, the students could pass even if they never opened the texts. Recently I discovered that barely half my students were even buying the assigned books, they were sure that they would not have to read them.

I assign the readings and then provide lectures that either frame the readings as I wish them to be or disagree with the position of the author. I do not cover the readings but make clear that I will answer any questions that arise from the readings. I think that a lecture to a well-prepared group of students can create a thrilling and stimulating experience in the intersubjective zone where learning takes place, but if students are not prepared for the lecture's content and are not actively participating within the zone a lecture makes no sense at all. I have lectured for years to seas of silent, immobile, expressionless faces without remembering that when I was an undergraduate and tried to listen to words that had little or no meaning I watched the clock and prayed for the time to pass quickly. I will no longer engage in such madness. If students have read the material, or are expecting to, then a lecture on the material makes sense. Listening as an active experience only takes place in a zone of development where the student is induced to be active as a general principle governing the co-construction of the zone.

I am convinced that students must read preceding every meeting with the instructor to assure that they are active co-constructors of the intersubjective space between the various participants. If there are no questions on materials read or discussed, and these questions must reflect some genuine effort of the students to have assimilated the material on their own, I regularly fall silent and after a while ask my class what it is they might find useful to do for the rest of the hour. I will not, in any circumstances, play the role of an entertainer or fill in the hour while the students sit passively. (I do believe it is important for teachers to be entertaining in class but this is only secondary to their educative function. I do not believe that being entertaining by itself defines a good educator.)

If reading is important to a student's academic adaptive development, then writing and expressing themselves about what they are struggling to learn is even more important. In most classes I require that students keep a daily log in which they outline and summarize all that they have read or heard in class, as well as their own personal reactions to any of the material that they feel resonates with any aspect of their own lives. It is with this activity that I hope to arouse reflection on their own personal narratives that relate to the topics and activities of the course. At regular intervals I have my students summarize their logs and write a more formal paper for me that simultaneously asks them to select those topics that were of interest to them, summarize the topics in their own words and then write their personal reasons for having chosen those topics. I do grade these papers, however, I allow students the freedom to rewrite anything that they wish to, especially if they were unhappy with the grade received.

I make clear that I wish to see the manner in which these topics have transformed their interpretations of their personal material, which now is acting as examples of the topics. I am not interested in learning primarily about their lives or having them reveal personal and intimate details of their lives. Similarly, I do not wish them to write biographies or exposes of friends and relatives or autobiographies of themselves. They are using their lives to illuminate topics in the course curriculum (which one way or another will include materials from the preceding chapters of this book). However, by seeing the incidents of their lives in the light of their formal studies, by reading and writing about the topics in relation to their lives, their perceptions of their lives must change and the topics become assimilated into their own personal narratives. Student's personal narratives change as they are accommodated to the demands of reading and writing about the course's content and the topics are transformed from information into living knowledge as they are assimilated into the narratives. This set of activities has become the heart of my teaching technique.

Requiring students to write about personal life experiences is a contentious issue, especially in a university setting where such activities have little historical precedent. They are also an issue in New York City, the mind your own business capitol of the world. Many students resent the process because they feel uncomfortable revealing personal information to a stranger (for many of my students any information revealed is too personal and this literally includes their names) and because it often means exploring material that is painful to think about and write down. Many students object to this exercise because it means extensive writing and writing seems to have been required even less in their educations than reading. I allow students to integrate topic material into the lives of others they know or even fictional characters. I generally have my students read fiction that fits the class material and show films that relate as well that can provide meaningful human material to analyze in relation to the class topics.

It is interesting to me that once reticent students realize that they have a choice and that their fellow students are enjoying exploring personal material, most begin to explore personal past themes, even those painful to recall. Many of my students have been voiceless all their lives and like all human beings find great pleasure and urgency in being heard by others. For some, the ability to bear witness to past injustices becomes a compelling motive to accept the assignment of integrating personal narratives with the master narratives of psychological theory.

I would like to further justify my desires to get students to write and even read their papers aloud in class and share the themes of their lives as they become transformed by this process. Many of my students have spent too many years as victims of the psychotic landscape. Their adaptive consciousness is shaped by a variety of defenses which include withdrawal from many aspects of life including the memory of much of their past. If people believe that they are defective then it makes sense to give up any hope of being loved and accepted. If the world is seen as essentially harsh and punitive then sitting absolutely still, numb, silent, and invisible also makes sense. If intellectual or other types of failure are preordained then there can be no legitimate reasons to try to succeed. If the past is remembered with the same preoperational appraisals and the same emotional pain as when the original painful events took place then a person only has reason to avoid looking at the past. The problem with these defenses is that their needs to be loved, heard, accepted, and to come to grips with the past might still be intense and causing them much suffering in spite of the defenses being utilized to protect themselves. Moreover, as we have already discussed, these defenses bring about an intensification of the very pain they are trying to escape. To be ones past is to continue living ones past. Moreover, it can lead to a structuring of the future that is, in one way or another, a replica of the past. But the most serious problem that these defenses pose for me as a teacher is that they prevent learning from taking place. The narratives course material is to be assimilated into and the accommodations to new processes which define the adaptive problems that the student must solve neither exist or are in fixated form and frozen in time and space. The student is either disengaged, in a state of heightened alert not far from terror, or just feeling plain stuck.

I do not wish my students to grapple with painful pasts, to be healed as is the goal of the mental health establishment, or to form closure, as cheap a term as has ever emerged from the new age, fairy tale philosophies to afflict our already too afflicted lives. The past is the past and while it cannot be altered it can be described instead of judged and understood from a variety of perspectives. My goals are educative even if the techniques are derived from my clinical experiences. I want to help my students have their history rather than be embedded in them. I want them to examine their history in the light of history, sociology, and psychology. I want them to evaluate their lives and the events that have shaped their consciousness with formal rather than preoperational logic. I try and provide exercises for them to write about in their logs that will allow them to see where they are embedded and where they might want to psychologically move.

I hope these moves allow them to feel less fear, less stuck, and more capable of defining themselves as not only members of their family, race, religion, gender, country, and culture but also in terms of the differences that make them unique. It is important for all of us to feel pride in our social history and the cultural roles that are necessary to define our identities, but not from a defensive posture that leads us to see ourselves only in terms of our race, gender, religion, or nationality. I want to help them feel empowered to be the author of their own story to the maximum degree to which the forces of history, sociology, biology, physics, and chemistry will allow them. I wish for them an ever-expanding personal narrative that includes the role that others have played in their lives politically and their ability to take charge of the politics of their own lives and relationships. I hope that they will be convinced to practice democratic politics based on humanistic moral and ethical principles.

I want my students to be able to create for themselves and others holding relationships that allow them to live comfortably in their own skins, to meditate on their own thoughts, and accept without hesitation their own emotions as sources of useful motivation rather than mental illnesses to be cured or sins to be avoided. I wish for my students to learn what arouses their interest and excites a sense of discovery rather than memorizing information that in no way relates to their lives. I hope they find or can create a place in which discovery and creativity mark their time on this earth. I would hope also that they might see that their selves and the relationships that define them, whether loving and holding, or hostile and destructive are all temporary and lacking in permanence no matter how hard they wish for or fear that they are so. I want my students to become aware of the vast flow of history and the myriad forces that they cannot control but to which they can contribute if only they allow their selves to dissolve as they concentrate on immersing themselves within that flow in order to understand it scientifically and reflect on it artistically.

I want my students to understand that time is change and that they are being changed by time just as they are influencing the course of time. I would hope that they could begin to see the interconnections and the reciprocal cause and effect relationship between the past and the present, themselves and the phenomena that exist at all different levels of organization. And if they cannot graduate from college at the standards that academic institutions must set, then let them be both glad that they tried and have begun a process of adaptive development that has left them different and better for having tried. Let them be in awe of the fact that they possess a life defined by a consciousness that exists both momentarily from the lens of history and in a way perhaps unequaled in all the universe and that this makes them precious. I hope that they learn to love more and better than many of them have up until this point in time and that they will love themselves, others in their lives, and the type of learning that can lead to a life of the mind.

There are more practical and prosaic reasons why I employ the diary or log assignment in my teaching. Most of my students stopped doing homework years ago, if in fact they ever started. I do not believe that the cognitive-affective changes I seek to induce in my students can ever take place if the only time in their day-to-day lives that there is intellectual engagement is during class time or if they do not develop clear strategies and effective habits of study. In their anarchic and authoritarian childhoods there were often no places to study at home even if such study was valued and reinforced by families and friends. My students have been telling me for years that most of their primary and secondary school teachers simply gave up trying to enforce rules relating to homework. The logs, with their emphasis on personal narratives, not only motivate many to write, often quite extensively, but force them to create strategies that improve written expression, critical analysis, the emergence of formal operations, as well as the ability to organize a stream of ideas into a logical and related whole. As with many of my colleagues, I discuss and try to demonstrate my own strategies for study and creative writing, but just as I believe that the philosopher Paul Feyerabend (1988) was correct when he inveighed against scientists imposing one method of inquiry on the field, so too must each student be free to develop whatever methods of study they find effective for themselves.

FACULTY DEVELOPMENT

I cannot close this chapter without discussing a bit of the structure of the college in which I work and the changes that I believe must take place if my dreams for my student's education are to be realized. If my student's conscious modes of experience are the products of authoritarian systems, then so are, for the most part, those of the faculty. While the college has elements of democracy and preaches humanism as its operating morality, an examination of faculty-administration and faculty-faculty relationships reveals much the same hierarchical ordering of power as those relationships that define teacher-student interactions. For the most part, the faces of the faculty, as they listen to administrative monologues, bear the same passive, expressionless visages as those of the students as they listen to the one-sided truths and monologues of their teachers. The students sit in their classes, isolated from one another, and sworn to secrecy not only from each other but themselves. The same silence often exists when faculty members are in the presence of administrators, and I imagine when the administrators are in the presence of their superiors. The students complain and moan about their teachers, the faculty about their administrations, but the complaints are made behind the backs of the feared authority. To the faces of authority, the students to the teachers, the faculty to administration, all too often only the most shameless of flattery is spoken. Flattery or silence. (I have become embarrassed by my students flattery and wonder why I could not see the instrumental nature of its existence earlier than I did. I sit in awe at the shameless flattery provided by various members of the faculty to various administrators and wonder what powerful needs of the administrator allow them to revel in these hollow, obsequious gestures.)

The students have been prevented from organizing themselves. In fact, the competitive system which places the power to reward in the hands of their teachers, teaches the students to enjoy the suffering of fellow students at the hands of teachers and never think of multiplying their power when dealing with teachers. I now regularly teach my students how to deal with those instructors from whom they feel abuse. I try and teach them how to approach authority with respect but in a unified group led by effective spokes people and describe their unhappiness with their course without blame or accusation. I teach them that they must listen to the teacher's responses and hope that these will be framed in the form of descriptions and not moral judgments that ascribe blame rather than define problems jointly to be solved. My students must learn that while they are human beings who lack the institutional power granted to their teachers, their teachers are no less human and are often unaware how powerless they feel in the face of their authority figures.

Finally, I teach my students the line of command within the college and how to proceed with higher authority if their attempts at conflict resolution fail with their teachers. Authority that engages in authoritarian politics, and this includes parents, teachers, and administrators, reward individuals for their obedience to power. The social organization and cooperation of children, students, teachers, and citizens are feared by the authority that seek to control and extend their power. It seems to me after being a teacher for more than thirty years that I wish I had learned much earlier these same lessons that I now teach my students.

I have been seeking to establish at my college for many years now, with varying degrees of success, both by myself and with like-minded colleagues who them-selves have worked alone or with others and with varying degrees of success, ongoing, interdepartmental discussions concerning the intellectual content of our specific disciplines, the methods of pedagogy that we have developed and dis-carded, and especially the politics of our mutual experiences. In short, I believe it is necessary for the faculty, just as with therapists, to discuss problems related to co-transference and the god-thing stories that justify selfish genes and selfish memes and which are inflicted on us by the authorities which, in turn, we inflict on our students in our classrooms. The curriculum that I now hold as essential for my students grew out of the curriculum that I developed in my role as therapist and which for me remains essential for anyone who works with people.

For many years I found myself as voiceless in relation to the power structure of my college as my students were toward me. I failed to see the humanity in my students who were often cast as lazy and unintelligent and failed to see the humanity of the administrators of whom I complained and labeled power hungry, dictatorial and other choice labels. I waited to be recognized and rewarded by the administra-tion without speaking out, demanding my due, exercising my own authority, or recognizing that they neither understood nor cared for my work or feelings any more than I cared for theirs. The administration and I did not know each other as thinking, feeling human beings any more than my students and I saw each other free of the labels and power inherent in moral hierarchies based on fear, inferiority, blackmail, and intimidation.

I did not understand until recently my own identity as it was expressed both in intrapsychic and social terms and how it related to my unhappiness at the college. I did not know that to survive as an artist and as a scientist I had to be in the world but not fully of it. I had to participate as a member of the power structure of any social organization of which I was a part but not identify with defensive transfer-ences of either those who held much power or those who held little or none. I could not become fully embedded in any relationship, or defined by any set of definitions in which I was not simultaneously a part of these relationships and definitions and separate from them. I had to be the same as every other human being but at the same time unique and unlike them.

When I looked up and felt a powerful administration demanding obedience of both my behavior and my beliefs, when I experienced that I would gain their favor only if I saw the world through their eyes, flattered them, and denied my own narrative I experienced the pull of the god-thing story. If I joined them I would have greater power and favor but the me that was separate would begin to die. I would not tell my story but theirs and I would have to deceive myself into believing that their story was mine. I would have eliminated from myself the responsibilities that come with having my own authority but lose my freedoms and liberties. I would be left with the illusion of freedom believing that I am free to pursue any objects as long as they are not the objects pursued by the authority. I can play in much the same way as a child until called to task by an adult. If I opposed these authorities I would be cast in the role of thing, become the it in an I-it relationship with those experiencing their own I as defined in godlike power in my life. To become it is to be despised and described with judgments that seek to discover what is wrong with them. It is to become the scapegoat and the victim blamed for the intellectual and moral failings of those in power. To identify oneself as an it, or thing, is to live in a state of rage, self-pity, self-hatred, and powerlessness and to see the authority not as human but as monsters in one's life.

Similarly, if I entered the god-thing story and looked down at my students as things I would experience what my administration experienced with me as I either submerged my identity in theirs or resisted them actively or (as is more often the case,) passively, sullenly, and resentfully. I wouldn't see my power with my students but the terrible responsibilities that come with playing the role of a god while remaining a human being. As my students increasingly depend on me I would not only have more power in their lives but an increasing and equal measure of the burdens that are no longer theirs but mine. I would feel increasingly helpless and find that I must have increasing power. I would be caught in a vicious cycle—the more power I had the less powerful I would feel.

I would also feel guilt and anger toward the very beings that I depend on but that I cannot depend on because I am constructing them as my lessors both intellectually and morally. I would begin to resent the demands my students made on me and see their desires for freedom as disobedience, disrespect, rebellious and a threat to my authority. I would not be able to delegate responsibility as I could not be dependent on those who are my intellectual and moral lessors. I would not seek in others debate and growth inducing diversity but mirror images of myself as well as agreement in all that I might conclude. As my students diminished in value as students I would resent my being forced to teach such inferior beings. I would conclude that the authority in my life was monstrous, therefore I become a monster in the eyes of my students. Life would become intolerable if I looked up or down, if I looked inside or outside. I would have constructed myself and those with whom I worked to be my own (and their own) worst nightmares.

How do we resolve these difficulties? How do we find a place within the power structure of our social institutions where we are in but not completely of the structure, where we can be embedded enough to enjoy the benefits of leadership and simultaneously depend on others? How do we collapse the authoritarian hierarchical structures that induce god-thing defensive narratives that increase the very structures that create our worst nightmares? How can we see each other as equals who differ in abilities and knowledge rather than stacked up with those above us as inherently superior and those below as inherently inferior? How can we create a situation in which we feel safe enough that the distinction between what is inside of us becomes congruent with that is external to us? I believe that we can never fully achieve such a situation but we can begin through the kind of peer supervision to which I now turn.

An implicit assumption in all clinical work is that supervision is necessary for success in the enterprise. Initially, supervisors evaluate their employees for their fitness in the field or progress in their specific jobs. Later, peer supervision replaces other forms of evaluation but the idea that professional development reaches some plateaus where improvement is unnecessary is totally alien to those in the field. There are simply too many stresses and too many areas where defensive adaptations can develop to consider that any therapist is no longer free of the need to discuss cases, techniques, and the changing theoretical perspectives in what is a volatile field of inquiry and application of skills. It is true that the supervisory process becomes authoritarian in the clinical field because problems of co-transference are interpreted as indications of the pathology of the therapist. Pathology or mental illness is in reality a moral judgment of unwanted, poorly understood behaviors; these implicit moral judgments increase the defensiveness of those participating in the supervisory processes. But when labels are not used, the kind of learning that go on with peers providing each other the best of their mutual wisdom in the privacy and security of what is essentially a holding environment makes for some of the most effective professional learning. I have long felt that our school environments would have changed if this type of professional development was built into the job specifications of educators.

Between 1979 and 1982 a colleague, who is also a clinician, and I succeeded in creating a peer supervisory process with an interdepartmental group of faculty. We met voluntarily for three academic years, with no requests for compensation, advice, or consent of the administration. (We might have been the only formally organized such group at the college since its existence in 1964 and through four administrations. Of course, informal groups and friendships have always existed at the college, but these are not formally constituted with clear professional objectives.) Our group swelled at times to more than a dozen and shrank at other times to six or seven but continued to meet until by common consent we could not continue our work without increasing our institutional power and therefore change more than our roles in the classroom.

One of the most important lessons that we learned from this activity was that our classrooms are not isolated from the world outside as many of us used to believe, and that the politics and structure of the classroom reflected their counterparts in the rest of the school and in society at large. (This same delusion also comforted me in my work as a therapist where I believed that I could help my patients change into more loving and honest people without changing the families and society that had shaped my patients and which still operated along the lines that I called pathological.) We had achieved much change in our professional lives but were still so embedded in our individual senses of institutional powerlessness that it never dawned on us to organize politically and reach out more vigorously to larger numbers of faculty. From the vantage point of my development at that time it seemed completely logical to simply disband the group. (As these words are being written, several of the graduates of the earlier group are again trying to reconstitute another peer supervisory group process but with clearly articulated political goals.)

It is neither necessary nor practical to try and describe our interactions specifically except to note that we did establish a holding environment in which we all felt safe and confident that we would be heard with respect and interest. Our group met the criteria for democratic politics and humanist morality. Our development, much to my surprise, began to follow the same trajectory as those of my patients when they realize that they are experiencing a recontextualization of adaptive skills and predictive assumptions. At first we all complained to one another about our individual powerlessness, alienation, guilt, and other negative emotions related to life at the college. It is inevitable it seems that the first step in any therapeutic process involves participants to be able to express their emotional pain and be heard without criticism or feeling that there is something wrong with them if they are hurting. The self-hatred and sense of being defective often derives from people being told that they are crazy, selfish, not appreciative enough among others when they assume that their parents or other authorities, (such as school teachers or administrators) either care or are capable of accepting complaints, demands, and other cries for help.

Once we are heard we cease to be our emotional pain and instead have it available for the kind of scrutiny that allows individuals to contextualize their emotions and understand them as reactions to various events as these have been appraised. The second stage of development usually involves a sharing of scenarios that paint each individual as a victim of insensitive, bullying and heartlessly cruel authority figures. "We are not bad, we are the victims of bad people." While it is emotionally easier to hate and be angry at authority figures rather than direct these feeling toward one's self, it is important that discussions continue and the feelings of rage and helplessness felt toward these disappointing authority figures be moved from defining the self to being examined by the self. Once individuals have their helplessness available for reflection they can begin to make plans and develop strategies to replace those adaptive patterns that are responsible for their feeling stuck in circumstances they find offensive. Finally, it becomes clear with still further development that even one's parents, teachers, and administrators are likely to be human and are being motivated not by meanness but by desires such as power, fear, sex, anxiety, shame, and guilt, just like the rest of us. It is at this point that our group began actively experimenting with new means of teaching and relating to our students. It was also at this point that I became aware of just how poorly trained I was as a pedagogue.

There are few skills more complex, or more important, than teaching except perhaps parenting. Complex skills are best taught as part of a system of mentoring in which mistakes can be made in the presence of a master who can help us reflect and best develop what we do and how we do it. Our parents are our first mentors, and in the process of raising us they prepare us for our own roles as parents. Our teachers in grade school and beyond also teach us to be parents by nurturing us and they providing us with lessons in living that are both part of and independent of the school curriculum. I often wish there had been more training for me in both my roles as parent and as teacher. I cannot conceive of a mechanism to teach parenting except perhaps therapy with a therapist who practices scientifically and humanistically and helps the patient understand a true holding environment, and perhaps a teacher who helps develop understanding of children as other than defective adults requiring authoritarian control. Learning to teach can easily be done in a mentored relationship and exists at all levels, except the college and university level, of the educational system

Most of the colleges and universities in this country's higher educational system demand that faculty members hold a Ph.D. before they are allowed into a classroom. A Ph.D. is, for most of us, a research degree; I was indeed provided ample mentoring into the skills of carrying out complex research designs. (I never developed an interest in conducting research since the positivist, laboratory contextualized paradigm I was taught seemed mechanical and artificial to me. It took me until recently to figure out that when I learned about my patient's or student's lives and used this knowledge to build and test my theories I was also doing valid research.) I was never provided an opportunity to learn to teach because it was assumed that my expertise in a field of knowledge was all that would be required to teach that knowledge.

It was also made clear to me and most of my colleagues that teaching was of a much lower order of importance than research. For most faculty members, especially for those teaching in four year and prestigious colleges, teaching does not lead to promotions or increased status. For many, the part of the job than involves teaching becomes a penance required in order to get on with the important activity of discovering new knowledge through primary research projects. The publish or perish mentality that faculty members work under is authoritarian and has led to much research that has little or no value except as another line in a faculty member's resume.

Some of us, however, take seriously the idea that the function of a college is to create and disseminate new knowledge. Even for those of us who love the classroom, training in research techniques outstrips the training in teaching skills. I invented my teaching techniques on my own, aided by what I learned as a therapist and as a parent more than anything I learned from other teachers. This book, is in part, my effort to share some of these personal inventions. (My skills as a therapist were also largely self-invented as there is no mentoring available in that field either. However, the justification for not providing mentoring involved the supposed confidentiality a therapist must maintain concerning patients.) No teacher should spend his or her career alone in a classroom but should be able to co-teach with a variety of other teachers. In this way teachers would have a variety of models to identify with and imitate and provide implicit reality checks on some of the things teachers say that are factually incorrect or which reflect the personal ideologies that are presented to our students as unalterably true. Teachers would also experience much less loneliness and alienation in the classroom and be able to demonstrate to students how to disagree and debate without becoming personally hurtful in the exchange of ideas.

I close this section suggesting that academics have much to learn and much to reorganize if schools are to change from authoritarian hierarchies and pseudofactories into democratic and humanistic institutions. We have much work to do if we wish to share with our students the joy of new discovery and creation. We have much to learn about ourselves if we are to counter Gregory Bateson's (1979: 8) criticism of teachers and answer the questions he raises when he writes: (Bateson believes that the critical insight education must provide its students is the ability to see the patterns which connect all phenomena.) "Why do schools touch almost nothing of the pattern which connects? Is it that teachers know that they carry the kiss of death which will turn to tastelessness whatever they touch and therefore they are wisely unwilling to touch or teach anything of real life importance? Or is it that they carry the kiss of death because they dare not teach anything of real life importance? What is wrong with them?"

EVALUATING MY METHODS

The next chapter contains narratives, and fragments of narratives, written by students in a number of different courses over the past two years or so. I have selected these essays according to several criteria. First, I wish to give the reader the flavor of the lives many of my students and what is demanded of them as they struggle to adapt to their lives and to school in the context of their lives. Second, I want my readers to see how the narratives that describe these lives are transformed as the students integrate new insights gained by assimilating various topics from the curriculum of human psychology that is integrated into every course that I teach. Finally, I hope to provide the reader with the vibrancy of these essays compared to the usually stilted prose provided by students when they write an essay to please a teacher for a grade. "What does he want me to say?" is an impossible question to answer unless the one who asks it can read minds. Writing with someone else's consciousness in mind does not enable an individual to play with their materials, experiment, and feel free to say what it is they wish to say and what it is only they can say.

Any reader with any research experience at all will know that my selecting essays in a subjective fashion hardly proves that either my method is superior to any other method or that the essays I have chosen might have been written as well by these same students if they had written them under different conditions. I agree with such criticisms. I have neither the interest nor the ability to set up a research project to prove either of the two contentions being questioned. If overall success of my method were measured by the number of students who pass my course as compared to the numbers passing the courses of other teachers using different methods then I doubt that my method would prove to be superior. I doubt that success could be measured by comparing the grade distribution of my students to students in other classes. In fact, I succeed in convincing only a minority of my students that I am not crazy or that my course is not much more difficult than their other, more traditionally run courses.

The freedom I give my students to read on their own, write on their own, write on topics of their choosing, rewrite as many times as they wish, and come to class prepared to discuss topics of their own choosing carries with it burdens of responsibility many of my students do not wish to have. Many of my students drop my course rather than engage the material and risk failing without having me to blame. Many students fail my courses because they simply do not do the work. I make a promise to every student that I will pass them if they demonstrate a genuine integrity in their work and produce more than they are used to producing. I probably give as many F's as any teacher who fails students based on failing grades on tests and if these numbers are added to the number of students who drop my courses I am probably averaging the same levels of success as any of those teachers who claim the superiority of traditional methods of lecture and examinations.

If success of my method is based on the feelings of cooperation and joy that I experience being in the classroom now that I am more a teacher and less a cop, judge, and jury, there is no question that my method is superior to any that I have used in the past or any used by faculty members who teach in a moral hierarchy in which their students are seen as victims or inadequate and undeserving of their place in higher education. Until I began to utilize the philosophy and methods described in this book I counted the years until early retirement. Now I genuinely dread the prospect! The narratives that I have chosen are only a few produced by students who seem to surprise themselves by the volumes of work they find that they are creating and the connections they feel toward me, their fellow students with whom they now share so much of their lives in a genuine community, and the school that they attend.

11

STORIES TOLD AND LESSONS LEARNED:
THE VOICES OF MY STUDENTS

STORY FRAGMENT 1: YOUNG ADULT FEMALE

Taking Psychology 32 (Human Growth and Development) was a very exhilarating experience. When the class first met our professor made it clear that we were not going to be spoon fed throughout the semester. We were given a syllabus that contained the reading material for which we would be responsible. Our professor told us that he was not going to give us notes that summarized what we were reading, but instead he wanted us to share our thoughts and views about what we had read. Immediately that freaked me out because I was so used to teachers assigning work which they would go over without knowing or caring if you read the assignment or not, so clearly this was a new situation for me and I was scared. I felt as if I was on my own and would have to do all the work by myself. I hated Professor Simon for doing this. I remember telling my friends that he was lazy and he did not want to do his job, which I felt at the time was to do my work for me.

We had an interesting discussion in class on our first day which had a big impact on me because it helped me realize that after all these years in school I was always memorizing things to get by and pass a class without actually learning. I went to primary school in Jamaica West Indies and the teachers there are allowed to hit you. So whenever I was given an assignment I would memorize it and make the teacher happy and myself happy for not getting a whooping, and in actuality I did not learn the things I memorized I only knew them for the time being, and that is not learning at all. When I came to the United States and the rules did not change I still memorized things to get by. I don't think I am a dumb person, however I am certain that if I was taught to learn rather than memorize I would be a lot more intelligent than I am now. Moreover, now that I am aware that there is a problem with me

In an effort to maintain the personal voices of my students, these narratives have received only minor editing.

memorizing instead of knowing I can better myself by reading for me and learning for me and trying to please myself first before anyone else.

STORY FRAGMENT 2: YOUNG ADULT FEMALE

I remember my first day at school. My mother dropped me off and I saw hundreds of kids my age crying and trying desperately not to enter the school yard. I was the total opposite, I enjoyed getting up early, getting dressed, and going off to school. The feeling came to an end because of my very first teacher, Mrs. B.

Up until this day I remember my first teacher, her attitude and my fear of her, and the fear she instilled in me. I sometimes wonder if I will ever have the power to overcome this feeling . . . one day she asked me to say the whole alphabet and the pronunciations to go along with the letters. Mrs. B. had a pointer and as she pointed to the letter I would say the letter and pronounce it. I said the wrong letter and was going ahead of her, she took the pointer and whacked it against the wall and grabbed my clothes until I felt my feet barely touching the floor and she said to me, "You are going to do it over and over until you get it right, do you understand me?" By this time all I could remember was hearing all the kids laugh at me and I felt this lump swell in my throat and my heart started to ache until my eyes filled with tears and I couldn't hold it back any more. Everyday since then I felt like a failure and was afraid to participate because I was afraid of being wrong, being yelled at, and above all being laughed at.

(Student then describes the escalation of her withdrawal throughout school and her growing awareness that this does not have to continue. She concludes her paper as follows.) Instead I sit in your class and want so much to participate and tell you what I think and share my experiences. Instead I just sit there and freeze up. This makes me feel like I'm in a bubble and I can't break through and I ask myself who put me in that bubble? It was Mrs. B. and all the other Mrs. B's I had as teachers, it's my junior high school, it's the bullies that made my life my childhood a living nightmare, and it's me for allowing them to control my life and keeping me in this bubble.

STORY FRAGMENT 3: YOUNG ADULT FEMALE

During the course of this psychology class, I have come across many interesting and challenging situations. However, it wasn't easy at first to know how valuable and helpful this course would be for me in the future. I would have to honestly say that I was very unhappy with this class at first. I found your way of teaching to be untraditional and unfair.

Untraditional in the sense that your teaching skills were none that I've ever experienced before in all my years of going to school, and unfair because you were aware that the majority of the class was used to a school system where students were taught to sit still, shut up, and copy off the board. However, Mr. Simon you wanted and you tried to get us out of the traditional way of learning. It was difficult at first for me to adapt to this environment for teaching especially because I was unaware of what you were trying to do. I feel it would have been a lot easier if only the students were aware of your intentions. Nevertheless, I'm not blaming anyone or pointing the finger, because the fact of the matter is no one can make another person do something if they're not comfortable doing it. And as the saying goes, "You can lead a horse to water, but you can't make it drink," stands very clear with me. In the past when I was being led to the water I was told when to drink, how to drink, and how much to drink. However, you left me alone to decide on my own when, how, and how much to drink. At that moment on, I realized that this course would be a whole new experience for me.

I was born on the Island of Jamaica. It was not until I was ten years old that I came to the United States. In Jamaica all the schools are privately owned schools that required students to wear uniforms. The school teachers are very strict and demanding. They make sure all their students pay attention and that they work. And if you didn't do what you're expected to do you were slapped a couple of times in the hand with a ruler. Teachers are very authoritative in Jamaica.

STORY FRAGMENT 4: YOUNG ADULT MALE

My name is B____ E____, but my friends call me Billy. I use that name outside legal matters because no one can pronounce it correctly. You might not even know who I am because I never spoke up in your class, although I absorbed all the information and discussions and used them to my advantage. I truly feel that I have learned a great deal in your class. All the things that have been hiding in my subconscious, thoughts, and hopes that were waiting to come out. You invoked and forced my fears to surface, pushed me to take a stand and control my life, instead of having my life control me, and they didn't make sense. I was an obedient zombie. I was literally pretending to be alive. In school I would just stare at my professors, going home I would occupy myself by getting lost in the scenery, and at home, I would disappear in the TV.

One of the things that I never gave much thought to, in class, is the fact that I didn't talk. I thought that was normal. In your class, if students had nothing to say, there would be no lesson so I tried to talk in class, but for some reason I couldn't get myself to say a word. I became angry with myself because I was trying to participate and I couldn't do it. I wrote about it in my narratives to try to figure out why I had this feeling of anxiety when it came to participating. I finally remembered something that happened to me a long time ago that I blocked out of my memory. I was in the fifth grade. I just came to this country and I didn't understand a word of English. I remember asking my teacher and my classmates questions but they would laugh at me and call me names. I was asking questions that I thought were appropriate at that time, but I got made fun of because my words didn't come out right. I remember feeling hurt and confused. I also felt stupid because I didn't understand and they did! I think that played a big role in the fact that I don't speak in class today. I feel better that I remember that part of my life because now I could deal with this problem. There is still a couple of days left in this semester. I hope I can surprise you and myself as well.

STORY FRAGMENT 5: YOUNG ADULT FEMALE

We tend to take people for granted. I just want to thank you for showing me the light. Helping me see the world in a different light. The book was a big guide. It also described things that were even hard to put into words. The part of the book that also helped me sort out my feelings was learning the "conscious" and the "unconscious." It helped me understand what it was I was feeling. Furthermore, I began to realize what I was feeling and why I was feeling it. The more I thought about it, I began to uncover that I was feeling things without knowing why at the moment. As I started to read the book I began to understand why I had so much hurt inside. It was all there, all the pain that had been put aside.

Judgments are strong words. I never took the time to think that judging a person and putting a label on them can affect a person. When we put labels on people we forget one little thing. The fact is we are hurting the persons feelings and more importantly we are hurting the person's soul. When a person puts a label on someone, they don't understand that they are making the person feel stuck. What I have seen with myself and other people around me is that we start to believe we are that judgment, and we can't escape it. After a class discussion Dr. Simon explained to us that we are not the labels we are given. . . . I understand now how it feels to be labeled and try and change that label.

(She then describes how her father has been labeled sick and crazy.) If he says he feels this way then he must feel sick. Nobody understands him. My father is probably stuck and doesn't know how to get out of the stage he is in now.

In conclusion, this narrative was time consuming but very worthwhile. we have been given the opportunity to write our story and the things in our lives that are important to us. The course helped me take a look at some of the ways I have been telling my narrative and change the things I always wanted to change in it.

STORY FRAGMENT 6: ADULT FEMALE IN EARLY THIRTIES

The worst experience that ever happened to me was being raped by my mother's husband, C., from about seven to nine years of age. Throughout my life this has caused me great harm. Harm with my relationships with men, and in dealing with my children. If I could would I erase the rape from existing? Yes, I would because it has affected me in so many ways.

Due to the fact that I was abused I have always felt guilty. Although I was very frightened by the action, my body was stimulated by his touch. The thought of this makes me sick (meaning I want to throw up). I also felt that I was "the other woman" and my mother would hate me. I told my older bother and he didn't believe me, so I knew Mom wouldn't believe me either.

In class, I learned that the body responds to touch. Although it felt good, it was a normal biological response my body had to touch, not that I was responding to him. It brought such a relief to have heard it in a class discussion. . . .

In a class discussion I realized that people only use verbal abuse and yell when they are threatened, or when their argument is weak. Instead of addressing the problem at hand, they fight about all the little things that have nothing to do with the problem itself.

Last week, I was upset at my husband because I needed help in the house. One evening we sat down and I told him exactly how I felt, and we discussed our feelings and came up with a solution without arguing. . . . I also learned when dealing with people that I should take into account the person's zone of proximal development; to deal with them at a level where they can understand and interact so they will feel comfortable. When a person feels comfortable progress can be made.

STORY FRAGMENT 7: YOUNG ADULT MALE

I was considering dropping the class when I was told of the easier classes I could take being that the credits are going toward electives, but my mind was changed halfway through the first class. In the first class we were asked to write down what we would change about our lives if given the chance. For me it was the death of my father, which was a painful experience for me being that I was only seven years old at the time of his death. At this age I really didn't understand fully the concept of death. I found it hard growing up with only my mother being a parent figure and at times I was often envious of the other children around me having both of their parents. We discussed in class the importance of having both a mother and a father to influence them in their childhood and I took great interest to this due to my experience and the feelings of emptiness I have. A part of me that will never be filled and which I will carry with me my whole life. I found it hard making it through that first class without crying.

My mind was changed when Dr. Simon told us about the experience in his life that he would have changed, which was the death of his father. Then he went on to say that he wouldn't change this because then he wouldn't be the same person he is today. This made me feel different about my situation because I am very happy with the person I have become. I am also proud of the job my mother has done in bringing up me and my sister, who was four when our father died and with whom I have never spoken two words about his death. Now that I am older and have matured I realize that after all the hard times we experience in our lives the important thing is that when these challenges are dealt with we become stronger people. . . .

We also discussed the idea of phony teachers which I took an interest in because my academic career has been plagued with them. In high school I was told that I was being prepared for college, yet in four years I didn't have to read one book or write one paper. I breezed through four years of college by finding three teachers that inspired me. These are the classes I really learned in. *Due to many years of having so many phony teachers I became a phony student and now it is hard to take any of my classes seriously* (emphasis is the author's).

STORY 8: YOUNG ADULT FEMALE

I used to think that I had a mental illness. I wasn't sure which one but I felt that I was not normal. When life circumstances became too much for me to bear I would go out, get very drunk and high, and try to forget. Sometimes, I would snap and yell at my friends and family who had done nothing wrong. Other days I would kick something (usually my bedroom wall) about a hundred times or until it broke. I remember crying to a dear friend one day, telling him I didn't know what was wrong with me. I was losing it, I told him. I couldn't afford psychotherapy or drugs, so I figured I would take this class and somewhere in the DSM would be the answer I was looking for. The answer, however, would not come from a book of illnesses and their symptoms, but from Dr. Laurence Simon, the professor of this class, his book *Psycho "therapy"* and another assigned book *Madness, Heresy, and the Rumor of Angels* by Seth Farber.

The first thing Mr. Simon told us was that if we were there to learn about chronic hand washing and multiple personalities we were about to be disappointed. He was going to teach us why, in his view, mental illness is a myth. What? Is this guy mentally ill? What about all the murderers and deviants and people like that Gigante guy who wanders around the streets of New York in a bathrobe talking to himself? What about me? If I wasn't mentally ill, then what was I? Why had I been acting so strangely, so irrationally? He began to explain and it all started to make some sense.

First, he explained from a medical point of view, there can be no such thing as a mental illness. Consider these illnesses: cancer, diabetes, and the common cold. All have real, tangible symptoms. . . . Mr. Simon gave us an example from the DSM called Oppositional Defiant Disorder. The symptoms of this illness were: often loses temper, often argues with adults, often does not follow rules. These are not medical symptoms which would constitute an illness, but the moral judgments of a therapist. Who is to say what is often? Don't all kids argue with adults? Who decides that these are symptoms of a mental illness requiring prescribed drugs that often just numb the patient's brain so that they will not only stop their previous behavior, but in most cases not want to behave in any way at all.

From the medical point of view, there can be no such thing as a mental illness because an illness requires symptoms and the symptoms in the DSM are only moral judgments. The behaviors which some of us engage in, such as wall kicking and sudden outbursts, are not signs of a mental illness but simply unwanted behavior labeled "abnormal."

I think I have explained why mental illness is a myth according to science. But there is a second part, a very tricky one. Not only, Mr. Simon said, is mental illness not possible medically, but is also morally wrong. If I had the money that day I was crying to my friend, I would have gone to a shrink. I would have said how depressed I was feeling, how lazy, how lonely, how quick I was to snap. I would have said that deep down inside there is a glowing person who is capable of feeling and doing wonderful things, but that lately I just didn't feel like doing anything. In return for sharing my deepest of feelings, he would have stamped my file MENTALLY ILL. . . . Stamping people mentally ill is morally wrong because it takes away people's liberties without a trial. What makes us most human is our ability to choose. The mentally ill person no longer has that right because it was taken away the moment they were labeled as such. All of their thoughts and feelings do not matter anymore because they are the thoughts and feelings of a crazy person. All this is not decided by God, who should be the only one with such authority, but by some psychiatrist, who, at some point in their life felt the same exact way as I or countless others have. . . .

I look back on that day, the day that I was crying and on the edge. I look back and I am so happy that I had no money. Maybe nothing would have happened. Maybe I would have just talked. But I will always know that there was a chance, a possibility that I would have been misunderstood, judged, and medicated and life as I know it and people as they know me would never be the same.

STORY FRAGMENT 9: YOUNG ADULT FEMALE

Lately I've had to face up to many issues in my life that all a long I tried my best to avoid. From the first day of this course, I have been trying to re-evaluate the circumstances of my life. In the first day of classes you asked a question on whether there was an event that we wish we could go back and change and I had chosen my mother's death. At the same time the question was asked, all I could think about was how much better my life would be if she were alive. Before my mother died she was my security, and with her presence I felt that nothing bad could ever happen to me. Since her death, I constantly live in fear as if at any moment without warning something horrible is going to take place which I may never recover from. On the other hand, because of her absence, I have had to become a very independent person and for the first time in my life I have been forced to take responsibility for my own actions.

Although I've assimilated the responsibility of having to fend for myself, I haven't quite accommodated to these new changes. I have a scary feeling not having someone around to pick me up in case I slip. Although I would love my mother to still be alive, I don't think that I would be the person that I am today if she were around. Being able to provide for myself is an accomplishment that I am very proud of. I do believe that I would have eventually gotten to this point but I am afraid to think of how long it might have taken me.

The discussion we had in class about having and making choices led me to reflect on my own relationships. For the past two years I have been in a relationship which has not been beneficial to me emotionally to say the least. I have been blaming the other person for making me feel sad and doing things to hurt me, while all along I knew that I had a choice whether to stay in the relationship or not. It was much easier to blame him for my lack of control over the situation than to come to the realization that I was as much at fault as he was. I now realize that my choice to remain was mine and mine alone and the fear of loneliness that I would endure stopped me from moving on. The option to leave seemed too unbearable. Though I knew that leaving this man in the end would be the best thing for me, I felt compelled to stay out of the hope that it would eventually get better. I try not to focus so much on choices that I don't have, but rather to devote time to carrying out the ones that I do have.

In connection to this subject is my new understanding of emotional bonds. While you were conducting the lesson it was as if you were reading my life. Besides my mother's love and emotional bond to me, I've always had a hard time believing that anybody can truly love me. Now that I am trying to get out of this non-productive relationship, I am trying to analyze my feelings for this person. I came to the conclusion that if an emotional bond must contain all of the components involved being true, such as a person being irreplaceable, distress, etc. then I did not really love this guy the way that I previously thought. I do believe on the other hand that we have a mutual dependency, perhaps stronger from my point of view, than any emotional bond. From the start, our relationship began for me because I needed someone to help me escape my daily struggles with life, someone to listen and comfort me in my time of need. He provided all those needs at first. I was so afraid of being alone that I settled for a relationship that I always knew in my heart would never last. Often, throughout our relationship I questioned whether I loved him or not, because I felt those overwhelming feelings that I had experienced before when being in love. Nonetheless, I couldn't end the relationship because I felt this emotional void in me. I wanted someone to replace and give me all the love and support my mother did. At times, I even suggested to myself that I was trying to replace my mother with a man. And at that time I seemed so ludicrous. . . . Now that we have separated the terror is back, constantly there to remind me that I am alone.

Prior to my mother's death, I had no true identity. Most of my decisions were made for me by my mother. I didn't go through Erikson's adolescent stage of Identity versus Role Confusion. Psychologist James E. Marcia talks about how adolescents have to experience crisis and commitment to develop their identity. Throughout my adolescent years, I didn't have to make serious decisions about my life because they were made for me. During my high school years, I had decided to go away to college but my mother persuaded me to stay home because she would worry about me too much, and since I am the only child she would be lonely.

For me to fully understand my mother's extreme involvement in my life, I had to take a closer look into her upbringing. She was an orphan at the age of three, the youngest of nine children. She was basically raised by her older brothers and sisters, who I may say didn't provide her with much love and affection. My mother used to call me mommy and when I asked her why she would say because she never got to call anyone by that name. She was very attached to me and wanted to shower me with all the love that she never received. That bond was partly attachment and part dependency. I feel that in her quest to shower me with love and attention, she did not give me the space I needed to experiment life for myself. In turn I grew dependent on our attachment and overindulged in it. . . .

I am learning more and more about myself, the way I am, and some of the reason why. My adaptation has been a long and tedious process but I would say that in the past six weeks I have learned more about myself and the people around me than that any other time in my life. I can stop thinking that there is something wrong with me for not feeling the same about certain people and not finding much interest in some of the things I used to cherish. Because I know that growth is essential to life and is an ongoing process.

∽

The following story fragments were all written in the fall semester of 1997. I taught a small psychology class of honor students, and was permitted to construct the context of the class. The course was entitled "Contemporary Issues in Psychology." There were no exams and all the assignments were papers drawn from the student's logs. I even allowed the students to choose the topics they would write on as long as the material related to classroom discussions and their readings. I wish space existed for me to print all three of their essays; instead I present fragments drawn from more than one of their essays.

STORY FRAGMENT 10: YOUNG ADULT FEMALE

Who am I? That is one question I thought I knew the answer to. If someone had asked me the question I would have replied, "I am L.A." and I would have thought that answered the question. Now as I think about it I realize I never sat down and thought about who I really am. Who is L.A. A better question is *what* is L.A.? Is L. my soul? Is L. my body? Is L. my mind? Is L. my consciousness? I just don't know the answers. Everything I thought I knew is gone and in its place is great confusion.

I once believed that I was a constant in the universe. I believed I had a soul that could never and would never die. I thought that I was more than just a body with a mind. Now I'm not so sure. I have been presented with too much evidence that proves the opposite. I have been presented with questions that I can not answer. For example, what happens to me when I sleep? Where do I go? Why can't I account for all the passing hours? These questions I cannot answer.

In 1993 I had surgery performed on my eye. I remember walking into the operating room and being scared to death. I was sure that it was going to hurt. My doctor assured me that I would feel nothing, but I didn't believe him. I was put under anesthesia. I closed my eyes for what seemed like one moment and then asked when the operation would begin. I was shocked to learn that the operation was finished for a few hours. I put the whole experience behind me until now. Now I can't stop wondering what happened to me during that time. Where was I? Did I even exist during that time? I can't explain what happened to me and that scares me more than I express. To me this is proof that I am not a constant in this universe. I am left with so many questions now such as. . . . If I am not even constant while I am alive then how is it possible that I can be constant after my death? The only conclusion that seems reasonable now is that I am not a constant. When I die will it be just like that surgery except I won't wake up at all?

All my life I have been told that there was more than this life. I was taught to believe that I was a human being with an undying soul. I was made to believe that I was created in the image of my God and, therefore, I was more than simply an animal. Now as I think about the facts it occurs to me that the reasonable conclusion suggests that I am no more than a highly evolved animal. There is evidence to link me to animals but no real proof of my undying soul. . . .

In the past few months my view of many things has changed due to my lessons in psychology. I feel as though I was blind to so many things that I now see. One of the most important lessons I have learned is the one regarding mental illness. In this paper I want to explain why and how this lesson has changed my life.

For many years I was convinced that I had a full understanding of mental illness. If anyone had asked me about it I would have said with complete confidence, "mental illness is simply a chemical imbalance that can be treated by administering certain drugs." I was so convinced that I knew what I was talking about because I had lived my life with someone who suffered with "mental illness." To be fully honest this someone is my mother. In 1983 when I was only five my mother had a "nervous breakdown." I remember my mother being violent and irrational. I remember being confused and scared because she was different than the woman I knew as my mother. My grandmother was forced to call the police because she feared my mother would harm herself or someone else. I remember the police dragging my mother away. At that time it was explained to me that my mother was sick. I didn't understand many of the things that I was told but I remember being told that my mother was schizophrenic. After one month of treatment my mother returned from the hospital. I was told that she was better again, but even at my age I realized that she wasn't the same as she had been before the "breakdown." I found that she was not the happy, loving person that she was before the drugs, but I was happy that she seemed rational.

As the years passed my mother had more "breakdowns." Sometimes she would be totally irrational and "crazy." At other times she would be sad and depressed. I lived through her ups and downs. I took care of her and tried my best to keep her from harming herself. It was as though I was her mother. She resisted her pills and I tried to make her take them. I believed that the pills were the only thing that would help. As I look back now I realize that I didn't want her to take the pills for her, I wanted her to take them for me. Somewhere deep inside I knew the pills didn't help the way that she felt, but I knew that if she took them I wouldn't have to deal with her "crazy" behavior.

In 1989 my mother had a very serious "breakdown." . . . She had to stay in the hospital for five weeks and when she returned she had a new diagnosis. What the doctors said that she had was "Bipolar syndrome" or "manic-depressive disorder" not schizophrenia. She was given new pills (lithium) and they seemed to work. . . . Since she is taking lithium my mother has been what (up until recently) I believe to be cured. My mother herself is even convinced she is cured because she has been back to work for over eight years now without a problem.

When I began studying psychology someone told me that my professor didn't believe in mental illness. I was filled with rage. I felt that anyone who believed that mental illness didn't exist was denying the life I led. I planned to hate my psychology professor. (I mean no offense). . . . My professor explained that drugs take away the unwanted behavior and doctors say that the patients are cured, but the sad fact is that the problem that caused the symptoms never gets fully dealt with. He went on to explain that the only thing the drugs do is confuse the brain chemistry to get rid of behavior considered unacceptable by society.

I thought about my professors words every day and the more I thought about it the more it made sense. I sat down with my mom and we had a really long talk about her life and her illness. She told me about the abuse she took from her mother, her husband, and society in general. She was beaten and told she was worthless throughout her life. The story she told me was sad and made me realize my professor was right. She isn't "crazy." She isn't schizophrenic, manic depressive or anything else. She is just a healthy person with a normal brain chemistry who took a lot of abuse. . . .

I have learned another interesting way of looking at who I am this semester called social constructionism. The idea states that personality does not come from within a person, but instead people invent one another. In this idea a person only knows someone by the effects they have on that person. People invent and reinvent themselves for each relationship. The moment I heard this idea it made total sense to me. I have thought for a long time that there have been many people inside of me because I am different in different situations. There is the L. who is a student, there is the L. in the work place, there is the L. I am with my parents, and there is the L. I am with my friends. They are all different because the situations and people involved are different.

I see my life in a new light after taking this class. I realize that I have been living most of my life to please others instead of writing my own narrative. I mentioned in class one day that I wanted to be an actress and was asked why I didn't pursue it. I gave all sorts of reasons why I didn't. After thinking about it I realized that my words in class that day were not my own. I was regurgitating my mothers words from our scripted arguments. She convinced me that I wasn't good enough to make it as an actress. It may be that I won't make it as a movie star, but if I try I will be closer than if I stand still. I have decided to pursue my acting. I will continue to try and assimilate the necessary skills in order to be an actress.

STORY FRAGMENT 11: YOUNG ADULT MALE

"Your enemies got you the moment you start to judge yourself by the bad labels of you." Strong words spoken by my mentor, Dr. Simon. Those words will forever stick with me throughout my life. My dream is to affect someone else's life as you have mine. I was asked to write a paper on what I learned in class. Where to begin there is just so much. I have put together chunks of information on what I *really* learned in class.

The Mind

The mind is to me where sanity lies. Emotions, experiences, and the innate willingness for survival all live here. Everyone has a mind but not everyone knows how to use it. My mother suffers from deep depression and is labeled "mentally ill" or as my grandmother refers to it, "sick." I always knew she had problems but I never believed she was "sick." Who in this world can define normal or abnormal? Just because society cannot relate to one's situation caused by one's own experience, one's own mind does not make one sick, rather it makes one different. We are all different as individuals, are we not? Our ability to communicate in a "normal manner" has determined what's normal and mentally ill in our society. In regards to my mother, I strongly believe she has lost the ability to communicate with herself and, in turn, with others. We fill our mind with emotions and experiences. Some of it sticks and some of it doesn't. The emotions and experiences that are important to us stick to what we call the unconscious.

Hello, my name is the unconsciousness. Here is where all my past thoughts and experiences lay and when you need me just feel a certain emotion or experience and I will appear. If you live in your unconsciousness than you cannot live in your consciousness. In other words, you cannot experience new stimuli if you are caught up in the storage of your past stimuli. The problem of living in the past (unconsciousness) does not allow one to experience new stimuli (consciousness). The unconsciousness must be filtered with new consciousness. Everyone has his or her own way of filtering old consciousness. For my filtering, I use school. For my mother, I wish I knew.

Facts and Judgments

What is a fact? Fact to me is concrete, a definite, and a must. Son, brother, lover, students are all facts. On the other hand, caring, loving, sensitive, smart, or stupid are all judgments. Judgments are personal opinions that establish worth or value, not factual worth or value. We as moral animals have learned to respond to each other and ourselves by judgments, not facts. I cannot change the immorality of people's beliefs, rather I can change my own.

My girlfriend is black and I am white. This is a fact. She is Catholic and I am Jewish. I invited my girlfriend over for the holiday. I then received a call from my father saying that is was inappropriate to bring my friend, teacher, and lover to dinner. I asked why she was not worthy of coming. He could not give me one factual answer. All he gave me were judgments. "What will people say about me" or "It is not allowed by Jewish law to make blessings around a gentile." I hate that word gentile, so grossly offensive. My response to all my father's judgments was that this is what you believe but I will not give in to ignorance, the fear of the unknown. If being Jewish means I must judge people I love, then I am not Jewish. Jewish is a religion, a culture, a belief, and not a person. I am H. the person, not the Jew. If the only thing you see in me is Jew, then all you are is a slave of yourself. In other words, you will never be able to look beyond yourself.

I arrived at the end of the dinner but I stayed with my love, my friend and my confidant. I had never felt more alive in my life. I truly believed in something, myself. I am who I am because of my girlfriend. She is a part of me like my father. However, she did not have me choose her over my father—that's a fact. I have been taught to be the author of my own book, I must write my own scripts and not allow others to write it for me. I am evolving into someone else, someone better. All that "I" ask for is someone or something worthy of "me."

STORY FRAGMENT 12: MID-TWENTIES ADULT FEMALE

In the process of trying to discover my own identity and what molds who I am, I have learned that nothing is constant—not even me. Wow, what a realization! Can this be true? What about God and the religion that promotes such a deity? What about the afterlife that most people live their whole life preparing for? What about culture and the traditions that create for most of us the foundations of everyday living? Suddenly, I feel suspended in midair with no direction to go to. I experience the feeling of loneliness, maybe even alienation.

A difficult concept to accept for it opens up the door to the world of the unknown. The world of the unknown where throughout history narrative or academic, we have been taught to fear. Interestingly, I often wonder why? We are surrounded by so much that we don't understand in the world we exist in. So why dismiss it?

In any case, along with the anxiety that goes along with the realization that nothing is constant, I feel a sort of freedom. Almost a creative freedom that allows me to ask questions. This is important—I believe especially because most of us are not allowed to discover the truth. A freedom as Dr. Simon states that narrates our own intentions, experiences, solutions to problems, analysis of our relationship to the world in which we exist. Sometimes I feel as if few are allowed—given permission to take over narrating people's lives. Even more devastating I have discovered many allow this to happen. Finally, a freedom that celebrates the idea of uniqueness. What I mean by this is the concept that none of us are the same, or even perceive the world in the exact same manner, fascinates me. What a beautiful feeling! Ironically, I feel some level of stability in this anxiety because I experience being an active participant of my own life, rather than a passive observer shopping for who I can ask for advice.

STORY FRAGMENT 13: YOUNG ADULT MALE

One of the topics I found to be the most thought provoking this semester was the definition of the self as the hereness in the thereness. It is interesting to think of myself as a small part of this universe where my hereness is irrelevant to the majority of the world. When we first discussed this topic I had some trouble understanding how I would go about making desired things from my thereness become part of my hereness. For example, I have long felt that I haven't had enough good, true friends. It seemed to me that most people were part of my thereness even though I wanted them to be part of my hereness. Often I felt that my own family was in some ways part of my thereness. At first I didn't understand how to remedy this problem, but then I made a connection between the lessons on hereness and thereness with an earlier topic on adaptation. I realized that I had a problem and I found that through assimilating certain people skills I was able to adapt and overcome my problem with people. I have made a great deal of friends this semester, several of them from this class.

Another concept I have learned which means a great deal to me is D. W. Winnicott's concept of holding environments. A holding environment is defined as a place where a person (being myself) can feel safe and "play." I realize through my childhood I never had a totally complete holding environment, a place where I truly felt safe. There were things I would never tell my parents, whereas my complete safety is in the hands of my girlfriend. I have come to the conclusion that my girlfriend is my true holding environment. I look back on my childhood and I wonder what could have been done differently to make my holding environment more complete? I hope to further understand the holding environment and how to create one for my future children.

We also discussed "blind spots" as defense mechanisms. We have trouble seeing the viewpoint of our significant others, be it our parents, siblings, friends, etc. We are egocentric as well as egotistical in our way of thinking. We get caught up in our own way of doing things or what is best for us. We don't worry about the consequences no matter how significantly or insignificantly they will affect someone else. After time we create scripts with these people. We fall into the same arguments over and over with no solution because we are embedded in only one way of being. In order to throw ourselves into another area of more sophisticated methods of dealing with these reoccurring situations we have to adapt to what we expect of ourselves. Using this class as a stepping stone, I can sit back and reflect on how I get involved in these metaphoric scripts. I now try and change the script as best I can. I don't take the defensive. I tell my girlfriend how I feel and what's causing it before I blame her for making the situation uncomfortable for me. I knew no one had the ability to make you feel anything before you mentioned it; I was glad that someone else realized it too.

STORY FRAGMENTS 14: YOUNG ADULT FEMALE

"My Second Essay"

As ridiculous as it may sound, or at least in my opinion, I am writing an essay on why I did not write my first essay. I am supposed to write my reasons from a psychological viewpoint, as opposed to a moral one. I am not really sure what that means exactly, but I am willing to try. Besides, it should be somewhat easy, considering that my reasons for not writing my original essay are mental challenges.

First off, I would like to say that I was enthusiastic about writing the first essay. The assignment was to choose a topic from my logs and write on it. I thought this was a great opportunity to evaluate my current situation and to finally confront a damaging personal problem of mine. Almost immediately, I knew to pick the strongest issue in my logs, my so-called "obsessive-compulsive disorder." Obsessive-compulsive disorder is an issue that holds great meaning in my life because I had been diagnosed with this "mental Illness." I had excitedly planned out my essay in my head, but when it came down to actually writing it all down, I was unable. . . . Attempting to write down the previous essay only brought up the experience of haunting memories and unachieved goals. My essay would have revolved around one basic question—is my obsessive-compulsive disorder caused by mental or physical influences? Unfortunately, the factors surrounding this life altering question were too difficult to handle.

Attending the first day of your class was an action that shocked my life. Your views on mental illness were fascinating and ones I had never heard before. I recall specific comments such as "doctors label people as mentally ill and fill their bodies with harmful drugs."When I surprised myself by having the courage to speak to you about my obsessive-compulsive disorder, you told me it was all "bullshit." For the first time, a person who was experienced and skilled in the psychiatric field was informing me that I was not chemically imbalanced. Wow—it was like a bolt of lightening pulsating through my body. It was very possible that my behaviors were the direct result of my traumatic childhood and that they could actually be changed. It was certainly not necessary to harm my body with drugs that, as you phrased it so clearly, were making me high. Wow—another bolt of lightening. There was only one problem. I was nowhere ready to confront my growing dependency on my medication or my conflicts concerning my abusive childhood.

When I finally began to see a psychiatrist, I was happy. When she informed me that I could possibly have obsessive-compulsive disorder and that she could recommend me to a doctor who prescribes drugs, I was thrilled. And when he told me I had a chemical imbalance, I literally bounced off the wall. I desperately wanted my condition to be physical and not mental. I lived in fear of being labeled "crazy." So with my mind, body, and soul intact I scarfed down my precious Zoloft with complete ease. After all, I was not "crazy." I lived my life as anyone else would, except I awoke each morning to headaches and nausea. However, I remained grateful for Zoloft because I was under the impression it was evening out my chemical imbalance. It was not until the first day of your class that I decided to discontinue my medication. I remained "normal" for a couple of days, until I was plagued with anxiety, interfering obsessions, as well as compulsions and a hopeless depression. . . . So once again I was popping Zoloft in my mouth like candy.

I cannot endure the pain that comes along with rehabilitation and recovery. Recovery from depression, fear, panic, anxiety, and obsessive-compulsions. All of these feelings are destructive to my very existence. Zoloft protects me from destruction. During one class discussion you stated that medication was a "band-aid," it in no way cured the problem it only covered it up. I now realize that this is true, which makes my situation even sadder. I know Zoloft is wrong for me, so why do I continue to take it? The answer is—I am a failure, or at least I feel like one at this moment. And this is one reason I did not write my first essay. I was scared to admit it, confront it—you name it, I was scared of it.

When I first spoke to you about my obsessive-compulsive disorder, you said it was a direct result of my dysfunctional childhood. Although it makes perfect sense, it is an idea I had never given much thought. In fact, my childhood is a memory I try rarely to reflect on. And this is another reason I did not write the original essay, I did not want to deal with my past. As a matter of fact, I am having an intensely difficult time writing this sentence and the one before it and most likely, the one after it.

At 4:00 P.M. our internalized fear would clock itself in. Any minute now . . . my stepfather stumbles into the living room, the embodiment of liquor. We all expected him to be intoxicated, we predicted the chosen argument, but his occasional blackouts were becoming all too frequent. As he screamed at my oldest sister, known as "the provoker," my mother—the neverending mediator—tried to calm them down. The glass shattering screams and the breaking of household objects grew worse and my only hope for protection, my brother, was forever absent from these torturous nights. My other sister, the hidden one, runs under the table or makes a dash for the roof. And I, the youngest child, grab a strong hold on my stepfather. I hang on his arm, tears staining my red face, pleading pathetically for it all to end. I was foolish. He was an unbeatable force who continued to torment us over and over, unaware that I was still dangling from his arm as he leaps for my sister. . . . I pray for tomorrow to come when I am able to go to school and play with my friends. I could pretend to be "normal," at least until 4:00 P.M. . . .

"I Have My Childhood"

My first essay focused on my obsessive-compulsive behavior and from where it originated. "Are my rituals and depression the result of physical or mental influences?" was the second question I asked. As I wrote my first essay entitled, "My Second Essay" I noticed my attention was gearing more towards the different elements that created my abusive childhood. In order for me to answer the above question, I need to evaluate my childhood from a psychological viewpoint, rather than a moral one.

I am an adult who recalls her dysfunctional childhood through the eyes of an adult, what a fascinating concept. It is an intriguing concept, yet completely foreign to me. How on earth will I remember the drunken look on my stepfather's face without cringing. To visualize him in his entirety and not feel intense fear is extremely difficult. Am I prepared to conjure up forgotten memories of his frequent blackouts accompanied by frequent threats that my family and I will "all be dead in the morning," without wanting to cry my terrified heart out. It almost seems inconceivable. Will I ever be able to recognize my childhood fears without being embedded in them? My most important goal at this time is to realize that I have a childhood, as opposed to I am my childhood. . . .

As a child, I lived with the fear of being labeled "not normal." . . . All of the lessons of my life combined concluded one gigantic lesson I lived by—DO NOT UNDER ANY CIRCUMSTANCES REVEAL YOUR EMOTIONS!!! . . . I am extremely loyal to my mother, I love her with all that I am, but I am so angry at her and accept that I may always be. . . . I need to realize that I was in no way responsible for his actions. I literally had no control over the situation. My childhood happened to me, it should not become me.

Although I have extreme anger and sadness over living with an alcoholic, I am also extremely grateful. Strange, isn't it? I am grateful that I had a dysfunctional childhood because it made me the person I am today. In fact, every experience I have had in my life has created the person I am today. The day I fully am aware I have my childhood, as opposed to I am my childhood, is the day I truly have me again.

～

I close this book with heartfelt thanks to all my students for sharing with me their lives and their stories. I wish them all ownership of their lives and the experience of telling stories that will enrich their lives and the lives of the rest of us for many healthy and joyful years to come.

REFERENCES

Adler, Alfred. 1968. *Understanding Human Nature*. Translated by Walter Berger. London: George Allen and Unwin.

Ainsworth, Mary. 1985. "Attachment across the Life Span." *Bulletin of the American Academy of Medicine*. 61: 792–811.

———. 1989. "Attachment Beyond Infancy." *American Psychologist* 44: 709–716.

Atwood, George, and Robert Stolorow. 1984. *Structures of Subjectivity*. Hillsdale, N.J.: The Analytic Press.

Azar, Beth. 1997. "When Research Is Swept Under the Rug." *APA Monitor* 28: 1.

Barkow, Jerome, Leda Cosmides and John Tooby. 1992. *The Adapted Mind: Evolutionary Psychology and the Generation of Culture*. New York: Oxford University Press.

Barnett, Lincoln. 1957. *The Universe and Dr. Einstein*. New York: William Morrow Co.

Bateson, Gregory. 1979. *Mind and Nature: A Necessary Unity*. New York: E. P. Dutton.

Becker, Ernst. 1973. *The Denial of Death*. New York: Free Press.

———. 1975. *Escape From Evil*. New York: Free Press.

Beit-Hallhami, Benjamin. 1974. "Salvation and Its Vicissitudes: Clinical Psychology and Political Values." *American Psychologist* 29: 124–130.

Benjamin, Jessica. 1989. *The Bonds of Love*. New York Pantheon.

Boesch, Ernst. 1997. "The Story of a Cultural Psychologist: Autobiographical Observations." *Culture and Psychology 3*: 257–276.

Bowlby, John. 1969. *Attachment and Loss*. Vol. 1: *Attachment*. New York: Basic Books.

———. 1973. *Attachment and Loss*. Vol. 2: *Separation: Anxiety and Anger*. New York: Basic Books.

———. 1979. *The Making and Breaking of Affectional Bonds*. London: Tavistock.

———. 1980. *Attachment and Loss*. Vol. 3: *Losses: Sadness and Depression*. London: Hogarth Press.

———. 1988. *A Secure Base*. New York: Pantheon.

Breggin, Peter. 1991. *Toxic Psychiatry: Why Therapy, Love and Empathy Must Replace the Drugs, Electroshock and Biochemical Theories of the New Psychiatry*. New York: St. Martin's Press.

Bridgman, R. W. 1927. *The Logic of Modern Physics*. New York: Macmillan.

Bronowski, Jacob. 1963. *The Common Sense of Science*. Cambridge, MA: Harvard University Press.

Bruner, Jerome. 1966. *Toward a Theory of Instruction*. Cambridge, MA: Harvard University Press.

Buber, Martin. 1990. *Pointing the Way: Collected Essays*. Atlantic Highlands, NJ: Humanities Press International.

Buss, David. 1994. *Evolution of Desire: Strategies of Human Mating*. New York: Basic Books.

Carnap, Rudolf. 1966. *Philosophical Foundations of Physics: An Introduction to the Philosophy of Science*. Edited by Martin Gardner. New York: Basic Books.

Chalmers, David. 1996. *The Conscious Mind: In Search of a Fundamental Theory*. New York: Oxford University Press.

Chein, Isidor. 1972. *The Science of Behavior and the Image of Man*. New York: Basic Books.

Chodorow, Nancy. 1978. *The Reproduction of Mothering: Psychoanalysis and the Sociology of Gender*. Berkeley: University of California Press.

Chomsky, Noam. 1972. *Language and Mind*. New York: Harcourt, Brace and Javonovich.

———. 1975. *Reflection on Language*. New York: Pantheon.

———. 1980. *Rules and Representations*. New York: Columbia University Press.

Cohen, David. 1990. *The Journal of Mind and Behavior* 11, no. 3 and no. 4.

Cohen, I. Bernard. 1985. *Revolution in Science*. Cambridge , MA: Harvard University Press.

———. 1994. *The Journal of Mind and Behavior* 15.

Cushman, Philip 1995. *Constructing the Self, Constructing America*. New York: Addison Welsley.

Damasio, Antonio. 1994. *Descartes' Error: Emotion, Reason and the Human Mind*. New York: Grosset and Dunlap.

Danziger, Kurt. 1990. *Constructing the Subject: Historical Origins of Psychological Research*. Cambridge MA: Cambridge University Press.

Dawes, Robyn. 1944. *House of Cards: Psychology and Psychotherapy Built on Myth*. New York: Free Press.

Dawkins, Robert. 1976. *The Selfish Gene*. New York: Oxford University Press.

De Jong, Huib Jooren. 1995. "Ecological Psychology and Naturalism: Heider, Gibson and Marr." *Theory and Psychology* 5: 251–270.

Degler, Carl. 1991. *In Search of Human Nature: The Decline and Revival of Darwinism in American Social Thought*. New York: Oxford University Press.

Dennett, Daniel. 1991. *Consciousness Explained*. New York: Little, Brown and Co.

———. 1995. *Darwin's Dangerous Idea*. New York: Simon and Schuster.

Dewey, John. 1929. *The Quest for Certainty*. New York: G. P. Putnam.

Erikson, Erik. 1968. *Identity, Youth and Crisis*. New York: W. W. Norton.

Farber, Seth. 1993. *Madness, Heresy and the Rumor of Angels*. New York: Open Court.

Fausto-Sterling, Marie. 1985. *Myths of Gender: Biological Themes about Men and Women*. New York: Basic Books.

Fernald, Dodge. 1997. *Psychology*. Upper Saddle River, NJ: Prentice-Hall.

Feyerabend, Paul. 1988. *Against Method*. Rev. ed. London: Verso.

Foucault, Michel. 1965. *Madness and Civilization*. New York: Pantheon Books.

Frankel, Jay. 1998. "The Play's the Thing: How the Essential Processes of Therapy Are Seen Most Clearly in Child Therapy." *Psychoanalytic Dialogues* 8:149–182.

Freud, Sigmund. 1957. *A General Introduction to Psychoanalysis*. Translated by J. Rivera. New York: Perma Books.

——. 1966. *The Complete Introductory Lecture in Psychoanalysis.* Translated and edited by James Strachey. New York: W. W. Norton and Co.

Frijda, Nico. 1986. *The Emotions.* Cambridge: Cambridge University Press.

——. 1988. "The Laws of Emotions." *American Psychologist* 43:349–358.

Fromm, Erich. 1947. *Escape From Freedom.* New York: Holt, Rinehart and Winston.

——. 1950. *Psychoanalysis and Religion.* New Haven, CT: Yale University Press.

——. 1980. *The Greatness and Limitations of Freud's Thought.* New York: Harper and Row.

Fukuyama, Francis. 1992. *The End of History and the Last Man.* New York: Free Press.

Gardner, Howard. 1983. *Frames of Mind: The Theory of Multiple Intelligences.* New York: Basic Books.

Gergen, Kenneth. 1985. "The Social Construction Movement in Modern Psychology." *American Psychologist* 40; 266–275.

——. 1991a. "Emerging Challenges for Theory and Psychology." *Theory and Psychology* 1: 13–36.

——. 1991b. *The Saturated Self: Dilemmas of Identity in Contemporary Life.* New York: Basic Books.

Giddens, Anthony. 1984. *The Constitution of Society.* Berkeley, CA: University of California Press.

Gilligan, Carol. 1982. *In Different Voices: Psychological Theory and Women's Psychology.* Cambridge, MA: Harvard University Press.

Giorgi, A. 1970. *Psychology as a Human Science.* New York: Harper and Row.

——. 1994. "The Idea of a Human Science." In *The Humanistic Movement: Recovering the Person in Psychology.* Edited by F. W. Wertz. New York: Gardner.

Goffman, Ervin. 1961. *Asylums: Essays on the Social Situation of Mental Patients and Other Inmates.* New York: Anchor Books.

Greenspan, Stanley. 1979. *Intelligence and Adaptation: An Integration of Psychoanalytic and Piagetian Developmental Psychology.* New York: International Universities Press.

Greenwood, John. 1989. *Explanation and Experiment in Social Psychological Science.* New York: Springer.

Grünbaum, Adolf. 1984. *The Foundation of Psychoanalysis.* Berkeley, CA: University of California Press.

Hacking, Ian. 1981. *Scientific Revolution.* Oxford: Oxford University Press.

——. 1995. *Rewriting the Soul: Multiple Personalities and the Science of Memory.* Princeton, NJ: Princeton University Press.

Hamilton, William. 1964. "The Genetical Evolution of Social Behavior." *Journal of Theoretical Biology,* 7: 1–52.

Harré, Rom. 1986. *The Social Constitution of Emotions.* Oxford: Basil Blackwell.

——. 1992. "What Is Real in Psychology: A Plea for Persons." *Theory and Psychology* 2: 153–159.

Hartmann, Heinz. 1958. "Ego Psychology and the Problem of Adaptation." Translated by David Rappaport. *Journal of the American Psychoanalytic Association.* Monograph no. 1. New York: International Universities Press.

Helme, William. 1992. Reformulating Psychology as a Human Science." *Theoretical and Philosophical Psychology* 12: 119–136.

Hernnstein, Richard, and Charles Murray. 1994. *The Bell Curve: Intelligence and Class Structure in American Life.* New York: Free Press.

Himmelfarb, Gertrude. 1994. *On Looking into the Abyss: Untimely Thoughts on Culture and Society.* New York: Alfred A. Knopf.

Hofstader, Richard. 1963. *Anti-Intellectualism in American Life*. New York: Alfred A. Knopf.

Holzkamp, Klaus. 1992. "On Doing Psychology Critically." *Theory and Psychology* 2: 193–204.

Hook, Sydney. 1987. *Out of Step: An Unquiet Life in the 20th Century*. New York: Harper and Row.

Horgan, John. 1996. *The End of Science*. New York: Addison Wesley.

Horney, Karen. 1950. *Neurosis and Human Growth*. New York: W. W. Norton.

Howard, George. 1991. "Cultural Tales: A Narrative Approach to Thinking, Crosscultural Psychology and Psychotherapy." *American Psychologist* 46: 187–197.

Husserl, Edmund. 1962. *Ideas: General Introduction to Pure Phenomenology*. Translated by R. Boyce Gibson. New York: Collier Books.

Idhe, Don. 1986. *Experimental Phenomenology*. Albany, NY: State University of New York Press.

Izard, Caroll. 1977. *Human Emotions*. New York: Plenum.

———. 1979. *Emotions in Personality and Psychopathology*. New York: Plenum.

Jaynes, Julian. 1976. *The Origins of Consciousness in the Breakdown of the Bicameral Mind*. New York: Houghton Mifflin.

Kagan, Jerome. 1984. *The Nature of the Child*. New York: Basic Books.

———. 1994. *Galen's Prophecy: Temperament in Human Nature*. New York: Basic Books.

———. 1996. "Three Pleasing Ideas." *American Psychologist* 51: 901–908.

Kegan, Robert. 1982. *The Evolving Self*. Cambridge MA: Harvard University Press.

———. 1994. *In Over Our Heads: The Mental Demands of Modern Life*. Cambridge MA: Harvard University Press.

Kelly, George. 1955. *The Psychology of Personal Constructs in Theory of Personality*, Vols. 1 and 2. New York: W. W. Norton.

Koestler, Arthur. 1967. *The Ghost in the Machine*. London: Arkana.

Kohlberg, Laurence. 1984. *The Psychology of Moral Development*. Vol. 2. San Francisco: Harper and Row.

Kohn, Alfie. 1993. *Punished by Rewards*. New York: Houghton Mifflin.

Kohn, David. 1997. "Charles Darwin, Science and Esthetics." Address Given at Baruch College Conference on Darwin and Darwinism, New York, NY.

Kohut, Heinz. 1971. *Analysis of the Self*. New York: International Universities Press.

———. 1977. *The Restoration of the Self*. New York: International Universities Press.

Kotré, John. 1995. *White Gloves: How We Create Ourselves Through Memory*. New York: Free Press.

Kuhn, Thomas. 1970. *The Structure of Scientific Revolutions*. 2d rev. ed. Chicago, Ill.: University of Chicago Press.

Laing, R. D. 1967. *The Politics of Experience*. New York: Pantheon.

———. 1969. *The Divided Self*. New York: Pantheon.

———. 1982. *The Voice of Experience*. New York: Pantheon.

Lawless, W. F. 1996. "Interaction Context Theory: The Interdependence and Mutual Exclusivity of Observation and Action." *Theoretical and Philosophical Psychology* 16: 141–161.

Lazarus, Richard. 1982. "Thoughts on the Relation Between Emotion and Cognition." *American Psychologist* 37: 1019–1024.

———. 1984. "On the Primacy of Cognition." *American Psychologist* 39: 124–129.

———. 1991. *Emotions and Adaptation*. New York: Oxford University Press.

Lerman, Hannah. 1986. *A Mote in Freud's Eye*. New York: Springer.

Lifton, Robert. 1979. *The Broken Connection*. New York: Simon and Schuster.

Locke, John C. 1993. *The Child's Path to Spoken Language*. Cambridge, MA: Harvard University Press.

Loftus, Elizabeth, and Kenneth Ketcham. 1994. *The Myth of Repressed Memories*. New York: St. Martin's Press.

London, Perry. 1986. *The Modes and Morals of Psychotherapy*. 2d ed. New York: Hemisphere Books.

Mahler, Margaret, 1968. *On Human Symbiosis and the Vicissitudes of Individuation*. New York: International Universities Press.

Mahoney, Michael. 1985. "Psychotherapy and Human Change Processes." In *Cognition and Psychotherapy*, edited by Michael Mahoney and Arthur Freeman. New York: Plenum.

———. 1991. *Human Change Processes: The Scientific Foundations of Psychotherapy*. New York: Basic Books.

Mancuso, James. 1986. "The Acquisition and Use of Narrative Grammar Structure." In *Narrative Psychology: The Storied Nature of Human Conduct*, edited by Theodore Sarbin. New York: Praeger.

———. 1996. "Constructionism, Personal Construct Psychology and Narrative Psychology." *Theory and Psychology* 6: 47–70.

Mandler, George. 1984. *Mind and Body: Psychology of Emotions and Stress*. New York: W. W. Norton.

Martin, Jack and Janice Thompson. 1997. "Between Scientism and Relativism: Phenomenology, Hermeneutics and the New Realism in Psychology." *Theory and Psychology* 7: 629–652.

Maslow, Abraham. 1968. *Toward a Psychology of Being*. 2d ed. Princeton, NJ: Van Nostrand and Co.

May, Rollo. 1991. *The Cry For Myth*. New York: W. W. Norton.

McAdams, Dan. 1993. *Stories We Live By: Personal Myths and the Making of the Self*. New York: William Morrow and Co.

McClellend D. C. 1953. *The Achieving Society*. New York: Appleton-Century-Crofts.

Merton, Robert. 1968. *Social Theory and Social Structure*. New York: Free Press.

Meyrowitz, Joshua. 1985. *No Sense of Place: The Impact of Electronic Media on Social Behavior*. New York: Oxford University Press.

Mitchell, Steven. 1992. *Hope and Dread in Psychoanalysis*. New York: Basic Books.

Mohanty, I. N. 1974. *The Concept of Intentionality*. St. Louis, MO: Warren A. Green.

Morris, Charles G. 1996. *Understanding Psychology*. 3rd ed. Upper Saddle River, NJ: Prentice-Hall.

Nagel, Thomas. 1980. "What Is It Like to Be a Bat?" In *Readings in the Philosophy of Psychology*, vol. 1, edited by Ned Block. 159–170. Cambridge, MA: Harvard University Press.

Orange, Donna. 1995. *Emotional Understanding: Studies in Psychoanalytic Epistomology*. New York: Guilford Press.

Orenstein, Robert. 1991. *The Evolution of Consciousness*. New York: Simon and Schuster.

Orwell, George. 1949. *1984*. New York: Harcourt Brace.

Piaget, Jean. 1950. *The Psychology of Intelligence*. Translated by M. Piercy and D. E. Berlyne. London: Routledge and Kegan Paul.

———. 1952. *The Origins of Intelligence in Children*. New York: International Universities Press.

———. 1954. *The Construction of Reality in the Child*. Translated by M. Cook. New York: Basic Books.

——. 1957. *Biology and Knowledge*. Chicago, IL: University of Chicago Press.

——. 1973. *The Child and Reality*. New York: Grossman Publishers.

——. 1975. *The Development of Thought*. New York: Viking Press.

——. 1981. *Intelligence and Affectivity*. Palo Alto, CA: Annual Reviews.

Pinker, Steven. 1994. *The Language Instinct: How the Mind Creates Language*. New York: Harper Perennial.

Plutchik, Robert. 1977. "Cognition in the Service of Emotions: An Evolutionary Approach." In *Emotions,* edited by D. Landland, J. R. Fell, E. Keen, A. Leshrer, R. Plutchik, and R. H. Tarpiz. Monterrey, CA: Brooks Cole.

——. 1980. *Emotions: A Psycho-Evolutionary Approach*. New York: Harper and Row.

Polanyi, Michael. 1958. *Personal Knowledge*. Chicago, IL: University of Chicago Press.

. 1966. *Science, Faith and Society*. Chicago, IL: University of Chicago Press.

——. 1967. *The Tacit Dimension*. New York: Anchor Books.

——. 1969. *Knowing and Being*. Chicago, IL: University of Chicago Press.

Pollster, Erving. 1987. *Every Persons Life Is Worth a Novel*. New York: W. W. Norton.

Popper, Karl. 1945. *The Open Society and Its Enemies*. Princeton, NJ: Princeton University Press.

——. 1961. *The Logic of Modern Discovery*. New York: Science Editions.

Postman, Neil. 1979. *Teaching as a Conserving Activity*. New York: Delacourte Press..

——. 1979. *The End Of Education: Redefining the Value of School*. New York: Alfred A. Knopf.

Postman, Neil, and Charles Weingartner. 1969. *Teaching as a Subversive Activity*. New York: Dell.

Puhakka, Kaisa. 1992. "Discovery As Seeing: Lessons From Radical Empiricism and Meditative Practice." *Theoretical and Philosophical Psychology* 12: 48–58.

Robinson, Daniel. 1991. "Might the Self Be Substance After All." *Theory and Psychology* 1: 37–50.

——. 1997. "Therapy and Theory as Civics." *Theory and Psychology* 7: 675–682.

Rogers, Carl. 1061. *On Becoming a Person: A Therapist's View of Psychotherapy*. Boston: Houghton Mifflin.

Rorty, Richard. 1979. *Philosophy and the Mirror of Nature*. Princeton, NJ: University of Princeton Press

——. 1991. *Objectivity, Relativism and Truth: Philosophical Papers*. Vol 1. Cambridge, UK: Cambridge University Press.

——. 1994. "The Unpatriotic Academy." *New York Times*, February, 13, 1994.

Rosen, Hugh. 1985. *Piagetian Dimensions of Clinical Relevance*. New York: Columbia University Press.

Rosenthal, Robert. 1992. *Pygmalion in the Classroom*. New York: Irvington Publishers.

Rossman, Neil. 1991. *Consciousness: Separation and Integration*. Albany, NY: State University of New York Press.

Rotman, Brian. 1979. *Jean Piaget: Psychologist of the Real*. Ithaca, NY: Cornell University Press.

Rotter, Julian. 1966. *Generalized Expectancies for Internal versus External Locus of Control*. New York: International Universities Press.

Rylchak, Joseph. 1997. *In Defense of Human Consciousness*. Washington, DC: American Psychological Association.

Sarbin Theodore. 1986. *Narrative Psychology: The Storied Nature of Human Conduct*. New York: Praeger.

Sarbin, Theodore, and James Mancuso. 1980. *Schizophrenia: Medical Diagnosis or Moral Verdict.* New York: Pergamon Press.

Sartre, Jean Paul. 1957. *The Transcendence of the Ego: An Existential Theory of Consciousness.* Translated by F. Williams and R. Kirkpatrick. New York: Noonday.

Sass, Louis. 1992. *Madness and Modernism: Insanity in the Light of Modern Art, Literature and Thought.* Cambridge, MA: Harvard University Press.

Schafer, Roy. 1980. *Narrative Action in Psychoanalysis.* Worchester, MA: Clark University Press.

———. 1983. *The Analytic Attitude.* London: Hogarth Press.

———. 1992. *Retelling a Life: Narration and Dialogue in Psychoanalysis.* New York: Basic Books.

Searles, John. 1995. *The Rediscovery of Mind.* Cambridge, MA: MIT Press.

Seligman, Martin. 1975. *Helplessness: On Depression, Development and Death.* San Francisco: W. H. Freeman.

Shanes Morris. 1992. "Intentionality and the Problem of Discovery in Scientific Epistomology." *Theory and Psychology* 2: 5–28.

Shotter, John. 1991. "Rhetoric and the Social Construction of Cognition." *Theory and Psychology* 1: 495–514.

Simon, Laurence. 1986. *Cognition and Affect: A Developmental Psychology of the Individual.* Buffalo, NY: Prometheus Books.

———. 1994. *Psycho"therapy": Theory, Practice, Modern and Postmodern Influences.* Westport, CT: Praeger.

Skinner, B. F. 1948. *Science and Human Behavior.* New York: Macmillan.

Slavin, Malcolm, and Daniel Kriegsman. 1992. *The Adaptive Design of the Human Psyche.* New York: Guilford.

Slife, Brent. 1993. *Time and Psychological Explanation.* Albany, NY: State University of New York Press.

———. 1994. "Free Will and That 'Stuck Feeling.'" *Theoretical and Philosophical Psychology* 14: 1–13.

Slife, Brent, and Richard Williams. 1997. "Toward a Theoretical Psychology: Should a Subdiscipline Be Formally Recognized." *American Psychologist* 52: 117–129.

Smith, J. A. R., R. Harré, and L. V. Langenhove. 1995. *Rethinking Methods in Psychology.* Thousand Oaks, CA: Sage.

Sowell, Thomas. 1995. *The Vision of the Anointed: Self Congratulations as a Basis for Social Policy.* New York: Basic Books.

———. 1996. *Migrations and Culture: A World View.* New York: Basic Books.

Spanier, Bonnie. 1993. "Natural Sciences: Molecular Biology." In *Rethinking the Disciplines: Biology,* edited by Bonnie Spanier, Sue Rosser, Joseph N. Muzio, and Edward Tucker. New York: CUNY Academy for the Humanities and Sciences.

Spence, Donald. 1982. *Narrative Truth and Historical Truth.* New York: W. W. Norton.

———. 1994. *The Rhetorical Voice of Psychoanalysis: Displacement of Evidence By Theory.* Cambridge, MA: Harvard University Press.

Sroufe, L. A. 1987. "The Role of Infant-Caregiver Attachment in Development." In *Clinical Implications of Attachment,* edited by J. Belsky and M. T. Nezworski. Hillsdale, NJ: Erlbaum.

Steele, Shelby. 1990. *The Content of Our Character: A New Vision of Race in America.* New York: St. Martin's Press.

Stern, Daniel. 1977. *The First Relationship: Infant and Mother.* Cambridge MA: Harvard University Press.

Sternberg, Robert. 1985. *Beyond IQ: A Triarchic Theory of Human Intelligence*. New York: Cambridge University Press.

Storr, Anthony, 1988. *Solitude: A Return to the Self*. New York: Free Press.

Strenger, Carlo. 1991. *Between Hermeneutics and Science*. New York: International Universities Press.

Szasz, Thomas. 1970. *The Manufacture of Madness*. New York: Harper Torchbooks.

——. 1974. *The Myth of Mental Illness*. Rev. ed. New York: Harper and Row.

——. 1978. *The Myth of Psychotherapy*. Garden City, NY: Anchor Press.

——. 1987. *The Therapeutic State*. Buffalo, NY: Prometheus Books.

——. 1996. *The Meaning of Mind: Language, Morality and Neuroscience*. Westport, CT: Praeger.

Tetlock, Philip. 1992. "An Alternate Metaphor in the Study of Judgment and Choice: People as Politicians." *Theory and Psychology* 1: 451–475.

Thomas, A. S., and H. E. Birch. 1968. *Temperamant and Behavior Disorders in Children*. New York: New York University Press.

Tillich, Paul. 1952. *The Courage to Be*. New Haven, CT: Yale University Press.

Trivers, Robert. 1985. *Social Evolution*. Boston: Addison Wesley.

Vonnegut, Kurt. 1988. *Welcome to the Monkey House*. New York: Dell.

Vygotsky, Lev. 1978. *Mind in Society: The Development of Higher Psychological Processes*. Cambridge, MA: Harvard University Press.

Weinberg, Steven. 1992. *Dreams of a Final Theory*. New York: Vintage Books.

Wertsch, James. 1997. "Introduction: Narrative Tools of History and Identity." *Culture and Psychology* 3: 5–20.

Wilson, Edward O. 1975. *Sociobiology: The New Synthesis*. Cambridge, MA: Harvard University Press.

——. 1992. *The Diversity of Life*. New York: W. W. Norton.

Wilson, Elizabeth. 1996. " 'Loving the Computer': Cognition, Embodiment and the Influencing Machine." *Theory and Psychology* 6: 577–600.

Wilson, James Q. 1993. *The Moral Sense*. New York: Free Press.

Winnicott, D. W. 1965. *The Maturational Process and the Facilitating Environment*. New York: International Universities Press.

Wright, Robert C. 1994. *The Moral Animal: Evolutionary Psychology and Everyday Life*. New York: Pantheon.

Yeats, William Butler. 1920. *Michael Robartes and the Dancer*. Churchtown, Dundrum: The Cuala Press.

Zajonc, Robert. 1980 "Feeling and Thinking: Preferences Need No Inferences." *American Psychologist* 33: 150–175.

——. 1984. "On the Primacy of Affect." *American Psychologist* 39: 117–123.

INDEX

Feyerabend, Paul, 33, 183
Fictional finalisms, 97
Fixation of development, 118–122
Frankel, Jay, 107
"The freedoms from," 141
"The freedoms to," 141
Freud, Sigmund, 24, 30, 73, 141
Frijda, Nico, 85
Fromm, Erich, 99, 124, 141
Future principle, 98

Gardner, Howard, 41
Gergen, Kenneth, 26, 55
Gibson, James, 94
Giddens, Anthony, 81
Gilligan, Carol, 55
Giorgi, A., 31
God-thing stories, 7–9, 11, 35
Goffman, Erving, 40
Grades, 174–177
Greenspan, Stanley, 90
Greenwood, John, 37
Grünbaum, Adolf, 132

Hacking, Ian, 29
Hamilton, William, 62
Harré, Rom, 55
Helme, William, 31
Himmelfarb, Gertrude, 51
Historical principle, 98
Holzkamp, Klaus, 68
Horgan, John, 79
Horney, Karen, 30
Human change processes, 24
Humanism: defined, 45–46; and free
    will, 47
Husserl, Edmund, 67, 77

Idhe, Don, 77
"I-It" relationships, 13
Intelligence, 41–42
"I-Thou" relationships, 13
Izard, Carroll, 85, 86

Jaynes, Julian, 56
Judgments: confusion with descriptions,
    36–42; defined, 43

Kagan, Jerome, 85, 99, 116, 132

Kegan, Robert, 32, 50, 85, 90, 101, 103–
    104
Kelly, George, 31, 55, 72, 83
Kohlberg, Laurence, 146
Kohn, Alfie, 175
Kohn, David, 33
Kotré, John, 92
Kriegsman, Daniel, 132
Kuhn, Thomas, 26, 29

Laing, R. D., 41, 92
Lakatos, Imre, 32
Lawless, W. F., 78
Lazarus, Richard, 55, 85, 91
Lerman, Hannah, 51
Locke, John, 64
Locus of control, 105
Loftus, Elizabeth, 92
London, Perry, 35

Mahler, Margaret, 41, 92
Mahoney, Michael, 21, 54, 55, 67, 84,
    85
Mancuso, James, 40, 55
Mandler, George, 85
Marx, Karl, 7
Maslow, Abraham, 30, 99
McAdams, Dan, 55
McClellend, David, 105
Memes, 65
Merton, Robert, 26
Meyerowitz, Joshua, 169
Mind-body controversy, 66–68
Mitchell, Steven, 92
Mohanty, I. N., 67, 77
Moral development, 146–148
Morality, defined, 45
Morris, Charles, 72
Myths, 11; of mental illness, 12; and sa-
    cred stories, 12

Nagel, Thomas, 57, 66
Nature-nurture controversy, 66–68
Nietzsche, Friederich, 15

Objectivity, 27
Orange, Donna, 92, 165
Orenstein, Robert, 56, 67
Orwell, George, 138

About the Author

LAURENCE SIMON is Professor of Psychology at Kingsborough Community College at the City University of New York and maintains a private practice in Bellmore, New York. He is the author of *Psycho "therapy"* (Praeger, 1994).

ISBN 0-275-96058-7

EAN

9 780275 960582

HARDCOVER BAR CODE

90000>